I'm Hungry, Daddy

I'm Hungry, Daddy

A TRUE STORY

CLIFF NICHOLS

BANTAM BOOKS
SYDNEY • AUCKLAND • TORONTO • NEW YORK • LONDON

I'M HUNGRY, DADDY
A BANTAM BOOK

First published in 2001 by Cliff Nichols
This edition first published in Australia and New Zealand in 2002 by Bantam

National Library of Australia
Cataloguing-in-Publication Entry

   Nichols, Cliff (Clifford), 1927–.
   I'm hungry, Daddy.
   ISBN 1 86325 383 1.
   1. Nichols, Cliff (Clifford), 1927–. 2. Alcoholics – New South Wales – Sydney – Biography. 3. Homeless persons – New South Wales – Sydney – Biography. 4. Fathers and daughters – New South Wales – Sydney – Biography. 5. Family relationships – New South Wales – Sydney – Biography. 6. Sydney (N.S.W.) – Social conditions – 20th century. I. Title.
   362.292092

Transworld Publishers,
a division of Random House Australia Pty Ltd
20 Alfred Street, Milsons Point, NSW 2061
http://www.randomhouse.com.au

Random House New Zealand Limited
18 Poland Road, Glenfield, Auckland

Transworld Publishers,
a division of The Random House Group Ltd
61-63 Uxbridge Road, London W5 5SA

Random House Inc
1540 Broadway, New York, New York 10036

Cover photo from the family collection of Cliff Nichols
Typeset by Midland Typesetters, Maryborough, Victoria
Printed and bound by Griffin Press, Netley, South Australia

Dedicated to Dian

I dedicate this book to my soul mate, Dian. Her deep affection has taught me the true value of love and has given meaning to my life. As my wife and best friend she has offered me safety from the storms of life, given me a sense of belonging, loved me for who I am and enabled me to love myself.

Contents

Acknowledgments

Sincere thanks to my boyhood pal, the talented star of stage and television, Mr Enzo Toppano, who, with his equally talented wife, the beautiful Peggy, was instrumental in motivating me to write and finally publish this autobiography.

My deepest gratitude to Dian Nichols, who, over a very long period, spent many days encouraging me to finish writing my story, then completed the typesetting and editing of my book.

A special thank you to Joanne Davidson for the hours spent assisting with the final editing and proofreading of the manuscript, and Jane Newling, respected journalist of Sydney, whose faith in the potential of the book motivated me to keep going.

Finally, my biggest thank you to Helen, who has been my reason to live so many times. Thank you for your unconditional love and neverending loyalty, and for making this book possible.

Don't Leave Me, Daddy

1963.

'Walk, you bastard! Stand up! Keep walking! Move your bloody feet! Come on, walk!' a voice bellows at me. The noise penetrates the numbness of my mind. 'That's it, keep moving! Don't go to bloody sleep. Wake up, you mongrel!'

My legs feel like jelly and I am walking on sponge. I wish the person in my head would stop hammering. I want to lie down. I don't want to open my eyes. I want to be left alone. I'm annoyed that this stranger won't let me die. Too weak to scream at him, I plead, 'Please don't yell, just leave me alone.' Perspiration oozes from my body. I wonder if I am waking up after a crazy nightmare.

'Here, drink this!' says the stranger. My eyes slowly open and the bright light pierces them like slivers of glass. Suddenly, the room starts to spin. I feel the stranger's strong arm around my waist, holding me steady. I sense

1

warmth in his voice as he lowers his tone and says, 'Come on, drink this.'

Looking down I see a large, chipped coffee mug in his hand. Steam is curling from its rim. He gently holds it to my mouth. I manage to swallow most of the warm, black liquid but some trickles down the sides of my mouth.

'Come on, you have to keep walking!'

'Please mate, let me sit down for a moment. No more!'

Lowering me onto a chair he asks, 'Can you see me?'

'Yeah, you and your twin brother!'

'You crazy bugger. I thought I'd lost you. Try and stand on your feet, son.'

Rising to my feet, I begin to shuffle slowly around the room. My first steps are very tentative. I sit on a chair to prevent myself from collapsing. Another hot coffee is placed on the kitchen table next to my shaking hands. I am afraid to pick up the cup because I know I won't be able to hold it. Gradually, the fog begins to clear and I see the outline of my saviour. He is a man of medium build, has thick grey hair and is about fifty years old. His face is warm and compassionate. Not knowing whether it is night or day I ask him the time. I'm not even sure what day it is.

He smiles. 'It's 10 a.m. By the way, my name is Jack.'

'Who?'

'Jack.'

'Why did you come here, mate?'

'You called last night. Don't you remember?'

'No.'

'You said you wanted help. The earliest I could get here was six this morning.'

'How did you get into the place?'

He grins and points towards Helen playing with her doll on the kitchen floor. 'Your little girl was sitting on the front steps with the door wide open. I asked her where her daddy was and she said you were asleep. I came straight in and found you stretched out on the kitchen floor.'

'Did you say you arrived at six?'

'Yes. I was on my way to work.'

'Does this mean you have been trying to revive me for four hours?'

'About that long, son. Just as well I came early this morning, otherwise I don't think you would have made it.'

I feel shocked and confused. A volcano starts to erupt just above my navel and I yell, 'Watch it, Jack, I'm gonna be sick!' He steps away gingerly as I hurry to the bathroom. I vomit on the floor and stench fills the room. I feel ashamed and worthless as he tries to clean up the mess. I cannot find a reason to keep going. My soul and spirit seem lifeless as I bury my face in my hands.

'All the pills I took last night were supposed to end this nightmare. I don't want to drink. Honest I don't. I just can't live without it. I even stuffed up killing myself. I can't take any more pain,' I tell him. He rests his hand on my shoulder for encouragement. He knows my mind is in a fog and that it is pointless saying anything. He understands my plight and I'm grateful he is here.

Helen comes over and places her tiny hand on mine. I sense the warmth of her touch as she asks, 'Daddy, are you sick?'

'Yes, love, but I'll be better soon. Go and play with your doll. Let Daddy sit here for a little while. I'll be all right.'

Jack realises that Helen is probably hungry. When he cannot find any food in the house he visits the local shop to buy sandwiches. Helen tucks into them with relish. I cannot look at food. Jack surveys the worn linoleum, stained walls and tarnished old furniture. He knows the place is a rough apology for accommodation and asks, 'Does any of the furniture belong to you, Cliff?'

'I only own a suitcase and a few clothes.'

'Come on, mate. The pair of you can't stay in this shit hole any longer. Let's pack and get both of you out of here. Come over to my place at Haberfield.'

Twenty minutes later Jack's wife, Ellie, warmly greets us. A smile comes over Helen's face as she nestles into the welcoming arms of this kind, caring woman.

'Are you hungry, darling?'

'Yes.' Helen is very shy around strangers but she always has a good appetite. A couple of hours ago she devoured three sandwiches and a cake. Now she eats Ellie's food with gusto. Food is my last priority.

'Here's a towel, mate. Get in the shower and clean yourself up. There's some fresh clothes on your bed in the spare room,' Jack says.

After days without showering, getting clean feels like a traumatic event. I am weak and have trouble standing but the warm water soothes my aching body. In the bedroom I smell the freshness of the clean linen. My head touches the pillow and I am asleep within seconds.

'Teena! Teena!' Helen is calling Jack's dog and her voice interrupts my sleep. The dog is barking. Helen is laughing and Jack is telling her to throw the ball. My mind is still foggy when Ellie appears in the doorway. I stretch my arms and ask the time. She tells me it is just after 9 a.m. and that I have been asleep for nearly seventeen hours.

These wonderful people play host to a man whose nerve endings are ripped to shreds. My guilt and disgust prevent me from sitting with them at mealtimes. Thank God they are patient and understanding. It takes a few days for me to feel human.

On the second day I manage a little breakfast. From across the kitchen I see that Jack has a serious look on his face. He says, 'Ellie and I have been discussing the future for you and Helen with our parish priest, Cliff. We're worried about the Welfare Department hearing about your situation and taking Helen from you. Father John has spoken to St Joseph's Home for Children and they have agreed to look after Helen for you. What do you think?'

I am shattered. The thought of losing my child causes me to remain silent.

I find myself hesitating as I look up and read the large sign: ST JOSEPH'S HOME FOR CHILDREN. I feel numb as I climb the circular steps leading to the large, double oak doors of the institution. Helen's face shows confusion and fear as she tightly clutches my trouser pocket with her tiny hand. She seems to be silently asking, 'What are we doing here, Daddy?' I try to comfort her by explaining the situation and cuddling her.

The door suddenly opens and we are greeted by a Catholic nun dressed in pure white. Panic and nausea cause my body to shake as she ushers us into a small office. Helen and I hide our grief by remaining silent. My head is shooting out arrows of confusion in many directions. I do not know whether to scream or faint at this moment of truth. I am frightened of losing Helen because I need her more than she needs me. She is my reason for living. She gives me the identity of being something human. She gives me fatherhood, dignity, safety, communication and unconditional love. I want to pick her up and run to the end of the earth. Instead, all I hear is Jack's words: 'Helen can't be exposed to the elements of skid row.' I know the only thing to do is to sign the paperwork. I feel like I am signing my own death certificate, because now I have nothing to live for.

Formalities completed, the nun informs me I should go. I walk through the doorway and turn to see the large, oak door slowly closing. My small child is standing alongside the woman in white. Helen's face is unmoving—no screams, tears or sounds. She appears to be frozen in fear. It is the child's eyes that haunt me. Her eyes say it all: 'Daddy, don't leave me. Daddy, I'll be good. Please don't go. Why are you going without me, Daddy?' The door slams shut. My legs almost collapse from underneath me as I walk away. The guilt is unbearable. I am failing the only love I have. I am abandoning my beautiful child.

Sixteen years of heavy drinking has cost a lot more than the price of alcohol. I have sacrificed the opportunity for a career in theatre and music. I have two failed marriages, and have lost two other daughters through those failures. Now my greatest cost is leaving Helen in an orphanage. At thirty-five I feel a total failure.

The Photo

1995.

Helen is now thirty-eight. She is a vivacious, witty, self-confident, attractive woman, who is a devoted mother of three. Many people often describe Helen as a replica of that great American actress, Bette Midler. The bond between Helen and I is strong. It was born during our journey of pain, which we travelled together and survived.

I open her letter and feel a warm glow inside. Within the letter is a small reprint of a photograph taken of Helen when she was five years old. On the back are the words, 'To Dad, all my love, your little girl, Helen xxxx.' The child in this photograph leaps out at me. She was always so trusting, accepting the circumstances of our lives. She was quiet and very patient with me. She never complained except when out of necessity she would utter the words, 'I'm hungry, Daddy.'

How she survived or understood the many horrific

situations we found ourselves in I'll never know. Even today I find it hard to believe that our journey through life has not damaged her. Sometimes when people ask her about her childhood she replies, 'I had a great childhood. It was never boring and I loved the variety. As long as I was with Dad, that's all that mattered. I always knew Dad loved me. He was a happy, kind drunk, who sang songs at three in the morning and other times bought me flowers.'

I gaze at the picture for a long time. Memories of the past come to life—the times of struggle, pain, hunger and being lost. I remember one particular Friday, in winter 1962. I find myself sitting on a grassy plot of land on the outskirts of the city. Darkness is closing in and the winter's chill is reaching my bones. Helen is wrapped in my old coat, sleeping soundly. I have been drinking for days and now begin to experience the horrors of delirium tremens.

My brain seems electrified, lightning flashes strike inside my skull, and the sour taste of fear is very real. My hands tremble. I'm scared and on the edge of going mad. Panic takes over and my breathing accelerates rapidly. My nose is running. I'm shaking all over. Madness makes me believe my head has exploded off my shoulders like a rocket. My thoughts are those of a crazy person. How come my tongue is stuck to the roof of my mouth? Why don't I have a head? Stark terror is my only emotion. Aimlessly, I run in all directions looking for my head and screaming to the heavens, 'No! No! Jesus Christ, don't do this to me! Please, God, don't destroy me!' I finally collapse in an alcoholic seizure.

Later, as I open my eyes, I find myself flat on my back lying in tall, wet grass. With glassy eyes I look up at the clouds. They reflect the glow of the outer city lights. Totally exhausted and defeated, sweat pours from every opening in my skin. It is the middle of winter yet all I can feel is heat. I feel so consumed with my own mortality and the devil claiming my soul that no other thought seems able to enter my head. Fear overwhelms me as I realise that I am going to die alone in this park. My instant need for human contact allows a split second of sanity.

'Helen!' I yell. Wild-eyed, I flounder through the grass until I find her. She is still sound asleep. I lower myself to the ground alongside her and lie down with my forearm across my eyes. I want the world to vanish. Wrung out and beaten, a soft moan escapes my lips as I fall into a deep sleep.

The cold, puny, yellow sunrise casts its sickly fingers of daylight across the lost souls of the night. Slowly, I sit up. The aroma of damp earth reaches my nostrils—the smell is a mixture of chilled death and fear. Helen is still in a deep sleep. My whole being is flooded with guilt and remorse as questions enter my head: How did I finish in this condition? Why am I like this? Why do I continually drink alcohol in this crazy way? How can I stop? How could I have done this to Helen?'

A murmur escapes Helen's lips and she awakens. She stands, rubs her eyes with the back of her hands, and looks at me with her angelic face, her large, enquiring blue eyes. 'I'm hungry, Daddy. Where's Mummy?' Her little body is still wrapped in the old coat. Her curly blonde hair is in need of a comb. I see her inner confusion as she wonders why we are in this dreadful place. Why isn't her mother here?

How can I look after this child? Where can I get money for food and shelter? Looking up to the heavens, I offer a small, pitiful prayer, 'God, or Jesus, or whoever you are, for Christ's sake help us.' I, too, am a small frightened child. I wonder if I close my eyes long enough will everything disappear. I close my eyes. I open them again, expecting that life will be beautiful and full of joy. It is not. Jesus, I need a drink, NOW! I'm starting to shake again. I fear another alcoholic seizure. I take hold of Helen's hand. 'I don't know where Mummy is. Let's get out of here.'

It takes about ten minutes to walk from the paddock of tangled green to Liverpool railway station. A mixture of rage, fear and pity runs through my being. I am on a journey to God knows where, to God knows what! The attendant on gate duty at the station is chattering away to a young woman, trying to impress her. I have no money for tickets, so we sneak quickly through the gates. Fortunately, he does not see us.

In the station waiting room's mirror the reflection of a complete stranger stares back at me. He is a derelict with dark, unruly hair plastered in all directions. He has swollen, red eyes and one week's growth of tar-black stubble on his face. His coat is crumpled and creased. The lapels of his coat are turned up in a fitting manner for a circus clown. His trousers have a busted fly and he has not bathed for some time. When I realise the stranger is me, I am shocked. I feel everybody in this room is looking at me, and draw my coat across the front of my trousers. My attempt to look human, by running my fingers through my dishevelled, damp hair, fails. Thankfully, our train arrives within minutes and I escape those glaring eyes.

We arrive at Central station. People are jostling and hurrying to get to their destinations. In front of me are three burly ticket collectors dressed in dark-blue railway uniforms; they are guarding the three exit gates. My heart is almost beating through my chest as I panic. How can I escape this lot? After studying the stern, official faces underneath the dark-blue caps, I know my only option is to run. I lift Helen up into my arms and tell her what I am about to do. She giggles and thinks it's funny. An elderly passenger is conversing with one of the ticket collectors. I realise this person can shield me from the burly bouncer. I take a deep breath and walk briskly through the exit gate.

Once through the gate I let out a deep sigh of relief. Helen is still laughing and she causes me to smile. Then a booming voice from the blimp in blue suddenly echoes throughout the enclosed walls of the station: 'Hey! You! You with the kid! Where are your tickets? Hey you! Come back here right now!'

Fear motivates me. I run through the underground station and don't stop until I reach the Haymarket. Here on the 'Mad Mile', the skid row of Sydney, I am swallowed up in a mass of people moving in all directions. Putting Helen down I suck in the air as my legs begin to tremble. Helen laughs again, thinking it is a wonderful game. It is quite novel for me to be running instead of staggering. Looking around for a friendly face, I see none. My silent plea comes from within: God almighty, will this nightmare ever end?

'Where are we going, Daddy?' my little child asks.

There is only one answer to Helen's question. 'Hell,' I mutter quietly to myself.

I almost drop the photograph of Helen as these memories send a shiver down my spine. Many people used to say, 'That Cliff Nichols is such a talented boy. He has the potential to put Glebe on the map!' Why didn't I put Glebe on the map? What went wrong? How did I end up an alcoholic? It is many years since I have been to Glebe. Maybe the walls of my childhood home can reveal the secrets of what happened and why I descended into the pit of alcoholism. Is that where it all started? Suddenly I need to know. I write a letter to the owners of 2 Jarocin Avenue, Glebe, requesting permission to visit.

2 Jarocin Avenue, Glebe

Before me is a lifetime of memories. The square glass panel at the top of the front door has the word 'ZARA' painted on it in gold letters. This is my old home and birthplace. Walking up to the front door I take a deep breath and knock. There is no response. Perhaps nobody is at home. I hesitate and knock once more. The door swings open and a young man in his thirties, dressed in a business suit, gives me a curious look. 'Yes, what can I do for you?' he inquires.

In a flurry of words I blurt out, 'My name is Cliff Nichols. I spoke to Kate on the phone today about having a look through my old home.' I suddenly feel rather stupid.

He smiles, then extends his hand, and I shake it gladly. 'Hello, Cliff. I'm Phillip, Kate's husband. Please come in. Kate is not home at the moment but you're more than welcome to have a look through.'

Relieved that Phillip is so friendly, I walk through the

14

front door and instantly know I am beginning a lone journey through a time tunnel.

It is winter. My mother Nell, Aunt Anne and I are sitting in the dining room in front of a blazing wood fire. In my hand is a long wire fork. I am toasting a thick slice of bread over the golden embers. My hands are still stinging after getting the cane today; I am always in trouble for not paying attention at school. The only way I can get mass approval is by being the class clown. The pain of getting the cane is not as bad as being unnoticed. There is a tiny explosion in the crackling firewood and a spark flies out onto the tiles. I jump and laugh in a rather nervous manner.

In the kitchen, the pantry is only partially filled because of the hard times. The only snack to be found is a piece of homemade apricot pie, made from lard because Nell cannot afford butter. For us and many others, the fashion of the day is poverty due to the Great Depression.

Saturday nights I go to Harold Park Paceway, which is just a five-minute walk from my home. I earn money by opening taxi doors for the patrons. Sometimes this earns me a penny, threepence or, if I am lucky, sixpence. I love to buy sweets or go to the movies with my hard-earned cash. The price of admission to the movies is threepence. Sometimes I see my favourite shows, such as Charlie Chan, the Chinese detective, my western hero, Hopalong Cassidy, and that man of the future, Flash Gordon. At eight, I start gambling and become a regular customer of the illegal bookmaker, Mr Furlong, who lives across the avenue. I have dreams of getting rich, and try to make my fortune backing racehorses. Occasionally the thrill of winning is mine.

It's the mid-thirties. The 'fairer sex' are not allowed to enter a hotel. My young mates and I are sent swaggering up the street armed with either a china jug, billy can or saucepan to purchase beer from the public bar. The Town Hall Hotel's draught beer is the cheapest and I pay for it with money my mother has safely tied in a handkerchief. I hate the embarrassment of these moments because everybody stares at me. They all know I am taking this contraband home to my mother and aunt, who are having a daily 'whistle wetting' in between household chores.

Home again, I open the small iron door on the front of the black fuel stove in our kitchen and feed pieces of timber into the flames. The fire heats the flat cooking surface and I can smell the aroma of curried neck chops for the evening meal. That is all the household budget can afford. In the adjoining room is a circular, bricked in, golden copper full of water. It is wash day and the water is being heated from underneath by a blazing wood fire. My Aunt Anne is doing the weekly wash. How I hate wash days! After she finishes washing, the leftover water is carried upstairs by bucket to the bathroom and I'm expected to bathe in it!

I hear Phillip greeting Kate as she arrives home, and I step out into the backyard to get some fresh air. Staring at the tiny yard, one of those frightening secrets I thought I could forget suddenly springs to life. I am nineteen years old and have just begun drinking. I decide to pay Nell a visit. It is coming on dusk and the front door is open. I walk through the house calling out, 'Anyone home?' I eventually find Nell standing in this small backyard. She is alone, intoxicated and swaying back and forth. I walk towards her, unaware of what is about to transpire. Alcohol gives me the courage to put my arms around her and hold her tightly. I am always wanting to do this because I have so much love to give her. I somehow want once more to become the unborn child within Nell, to start from the beginning again. Perhaps on my rebirth then I will have my mother, not just Nell the alcoholic. All I want is someone to call mother, and for her to love me as her son. Nell loosens my arms and pushes me away saying, 'What's wrong with you? Are you mad?' Feeling the ultimate rejection, which makes me empty and sick inside, I turn and walk back through the house. Outside, the street lights are being turned on. My footsteps lead me to the nearest hotel and oblivion.

Phillip introduces me to Kate when I walk back into the dining room. 'I guess the old place has changed considerably, Cliff?' Kate asks.

'Yes, Kate,' is my reply, knowing she is unaware of what I am seeing. What my mind is viewing was there twenty years before Kate was born.

After climbing to the top of the solid timber stairs I see the bathroom. The grey, iron bathtub is on one side, and standing like a sentry on guard-duty over the bath is the good old chip heater. I called it 'Puffing Billy'. Walking along the top corridor, Phillip and I pause at the closed doorway before us. Phillip's hand grasps the door knob and slowly swings the door open. I try to swallow the saliva that quickly floods my mouth. My breathing increases and there is a mixture of anticipation and fear as I wonder what the room is going to reveal. Nell has been dead for such a long time. Slowly, I enter my mother's bedroom.

My parents' lives come back to me as if I might truly find them here. My mother, Ellen Agnes Nichols, was known to all as Nell or Nellie. She and my father tried to conceive a child for ten years before my arrival. Nell was thirty-four when I was born. Photographs of her around the age of twenty years portray a lovely looking young woman. She was small and slim with shoulder-length, fair hair and twinkling blue eyes. Her face was so alive and beautiful that many advertising agencies and department stores employed her to model millinery. Nell spoke with a rich, modulated voice and in perfect English. She also had a wonderful sense of humour, which made her a popular companion for many.

Fred, my father, was also small, yet of solid build, with light-brown, hazel eyes and a soft, quiet manner. He had a large bald patch on the rear of his head, where thick black wavy hair once grew. His face portrayed his wonderful warmth and love. He was a rare, caring man. Fred was part of the original gallant force of Australian soldiers who landed and fought at Gallipoli in the Great War in 1915. While serving there as a stretcher-bearer, he collapsed with trench fever. Three days later he regained consciousness while on board a hospital ship sailing for India. He then realised the fever had caused most of his hair to fall out. After seeing the devastation of war, Fred was motivated by love and compassion for his fellow human beings, especially the underprivileged. He was often seen busking at local hotels, earning money to give people a helping hand. Later in life I was to become one of those people who needed his help.

Nell and Fred's marriage broke up in 1929. I was two years old. My mother's sister, Anne, had come to live with us and as the old saying goes, 'two's company and three's a crowd'. I did not understand how this caused the breakdown of their marriage, when all I saw was both of them always showing the greatest respect for each other. I never heard either one of them say a bad word concerning the other.

It had been common knowledge that Nell never, ever touched alcohol. In fact, she detested the stuff so much that she would not allow anybody to bring alcohol into her house. But in 1935 everything changed. It was a day of extreme heatwave conditions, and my mother was helping a neighbour, Elsie, with her ironing. The only airconditioning was a hand-held fan, waved to and fro across the face. Nell started to feel dehydrated and asked Elsie for a glass of cold cordial or ice water. Elsie opened the ice chest door and then realised that she had forgotten to buy cordial and there was no ice water. Then Elsie made a dangerous suggestion: 'Now don't get angry, Nell. The only thing cold in the ice chest is a bottle of white wine.' But Nell was so thirsty she accepted a small glass of the cold wine, her first taste of alcohol at forty-one. After the first drink, the desire for more took over. 'Elsie, pour me another one, please, and make it larger this time.' The compulsion to drink alcohol daily then became as common to Nell as other people having cups of tea. Unfortunately, more booze went down Nell's throat each day than the amount of tea consumed by others. Nell did not realise that I witnessed the ravages of alcohol abuse as a child and teenager. I began to detest and loathe alcohol as Nell once did. It was sad to see booze become Nell's master; it not only tore away the beauty of her face and body, but like evil acid it ate away at her mind, soul and, finally, her spirit.

'Who slept in this room, Cliff?' Phillip once more interrupts my thoughts.

'Actually, my mother and I shared this room up until I was about seven. She then arranged for me to sleep out there on the balcony.' I point to the area just off my mother's bedroom. I do not tell Phillip how isolated I felt sleeping out there after my mother started drinking.

Gazing around the bedroom I am astonished to see the old wooden mantelpiece on the far wall. I remember the little mementos of miniature pottery, tiny framed photos and bric-a-brac, which sat proudly on coffee-coloured lace doilies. I am a child watching Nell still sleeping in her four-poster bed. Daylight is about to filter through the window. I can smell acidic urine from the bucket under her bed and the linoleum floor is cold under my small bare feet. I am a young boy desperately wanting Nell's recognition and needing her love. I quietly drag a chair over towards the mantelpiece. I stand on it, reach up, slowly remove the eight objects and place each one on the floor. Looking to check if Nell is still sleeping, I tell myself to be quiet because I want this to be a surprise. I tiptoe along the hallway towards the bathroom, dampen a small cloth and return to the bedroom to wipe all of the ornaments. Replacing each one in its rightful place, I then proudly survey my finished work. I sit down on a chair and wait.

Time seems to pass so slowly. It is very quiet and cold. The only sound to be heard is the continuous tick, tick, tick from the small clock on my mother's bedside table. The silence is broken by little moans coming from Nell's lips. I know when Nell awakens the first thing she will see is the mantelpiece. When she notices my good work maybe she will put her arms around me and give me a big cuddle. Then she will tell me I'm a wonderful boy and that she is so proud of me.

Nell does not notice my cleaning. I perform this ritual another eight or nine times over the next six weeks before realising Nell will never ever notice. Each time my efforts go unrewarded, I shrug my small shoulders and say, 'It's all right. It doesn't matter.' The truth is, a small part of me dies inside. I feel I do not belong.

Holding back my tears, a strange feeling envelopes me. I am only eight yet I am aware that sympathy for my plight is coming from the four walls of this room. These walls have watched over me since infancy and have offered protection for mother and child. They have seen and held the warmth, comfort, laughter, music and love between my mother and I. Now the walls witness the death of this bond as alcohol enters my mother's life. The room is filled with so much sadness that the walls begin to weep at the sight of my abandonment.

'Many wonderful memories, Cliff?' Phillip intrudes.

Trying to hide my feelings, I reply, 'Yes, Phillip, lots of memories!'

We walk out onto the balcony off my mother's bedroom. It all seems too much for me, though I appreciate the fresh air here. Phillip senses the impact this visit is having upon me, excuses himself and goes downstairs. I am now alone on the balcony.

Boy on the Balcony

The rain is fine and misty, falling on the rooftop in a quiet, lonely way. At the far end of the open balcony I am safely huddled between two worn blankets. My face is pressed against the iron lattice railing and I stare at the street below. The fresh, clean rain is soothing. I have dark-brown eyes, which match the colour of my thick hair and olive skin. My build is small for an eight-year-old. I love to dance, sing and entertain but I am isolated as an only child, and I long for the companionship of a little brother or sister.

I have unfounded fears which sometimes mount to stark terror. I occasionally envisage a person with a hideous face and a huge knife, climbing up here to where I sleep. I know he is coming to get me. I keep looking down to the street below, knowing my killer will appear at any moment. My anxiety causes me to be violently ill at times and my mother, Nell, often tells people that I am highly strung. I have a strong need to be held warmly in my mother's arms for reassurance and safety. Unfortunately, this need is rarely met now she is drinking. I miss her warmth and love and lie awake for many hours being afraid of the unknown. Nell is downstairs drinking wine with my Aunt Anne. She will stumble through the door of her bedroom later and fall into a deep sleep. The only thing that seems alive is a lone wooden light pole rising from the glistening street below. My eyes are held in hypnotic trance by its leering, fat light-globe half hidden underneath its metal collar. My focus is challenging the lone globe in its attempt to illuminate the dead night surrounds. The misty rain creates a colourful rainbow dance around the little white light. The magic of intermingling colours and gentle swaying of the pole in the sweeping wind give me comfort. This is my companion of the night. How I wish my light pole could talk to me.

I eagerly look forward to the weekends. My father calls on Saturdays and takes me on outings to the movies, football, ferry rides to Manly and many other surprises. It seems to break the isolation and loneliness I feel.

I love it when he takes me to some of the many eating establishments in the city. He first introduces me to 'fine dining' at a café called Mason's, situated at the end of Elizabeth Street, not far from the Haymarket. We walk into this place early one Saturday morning. The first thing I notice is the odour and warmth of the heavy breathing coming from the many hungry patrons. The faces of these people have the look of defeat.

'Same as usual, Fred?' The young waiter knows my Dad.

'Yes, Theo, but make it for two. This is my son, Cliff.'

'Hello, Cliff. Won't be long.'

On the table is a high stack of thickly sliced bread. During the Depression, a large bowl of soup and all the bread one could eat cost one shilling. An old man with a bushy, dirty grey beard which is slightly ginger around his upper lip and chin keeps staring at me. His eyes are a watery, pale blue and seem lifeless. While I wait for my soup my young mind wonders if he may have fathered a son in the past and if he had, did the boy die or maybe he has not seen him for many years. His focus suddenly turns to Fred and his beloved guitar alongside him. I imagine he wants Fred to play and sing a love song from his past, or play his favourite tune of days gone by. My soup tastes good and so does the bread. As I gaze around the room I see many unloved souls slurping the hot liquid into their empty stomachs. The eyes of some are almost black and very hard and they give the appearance of some wild animal from the jungle protecting their kill. Even at this age I have an affinity with these people.

The Hole in the Wall is another landmark of the early thirties. This café is located in Eddy Avenue, adjoining Central railway station. A long counter runs the length of the room. On one side are approximately twenty mushroom-type stools. The clientele are a mixed bunch; train travellers, workers and battlers. The waitress approaches and in her customary manner says: 'Yeah, what is it?'

'Pie and peas, please.'

'Do you want gravy?'

'Yes, thank you.'

Her shrill, piercing voice is then heard as she places our order: 'Sky high for two with the lot!'

My favourite restaurant, though, is a place Nell takes me to. My mum holds my hand and we stroll for thirty minutes from Glebe, heading to Grace Bros department store. I am excited. It is Christmas Eve and I'm on my way to see Him. Our first port of call is to a fairyland of food known as Sargent's. As we enter this wonderland we are greeted by a young woman dressed in a long-sleeved black dress with white cuffs at her wrists, a small white apron around her waist and a dainty white lace tiara on her head. 'Table for two?'

My nostrils are working like radar and the wonderful signals being relayed to me are of tantalising fresh coffee, pastries and bread rolls—even the other aromas of lavender water and cigar smoke add to my excitement.

Once we are seated at our table I feel my heart will burst. Nell orders our meal and my eyes travel around the room and see little golden ceiling lights. The customers are all sitting up straight, dressed in their best clothes and are chattering away quietly. On our table is a vase filled with colourful wax flowers and directly in front of me is the shiniest knife, fork and spoon I have ever seen. I can even see my face in the spoon.

The meal arrives and before me is the ultimate in luxury, a connoisseur's dream is awaiting the test of my taste buds, rumbling sounds from my belly are saying,

'It's time!' On the large white plate sits a round, brown, flakey Sargent's pie. Nestled on one side of the pie is a large mound of snow-white mashed potatoes and on the other side is a mountain of emerald-green, mushy peas. The crowning glory arrives when the waitress places a crunchy hot bread roll on my smaller plate, accompanied by a wrinkled tube of butter in a shiny metal dish. At this moment I wonder if I am dead and have gone to Heaven.

The department store is a few minutes' walk away and we are soon in the elevator, slowly ascending. First floor, second floor, third floor. 'Manchester and Santa's Castle,' says the operator. I exit the lift and there he is right before my eyes. A jolly fat man wearing a bright red floppy hat, his beautiful white beard and a sparkling smile. Around his fat tummy is a wide black belt with a shiny buckle. Fascinated, I walk slowly towards Santa. Nell lifts me up onto his knee. I nestle in and tell him what I want for Christmas—a scooter. I am ecstatic.

Although I am thrilled to receive my scooter on Christmas Day, I still struggle with the feeling of being alone. The only thing that lifts my spirits sky high is the weekend visits by my Dad. Once a month on a Sunday Fred takes me from Glebe to the other side of the harbour to the Spit, down from the blue-ribbon suburb of Mosman. Cars are all lined up for about seven hundred and fifty yards from the water's edge, waiting to drive onto the large punt which will transport them across the water. Once they reach the other side, they'll continue their journey to the famous seaside resort of

Manly or further up the peninsula to other coastal destinations. Fred and his good friend Brownie always come here to busk. They play trumpets in duet and give the bored car drivers entertainment while they wait for the punt.

At eight years of age my job is to go up and down the line of cars with a collection box in my hand, rattling the coins inside and spruiking as Fred has taught me. 'Spare a coin. The players and I have to be fed.' This causes laughter from the drivers and many make remarks like, 'You look well fed to me' or 'You need more stretching than food, Shorty.' Nevertheless, the takings are always healthy, especially considering we are in a world depression; the money made in a few hours is usually equivalent to a week's wages. My dad always hands me almost half of his Sunday earnings. He changes the coins into notes, ties them up in a handkerchief and tells me to give the money to Nell. I admire him so much, and I miss him when he is not around.

One Saturday I arrive home from one of my wonderful outings with Dad, walk into the empty house and, like most kids my age, start looking for something to eat. Without warning, heavy knocking on the front door is accompanied by a strong male voice: 'Anybody home?' I freeze with fear and cautiously walk towards the front door. A man appears before me. He is in uniform with a peaked cap on his head. At first glance I think he is a policeman.

'Your dad home, son?'

'No, he doesn't live here,' is my nervous reply.

The man eases his cap to the back of his head and says, 'Well, who else is at home?'

'Just me.'

The man squats down on his haunches, his eyes level with mine and says, 'Son, is your name Cliff?'

'Yes,' I answer, wondering how this person knows my name.

The man stands up. 'You had better come with me to Prince Alfred Hospital. I'm an ambulance officer. Your mum has had a fall. Nothing to get too worried about, young fellow. After the doctor finishes examining her you will be able to bring her home. She keeps asking for you.'

I feel a sense of wonderment being chauffeur-driven in an ambulance—my feet are my usual mode of transport—and I enjoy my ride. I am oblivious to the world around me having been plunged into the Great Depression. I have no idea of its impact on the working-class people. I do not notice the long queues at the soup kitchens or understand the shame people feel when receiving coupons to get food. Few people own a motor vehicle or telephone. I am also unaware that for some the only escape from their poverty and hopeless situation is to drown their feelings in alcohol. I am just a boy, riding in an ambulance to pick up my mum. I see the pain on people's faces but I don't know what causes it.

On arrival I am led through the hospital corridor by the ambulance driver. We reach huge double doors and as they open I see what looks like a war zone. Within this huge room, about twenty tables are covered in white sheets and used as beds. Numerous men and women have assorted bandages on their bodies. Others have arms in slings or plaster casts on their limbs. This assortment of broken humanity groans, screams and sobs. Some even hurl angry abuse at the nursing staff. I feel sick and want to run out of here. The volatile smell of chloroform mingling with the repugnant body odours is too much for me. My head spins.

Suddenly, a loud, clear, familiar voice rings out, 'There's my Cliffy. That's my boy. The one and only after ten years of trying.' The blood drains out of me as I see Nell sitting on a table with her head swathed in a blood-soaked bandage. My mother is still drunk, her bruised knees are visible through gaping holes in her stockings and her dress is splattered in blood. This sight causes shame and disgust to fill my being. Controlled anger begins to burn deep within my belly. I feel as though my feet are nailed to the floor and it is impossible for me to run away. I try to disguise my identity by bowing my head as I walk towards her slowly. She puts her band-aged arm around my shoulder and continues telling the world, 'This is my one and only.' I want to die as the nursing staff and patients turn their heads to look at me. I feel like some sort of freak born out of 'ten years of trying'. What they see is a terrified, eight-year-old boy dressed in short pants and shirt, standing barefoot along-side his drunken mother.

Everyone among the carnage recognises that this is my mother. Her disgusting appearance, alcoholic stupor and behaviour cause me to feel like disowning this woman. My shame causes me to feel nauseated. I am ashamed of my mother's existence and something within me dies for all time.

It's 1937, I am now ten years old, and there's a whole world bustling beneath my balcony. I run downstairs and outside to watch the passing parade.

Saturday mornings see Glebe come alive. For most people it is time to relax and play after the dreary working week. In our small avenue, radios are blaring out information regarding the day's horse racing. Women are leaning on small picket fences, discussing topics like movies, recent operations and recipes. One woman comments, 'Isn't it sad that Miss Davis is in hospital recovering from consumption. She should never have caught that terrible disease because she comes from such a good-living family.' Up the street, sitting on hotel doorsteps, men folk are quaffing large glasses of beer and in serious conversation about the possibility of war in Europe. A tram screeches to a grinding halt. Its passengers alight and disperse in different directions. Some hold tennis racquets, others cricket bats and footballs. All are in a jovial mood, heading for their respective sporting grounds. The man with his small horse and cart calls out, 'Rabbit, Oh! Rabbit, Oh!' He is selling fresh skinned rabbits, which provide a cheap meal. Hot on his heels is the ice man calling, 'Ice! Ice!' He produces a large pair of steel tongs, which grip each side of the frozen block. Underneath the ice he holds a chaff bag to prevent water dripping onto the customer's freshly polished linoleum floor as he carries it to the family ice chest. The parade continues: 'Milko! Milko!' I run inside, grab the milk jug and money off Nell and return to order a pint of milk. At the rear of his cart is a tap jutting out from a large box. When the milkman turns it on I watch the creamy, ice-cold milk fill his measuring container. 'There you go young fellow. One pint.' He empties the contents into my jug. The bread carter is my favourite hawker. Nestled within his large cane basket are crunchy delights. The wonderful aroma of freshly baked bread excites my nostrils as he lifts the canvas cover. After buying bread, my friends and I love to pat the bread carter's horse. It stands patiently as many flies flitter around its bridled head.

Mick, Lloyd, Tiger and Billy are my closest friends. We are standing outside the local fruit shop and are about to experience history in the making. Suddenly, a large red truck, with white and black trim, stops just a few feet from us. Its full load of crates are stacked on racks at a forty-five degree angle and within each crate are row after row of small dark-brown bottles. Three men dressed in khaki uniforms and peaked caps leap from the truck. One of the men, who is clutching some of these bottles, heads straight for our little group. We are bewildered when he speaks to us in an excited tone. 'Here, boys, try the new drink sensation!' He reaches for a bottle opener, which is hanging on a chain around his neck. After flicking the caps off the bottles he hands each one of us a drink. In a flash he is gone across the road to a group of curious adults. Receiving something for nothing is unheard of in these hard times. We stare at each other, then start to giggle. Sipping from our little bottles, our eyes start to water from the fizzy taste. Lloyd lets out a thunderous belch that causes great laughter. Within seconds we are all performing our own 'Fizzy Belch Opera'. I look at the writing on the bottle and call out loudly, 'Hey boys, "Coca-Cola" is the name of this drink.'

Two other memorable events also occur this year. The first happens one winter's evening. I am chatting with my Aunt Anne and I hear Nell come home and call out, 'Where are you?'

'Upstairs,' I yell.

As Nell climbs the stairs my nose smells a very strange aroma. It is a mixture of barbecued meat and roast dinner, which grows stronger as my mother gets closer. Nell is holding three brown paper bags, each with a round grease pattern coming through the paper.

'What have you got?' I ask.

'It's a new American thing,' Nell informs me. 'I bought them at a new food shop in Glebe Road. Everybody is buying them. They cook them on a large hotplate in front of you while you wait.'

We tear the bags open. In front of me is a feast. I lift the top off the round, toasted, bread roll and see a thin slab of brown, cooked meat, slices of pink tomato, deep red beetroot and golden pieces of cooked onions. All of this is crowned with heavy shreds of bright green lettuce and a smear of scarlet tomato sauce. I extend my jaws, chomp down and taste a little bit of heaven. The juice from this wonderful food runs down either side of my mouth. 'Boy, this tastes good!' I exclaim to my mother. 'What do they call these?'

'Hamburgers.'

Aunt Anne, who has half devoured her hamburger, looks up and says, 'They don't taste much like ham to me. More of a beef flavour!'

Nell and I nod our heads in agreement.

My mum smiles at me. 'You are really enjoying this treat, aren't you, son?'

'Yes, Nell. I sure am.' The feeling of sharing these moments with my mum is heart-warming for me and we both chatter away as we continue to eat.

When Nell thinks it is show time she picks up a magazine and asks, 'Are you going to read from this, Joe?' Joe is Nell's nickname for me. She loves me devising humorous plays to make her laugh.

I pick up the magazine and read the various advertisements and make up my own dialogue. 'Do you suffer with body odour? If you do, then our soap will take it away if you swallow a cake every day! Are you a wallflower at the local dance because you are not tall enough? Well if you are, increase your height by having your legs pulled!' I see a picture of a skinny little man sitting on a sandy beach, which portrays a well-developed, muscular bully kicking sand into an unfortunate person's face. 'Do you wish you could fight back? You can if you take our three-month course on body development. You will then be so strong that you can drown the mongrel!' Nell laughs and tears begin to roll down her cheeks. I feel so close to her and continue my show hoping these intimate moments will last forever. Unfortunately they don't.

On another day Nell arrives home with yet another one of her discoveries. Among her grocery shopping is a small jar which contains something like solid black molasses. Aunt Anne stares at this weird item and asks Nell, 'What in the name of God have you got here?'

Nell, the 'Finder of Exotic Foods', replies, 'It's fairly new in the shops. See here on the label, it says to spread thinly on a slice of bread.'

We put this new wonder to the taste test. Aunt Anne is the first to react: 'I'm not too sure. It's unusual.' My reaction to this new product is to ask for a second helping. My mum takes one bite and then pushes the plate away. 'I don't like this at all. I'm sure this stuff will never be successful with the Australian public.'

Nell could not have been more wrong with her prediction. This 'stuff', as she called it, is today one of the most popular products to have ever graced the tables of Australian homes. It is a household name—Vegemite.

I love music, and this love is inherited from my father, who is a very good musician. He played trombone with the Cooma Brass Band as a small boy. Later in life he was a member of the Anzac Memorial Australian Army Band. I, in turn, at the age of seven, become a member of the Glebe District Silver Band. I start my musical career by playing the triangle and then progress to tenor horn.

One day I am passing the front door of the local delicatessen when I hear the most beautiful music coming from an upstairs room. I am compelled to walk into the shop and ask the woman behind the counter if I can see and listen to the person playing the music. Mrs Toppano introduces herself. She is a warm, kind Italian woman, who admires the courage I have for a nine-year-old. 'Just a moment and I'll check. Enzo!' she calls from the foot of the stairs. 'Enzo. Please come down here for a minute.'

A young, dark-haired lad about my age appears. He is shy yet very warm. There is an instant affinity between us. He spends so many hours practising his music that he is very lonely for companionship. When his mother says, 'This young fellow heard you playing your music and wants to know if he could listen and watch while you practise. What do you think?'

'Sure, that's fine with me. My name is Enzo. What's yours?'

'Cliffy.' For the next two hours I am fascinated by his passion for music and his flashing fingers. This is the beginning of a life-long friendship.

I am so eager to learn to play like Enzo that I tell my dad all about our meeting. Fred, who also has a passion for music, senses my excitement and approaches Enzo's dad to ask about purchasing a piano accordion for me. To help pay my instrument off, Fred takes a night-shift job at an engineering factory for two years. He wants his son to have the opportunity for the musical career that he longed for. I am excited to hold my own instrument and feel so proud. I love learning and practising with Enzo. Nell is tone deaf and does not understand why I continually practise the scales and exercises rather than play a tune. She does not know much about music.

I am a restless young fellow, who detests the regimented school routines. I prefer to play music rather than to study. In 1940 I decide to leave school. When I tell Nell she does not object even though my job prospects are limited. I manage to find work as a paperboy in Glebe, then as a lunch boy at an ammunitions factory followed by a labourer in a timber factory.

I remain in the Glebe band. At thirteen my friends and I spend most of our nights playing snooker in a sleazy, downstairs den known as the Crystal Palace Pool Hall, near Central railway station. One night, around 5 a.m. we finish playing pool, walk back to Glebe and sit on the footpath. We talk and wait for sunrise. Medical science could have coined the phrase hyperactive to describe me as a young lad. I have boundless energy. My pals are exhausted and horizontal on the footpath, staring at the stars. I come alive and start tap dancing on the road to my own accompaniment. Songs like 'Carolina in the Morning', 'When You're Smiling', and 'Bye Bye Blues' are my forte. Initially, my audience gives me a round of applause but after my sixth encore they are tired of my antics. They rudely interject. 'Drop dead, will ya, Cliffy. Piss off. Give us a break.' This is my cue to conclude the performance and slowly walk home.

Now that I am contributing financially to the household, Nell has extra money for additional luxuries. We can now afford to buy a chip heater for the bathroom. This gives us the luxury of hot running water. This is the year of celebration for our home. Progress at last! No more filling buckets with soapy wash-day water from the copper and carrying it up the stairs to the bathroom. Thanks to science, all I have to do now is light the wonderful chip heater to have instant hot water. I read the instructions on how to have my first bath. I add wood chips and paper and turn the cold water tap on. Then I light the chip heater as a steady stream of water passes through the pipes. At first nothing happens, then a strange sound of rumbling and gurgling occurs as the water is being heated. The steady flow of hot water commences. With this flow, a peculiar chanting sound of woof, woof, woof is heard. It is similar to a steam train picking up speed. My imagination starts to run wild. It sounds like a metallic volcano building up to a violent crescendo that will not only blow our house to bits but literally devastate the whole bloody Glebe neighbourhood. Fearfully, I call out, 'Nell! Is this thing all right?' She hurriedly comes and checks out what is happening and reassures me that I am safe. I then relax into a bath with hot water up to my armpits. It feels good to be wealthy!

Soaking in the bath, my thoughts go back to the hardship of the 1930s. These were very hard times, but though it was tough, my mates and I would always manage to find our pleasures—even in the simplest things. I smile as I remember my lunchtime ritual back in schooldays. The moment the bell rang, my mate and

I would hurry down to the local bakery and buy a three-penny loaf of Vienna bread. This loaf was about ten inches long and four and a half inches deep and we would get the baker to slice it in half. Then we would rush to the fish and chip shop where each of us would purchase one penny's worth of hot potato chips and two potato scallops costing one half penny each. Then we would prepare for our feast. Firstly, we would pull all of the warm dough out of the bread and then tip the pile of potato chips and hot scallops into the hole in the loaf. This was followed by the methodical shoving of the dough back into its rightful place, forcing it down onto the hot cuisine within.

Our hands would be quivering and our mouths watering as we anticipated eating our creation. We would then open our mouths as wide as we could and like a human guillotine our teeth would plunge into this ecstasy from Heaven. The hot, salty taste was wonderful and our cheeks would be bulging on either side. All my mate and I could do was smile at each other. No words were spoken. This ritual took about ten minutes. We used to say our bellies were full up to the collar bone. Our jaws would ache for another five minutes before we would say, 'That feels better.'

These were very hard times, though, and Nell always taught me to keep my dignity no matter what. Very few parents in the Glebe district could afford to buy fruit for their children, so it was a rare sight to see any child eating fruit at school. When a privileged lad produced a juicy, red apple he was instantly surrounded by young boys.

They would sit cross-legged in a half-circle near him and watch him chew his way through the juicy flesh of the fruit. Each of the audience would call out, 'Will ya leave us the core?' When the apple was eaten right down, leaving only a couple of dark seeds and a meagre wisp of apple, the 'Apple King' would then throw the core up into the air. The gathered throng would scramble to try and grab the prize. I never participated in this game, however, because of Nell's wonderful advice: 'Son, never settle for someone's leftovers. If they do not offer food or sweets prior to eating, never accept what is left after they have had their fill.'

Nell has learnt about people through her own humiliation and loss of dignity, and she has taught me about those people who represent everything in the character of a human being that she loathes—selfishness, lack of caring and thoughtlessness.

I begin to realise that despite Nell's compulsion to drink, her heartache and pain, she continually stands by me. Through her times of great struggle people want her to put me into a boys home. She refuses to do this because of her great love for me. I often see her on bended knees scrubbing and polishing other people's floors. I even see the ugly sight of her thumbnail being torn out as she catches it on the rough floor boards.

I also understand the indignity of this once proud Grace Bros model now ironing other people's clothes and being taken advantage of when she is repaid for her loyalty and hard labour with glasses of alcohol or a menial wage. All I want her to do is to stop drinking to save herself from the humiliation. Every time I see her drink another glass of alcohol I ask myself, 'Why doesn't she just stop?' I am very insecure and need my mother to be close to me. I want her to hold me and love me. I hate the thought of her becoming a distant stranger. I begin to carry the burden of her shame and feel guilty that I could somehow be responsible for her strange behaviour. Her existence seems to equate with that old saying: 'The other day upon a stair, I saw a woman who wasn't there.'

Eventually I comprehend that she is unable to stop. Even though Nell has an addiction to alcohol she demonstrates great effort to survive in the face of humiliation. She clings desperately to her life principles and manages to successfully impart these into my life. She often says, 'Son, if you can't say a nice word about someone, then say nothing at all', or 'Remember, Cliff, resentment, bitterness and revenge are wasted emotions.' She has a quiet faith in God and I often see her bless herself as she passes the Catholic Church.

Fred also equips me for life with his ethics. Like Nell, he also dislikes greed and frequently tells me, 'Cliff, never save up to go broke. The mental asylums are not just reserved for the poor.' He is also a person who sticks to his principles and says, 'Always keep your shoes shined and never lose your principles.' I, too, become like Nell and Fred. What I detest most of all in life is greed.

I become tired of watching my mother drink and a need to escape this degrading lifestyle begins to surface. I feel like I will suffocate if I stay in Glebe any longer.

I need to run away to breathe. I remember my days as a young boy on the balcony and my dreams about all the great things life has to offer me. I dreamed about being a professional footballer, winning at Wimbledon and being a priest and jockey. I heard the cheers of the crowd as I was crowned boxing champion of the world. I loved this fantasy world. It helped me escape from my fears and the reality of life with Nell. It put my mind at peace so I could sleep. Part of me wants to go back to the balcony yet the need to escape Glebe is stronger.

Man of the World

At last I have reached the mature age of fifteen, and it is time to go out and set the world on fire. Fortunately, I am unaware that I will not even get the match lit. When Nell and Aunt Anne learn about my leaving home to make my fortune, Nell's comment is, 'Wherever you're going make sure that you don't go near relations. They'll give you nothing!'

I know Nell is right. Her comment is based on her own disappointment. Two of her sisters are very wealthy women yet neither of them offers her as much as a loaf of bread during her struggles.

Leaving Glebe is exciting for me. As I wander down Glebe Point Road toward the city the 'Symphony in Steel' is bidding me farewell. Since the outbreak of World War II, a large engineering factory operates seven days a week near my home. It provides materials for the fighting forces. I hear the metallic clang, the bloodcurdling squeal when the cutting tools jam and the loud continuous boomp, boomp, boomp of the leather conveyor belts intermingled with the choir of workers' voices as they curse, give orders or yell at each other. Everybody is in a hurry to get their tasks completed. I am on a mission of freedom.

Armed with only an old suitcase, I venture out into the unknown, but not before visiting Mr Furlong, the local illegal bookmaker—he has a soft spot for me and graciously lends me some money. He tells me, 'If you put your mind to things and work hard, then one day life will reward you. It's good that you are getting away from this unhealthy environment. This is your opportunity to start a brand new life. You deserve a chance, son. Good luck!'

Central railway station is busy with travellers moving in all directions. Porters are wheeling trolleys laden with luggage. Loud speakers are blaring out information. There are hissing sounds as a large black steam engine belches out a great vapour of white-grey mist. Above my head, suspended from the interior ceiling of the railway station, is the largest clock I have ever seen.

I step up to the ticket counter and the man enclosed within his small cubicle asks me, 'Where to?' Uncertain of where to go I glance towards the large indicator boards to see the names of various towns the train passes through. One name stands out in bold black letters: LEETON.

'Well!' says the impatient ticket seller. 'Do you know where you want to go or not?'

'Yes, a single ticket to Leeton, please,' I respond

quickly. After receiving my ticket I notice that my train departs at 7.15 p.m.

The train is filled to capacity. Rather than sit in the cramped, smoke-filled compartment, I decide to lie down in the corridor and wrap my blanket around me. The long overnight journey is cold, tedious and uncomfortable, and it is impossible to doze in this draughty corridor, with the rocking and clacking of the old coal-burner train. Two hours later, a kind lady from a compartment nearby offers me a cup of tea and a sandwich, and her offer is gratefully accepted.

By mid-morning my weariness is forgotten as the train slowly pulls into Leeton railway station. I find myself amid the scramble of people grabbing luggage from the overhead racks and calling out to friends waiting on the platform. After being pushed and shoved by these anxious passengers, and squeezed between two red-faced, portly men, I am finally off the train. Eventually, I find myself in Pine Avenue, the main street of Leeton. A large sign on the side of a building beckons me. It reads, 'Snooker and Billiards Pool Hall'. Inside it is very quiet and semi-dark. The place seems deserted until I notice an elderly gentleman perched on a stool in a dark corner of the room. He is sipping a cup of tea.

'You the boss?' I ask nervously.

'Naa,' is his reply. With a jerk of his thumb he points to a door and continues, 'Nick Scanlon. He's the boss. You can find him in there.'

Nick Scanlon is a slim, dark-haired man about forty-five years of age. His very dark-brown eyes look straight into mine as he says, 'What can I do for you, young man?'

I try to puff myself up to look taller and larger than my jockey-like frame as I respond, 'I've just arrived up from Sydney. Maybe you can tell me the best place to get a room to stay?'

He looks at me in a puzzled manner and asks, 'How old are you, son?'

'I'm fifteen, Mr Scanlon.' I start to worry about whether I should have come here or not.

'You're only a little bloke for your age,' he says with a smile on his face.

'Yes but I'm strong,' I quickly defend myself.

He laughs. 'I bet you are.'

Mr Scanlon gives me directions and in no time I find myself at the front gate of Mrs O'Leary's guest house. Mrs O'Leary speaks in a loud, clear voice, and she is shaped like a barrel. Her grey hair is swept up and held together at the back of her head with a large brown tortoise-shell comb. She tells me she has a room available.

My single bed is the only one not within the main part of the house. It is situated on the enclosed ground-floor veranda. Prior to retiring, Mrs O'Leary gives me a candle to light my way. The little bedroom has no electric light and the night is bitterly cold. Making a desperate attempt to get warm, I huddle in a tent-like structure underneath the sheets. I hold the lit candle in one hand and support the sheet with my knees. All I succeed in doing is scorching the top of my sheet. Finally, I fall asleep.

I awaken to pure golden, country sunlight filtering

through the glass panels of my enclosed room. Sitting up, I stretch, then swing my legs out of the bed ready to devour a hearty breakfast. This is my first morning of rural life. 'What time is breakfast, Mrs O'Leary?' I ask when I find her.

'I don't supply meals, just accommodation,' is the stern reply. 'If you walk up to the main street you'll see the Wattle Café. They open early and serve a very good meal. By the way, are you looking for work?'

'Yes,' is my quick reply. She informs me that one of her lodgers is a contractor and he is looking for workers to fumigate the many fruit trees in the district.

The job interview is very short and my new boss tells me that I can start the following day. I feel chuffed that I have found work so quickly. Now I feel like a man of the world and know that money will soon fill my pockets. My part in this operation is to carry a five-foot long metal apparatus. I open its lid and pour either arsenic or cyanide powder inside. Two other workmen are ahead of me, covering the fruit trees with a large sheet of material. Placing the four-foot protruding snout of my machine under the sheet, I begin to quickly wind the handle of my contraption. Powder is blown under and into the orange trees. Row after row of endless fruit trees are fumigated like this and I am exhausted by the end of the work day. I am a naive, fifteen-year-old city boy handling deadly material and do not realise why my weekly wage packet is so healthy. The few able-bodied Leeton men who are not overseas fighting in the War have little to do with such toxic work.

In my opinion I am a man of the world now and I love my newfound freedom and independence. The working hours are from about 4 p.m. to 11 p.m., which allows me to have the greater part of the day to myself. I quickly repay Mr Furlong, posting him the money I owe. Many days are spent in Scanlon's pool hall and sometimes I play cards for money. In one of these gambling sessions, though, I learn the meaning of a new word: sensitivity.

An Aboriginal man opposite me is slowly shuffling the cards and chatting away to a fellow card player. It seems he is more interested in having a chat than playing cards. Impatience gets the better of me and I blurt out, 'Come on, Jacky Jacky, hurry up and deal the bloody cards!'

I barely complete my sentence when the man rears out of his seat. His hands are outstretched and his face is twisted with rage. 'You little bastard!' he roars.

Two of the other card players leap out of their chairs, grab hold of him, and manage to restrain him from choking the breath out of my little body. When peace is finally restored, one of my card-playing bodyguards informs me that an apology is in order. He also suggests that I should never, ever address any Aboriginal person by that name. I promptly apologise to the man— at least four times—I am grateful that I am breathing. It sure beats the alternative of being dead.

Five months pass and I am surprised when my Dad arrives at the guest house. He has made the long journey from Sydney to see if his boy is safe. Seeing his familiar face gives me a warm and wonderful feeling inside. This is the beginning of a magnificent bond between father and son. Like most children of this age, I take my father for granted. In my formative years I gave little thought to what type of person Fred was. I was usually concerned only about what I needed, and loved it when Fred called to take me on outings. He was Fred, the man they said was my father. The one who treats me to anywhere I want to go and anything I want to do. Now, as he stands in the doorway of Mrs O'Leary's home, I feel a sudden surge of love and respect for this wonderful man. He is my father and I want to be his friend.

One week after Fred arrives and knows that I am safe, he tells me that he is heading back to Sydney. I am feeling very restless and it does not take much encouragement for me to decide that I am sick of country living. I need to go back to Glebe, where I feel most comfortable. After saying my farewells, father and son board the train for Sydney.

Like many young lads I have a dream. The difference between my vision of the future and other people's is that I am very confused about what it is. I cannot make up my mind whether I should pursue a career as a jockey, priest or a Glebe gangster! It is Fred who clarifies the confusion for me. He suggests that a person weighing ninety pounds and being a mere five feet, two inches tall will not be a threat to a standover man or gangster. He also points out that with my knockabout education, the Vatican could disintegrate into turmoil if 'Father Tom Thumb' ever wandered into the flock. There is only one course of action to take. Fred organises an interview with a Randwick racehorse trainer, who decides to give me a three-month trial. He is going to assess my potential as a future jockey. It is 'Post Time'.

Clang, clang, clang. The sound of steel against steel. I wonder who on earth is making such a loud racket so late at night. The small bedside clock reads 4 a.m. and I realise that this is my first morning wake-up call. Suddenly, the room floods with piercing light and a voice calls out, 'Come on, boys, out of bed. There's work to be done.'

'This must be a mistake,' I mumble to myself. 'Nobody would get out of bed at this time of day.' Three other lads and I crawl out of our warm beds, which are situated in the hayloft above the stabled horses. In a trance-like state we all wander down the rickety steps and walk towards the house. In a snug, cosy kitchen we find our breakfast.

Our daily duties are very mundane. We feed and water horses, clean manure and old straw out of each stable, place fresh straw on the floors and hose the yards down thoroughly. This is far from my idea of a jockey's glamorous life. I believe that this life should involve arriving at the racecourse, being handed the colourful racing silks to wear, riding in the races, winning as many events as possible, then going home. Stark reality gives me a dreadful shock when I am required to constantly do these daily chores, returning every evening to the hayloft bedroom exhausted. I discuss with the other boys my future dreams of donning the rainbow racing silks for the first time, riding my first winner on the hallowed turf, listening to the cheers of the crowd and the presentation of the cup. When we tire of daydreaming, another sport is introduced: chasing the odd rat found lurking in the loft. This game is not one of my favourite pastimes.

The days drag on. Sometimes I go to the racetrack to tend one of the thoroughbreds but not to ride on the royal surface. Astride a pony, I occasionally lead a racehorse to the track, and it is then handed over to the jockey who is riding trackwork that morning. Things are not happening fast enough for me and the streak of impatience in my make-up becomes obvious. I do not understand that achieving my dream involves ten percent inspiration and ninety percent perspiration. After six long weeks I decide to say farewell to the sport of kings.

The tram stops outside the Glebe Town Hall and I heave my large suitcase onto the footpath. A sudden surge of failure sweeps through me and I feel like I have let everybody down, my mother and father, my neighbours and close friends. My turmoil within is not so much about walking away from the stables because of my own inabilities. I was told I had great potential. My enemy that runs riot within is impatience. Everything has to happen immediately for me. I am too impatient to complete my apprenticeship. I slowly walk along Jarocin Avenue. My head is down and my self-esteem is at an all time low. Looking up I can see Nell hosing the small front lawn of our house. She has a great wit and can see something funny in just about everything that happens. She sees me slowly walking towards her and calls out, 'Well, look who's coming. It's Billy Cook, Australia's champion jockey, back from India!' It is Saturday morning and a few neighbours' heads turn in my direction. I feel that they are all laughing at the failure carrying the large suitcase. My humiliation is unbearable. I do not see the funny side of Nell's comments. Walking up the front steps through the open front door, I ignore Nell's questions: 'What happened? What's gone wrong?' My only comment as I make my way upstairs to my bed on the balcony is, 'I will explain later.' I desperately want to put the matter behind me and have no intention of ever mentioning it again. I do not realise that my attitudes are my problem.

It does not take me long, though, to appreciate Nell's sense of humour again. The Second World War is in top gear and outside the newsagent's shop, people with sombre faces are reading the daily headlines; they are anxious to read about the Australian Imperial Forces engaged in a dire struggle with the enemy in the Middle East. 'Tobruk Taken', 'Middle East Invasion in Full Swing', '9th Australian Division Press Forward', the headlines say. One evening as Nell and I walk up the avenue we see a much larger crowd than usual outside the newsagent's. Softly spoken comments come from people in the crowd. One person says, 'Dear me, this is dreadful!' The headline that screams out in very large black print is 'Benghazzi Falls'. Nell burrows her way through the throng. After reading the headline, she immediately calls out in a loud, clear voice, 'Well, fancy that! I wonder if the jockey was hurt?' A great roar of laughter goes up and one man speaks for all when he says, 'Only you could get away with that, Nellie. Bless you for allowing me to laugh.'

Nell also has the ability to make herself and her own misfortune the butt of a joke. I remember the time she had just come out of the operating theatre after a serious operation. Aunt Anne and I are informed by the nurse that we can visit for a few minutes. My Aunt asks, 'How are you getting along, Nell?' She gives a sly wink and replies as quick as a flash, 'One leg after the other and making a living in between!' The spirit of this woman is strong, even though I know she is in great pain.

My newfound freedom is short-lived when I realise that nothing has changed in Nell's life. Her drinking still causes me to feel disgust and my means of escaping my home life are work and music. I find employment at a warehouse working as an assistant on a delivery van.

My passion for music, dance and comedy is once again ignited. I begin writing short plays and sketches, which are performed with my friends at various church halls of all denominations. These occasions are very exciting for me and I feel my future could be in this area. I rejoin the Glebe band and also play my piano accordian for radio stations and various other functions. I love being the centre of attention and the recognition I receive builds my self-confidence sky high. I lose my restlessness because my mind is occupied and I begin to focus on my future.

Booze and Brass

February 19, 1945 is my eighteenth birthday. World War II is still in progress and I am now old enough to enlist in the armed forces. I want to put an end to the hostilities and save the world. After being accepted by the Royal Australian Air Force, I know it will not be long before I am a fighter pilot flying high among the clouds. But instead of piloting an aircraft, the only machines I am given to operate are a decoder and typewriter. Instead of flying overseas I am located in the signal office here in Australia. The war ends in September 1945. In May 1946, my short-lived adventure ends and I am discharged.

Civilian life is very boring because I am no longer focused on my music and I am like a loose cannon rolling around on the deck of the ship of life. I go from one mundane job to the next. I decide to play in the Glebe District Silver Band on weekends. It fuels my passion for music once again. After six months of going nowhere I make a decision to enlist in the army. In November 1946,

I join Eastern Command Military Band, which is stationed at Victoria Barracks in Sydney. Nell is so oblivious to my career prospects that I could have told her I was joining an elastic band! On the other hand, Fred is thrilled. I am overawed by the wonderful talent of these musicians and I feel very honoured to be playing tenor horn and trombone with them.

The band, comprising thirty members, is treated quite favourably by the upper echelons of the army; we are granted leave when the band is not engaged and receive complimentary food and beverage at military functions. I am the youngest member of the band and the standard of these fine musicians greatly impresses me. Some members have an additional talent that is quite awesome: the ability to consume booze. The fluid intake would give a camel an inferiority complex. I am a non-drinker because I swore I would never touch the stuff after seeing it destroy my mother's life. I know that alcohol will never pass my lips.

In January 1947, I cross paths with Mick Lamrock, who is on leave from the Royal Australian Navy. Mick and I grew up together in Glebe and have been friends since I was six. Catching up is exciting and Mick suggests that he buy me a beer to celebrate. He sees the disapproving look on my face and immediately remembers my dislike of alcohol. 'Sorry, Nicko,' he apologises, 'I forgot that you never touch the stuff. Let me buy you a lemonade.'

But, caught up in the wild excitement of seeing my oldest friend, five words jump from my mouth. These five fateful words are to change my life completely: 'One beer won't hurt me.'

The first beer goes down my throat. Any tension I have is dissolved and my anxieties seem to vanish. Drinking the second and third beers allows Mick and I to solve the world's problems. Five and then six beers are consumed. This magic elixir makes me feel like an intellectual giant, seven foot tall and bulletproof. I grew up with the shame of the whole neighbourhood knowing that my mother was a drunkard. I am therefore normally a self-conscious, sensitive person and dislike myself because of the worthlessness I feel. When I see my reflection in the bar mirror I see a very handsome, suave, devil-may-care man in uniform. I believe the women serving behind the bar can't take their eyes off me. Life suddenly takes on a new dimension. I am free. I am wonderful. I am relaxed. I am pissed!

'Surely you've had enough,' says Mick after the sixth beer is consumed. I look at my friend and wonder why he wants to spoil my moment of euphoria. Reluctantly, I allow him to lead me out of the hotel. My legs feel like jelly as he escorts me back to Jarocin Avenue. It is not long before I am in bed and fast asleep.

The following morning I am relatively normal and only slightly the worse for my introduction to booze. Nobody realises I have tasted alcohol the night before. I am quite blasé about having my first drink despite having nausea, a dry throat and mild headache. It is a bright sunny day and I return to Victoria Barracks, where a large group of spectators are assembled early waiting for a traditional army ceremony. Surrounding the spacious, green parade ground is a circular roadway, bordered by bricked-in flower beds filled with colourful blooms. There are many dignitaries in attendance, politicians, church leaders, high-ranking members of the army, navy and air force and the general public.

The band has been rehearsing for weeks for this occasion, the day for the time-honoured presentation of the 'Beating of the Retreat', which requires the band to perform the difficult task of slow marching while playing their instruments. Each member is resplendent in his scarlet tunic with gold piping and shining gold buttons. Coats are buttoned all the way up to the neck. Trousers are dark-navy with a two-inch red stripe running vertically down the outside of each leg. The crowning glory is a large snow-white pith helmet with a gold chain chin-strap to hold the helmet firmly in place. The black boots have a mirror-like shine.

One hour before the appointed starting time the bandmaster informs us that we can relax. He orders us to report back thirty minutes before the ceremony is due to begin. Some of us wander over to the Greenwood Tree Hotel, opposite the barracks. We intend to just have one or two ales prior to commencing our arduous task. Unfortunately, there is a drastic beer shortage in our fair city. We initially have one or two small glasses of rum instead and then become foolish and overdo it. We eventually find our way back to the assembly point.

Our big moment arrives. The command is given: 'Band, by the centre slow march.' This we manage to do for four or five paces before the band starts to move into more of a swaying motion than slow marching. The music coming from our instruments is brilliant. Unfortunately, the bandsman on the front right flank holding a large metal bass is slowly moving to his right-hand side. I can see from the rear of the band that this man is actually starting to slow march or plod through the flower beds. Naturally, everybody behind is following him. The member on the front left flank playing a shining trombone is weaving to his left. He is almost plaiting his legs and leads the bandsmen behind him towards the large, open double gates at the main entrance to Victoria Barracks, twenty yards from the busy thoroughfare of Oxford Street. And all the while the drum major leading the band is unaware of the pantomime going on behind him.

I wonder what the distinguished members of the audience are thinking. Do they think this is a novel display the band is putting on? One half doing a tiptoe through the tulips and the other half endeavouring to cross Oxford Street to play Russian roulette with the traffic! Suddenly, the red alert button is pushed as outraged voices from all directions bark out orders. Whistles blare and one voice louder than the rest bellows, 'Get those men out of the flower beds. Bring those men in from the street. Band halt!'

A very red-faced officer stands alongside poor Lennie with the big metal bass and barks out an order: 'You soldier, get out of that flower bed.'

'Who, me?' says Lennie, looking down with bloodshot eyes and finally realising that his size-ten boots are firmly planted in among the pansies and petunias. Lennie hastily steps back onto the roadway. He straightens his white helmet, which was tilted to one side, and addresses the officer pathetically, 'Sorry, mate.'

Suddenly, the call goes out: 'Band fall in.' In true stiff-upper-lip tradition, we regroup. The exercise of 'Beating the Retreat' resumes and the band carries on to complete the task as if nothing has happened.

The following morning is judgement day for the bandmaster. He is ordered to report before high-ranking officers to give account of the previous day's display by his band. Bandmaster Pearson explains that both the soldier on bass, holding the right flank, and the other bandsman on trombone, holding the left flank, are returned soldiers who served in New Guinea during wartime. He claims that both men suffered malaria attacks simultaneously during the 'Beating of the Retreat', which accounts for their erratic behaviour. Remarkably, this explanation is accepted. Perhaps the panel prefers to believe this story rather than lock away members of their beloved band. This incident is swept under the carpet, though the powers that be insist a repeat of this performance will not be tolerated.

This threat goes in one ear and out the other. It is like water off a duck's back to me. The average soldier would have been fearful enough to take heed of this warning. I am not. Fear and threats have no meaning for me because my need to keep drinking is all I can think about. This is proven several days later when I am semi-intoxicated as the band leads a parade through the streets of Sydney.

At Martin Place thousands of people are lined up on both sides of the pavement, ten deep behind the wooden barricades. They are eagerly awaiting the start of the big parade.

Eastern Command Army Band are forming up at the top end of Martin Place. Today the band will lead the procession six abreast. The march will take us down a slight decline on this route, past a ten foot high pagoda-like toilet set right in the middle of Martin Place. Just prior to reaching this iron lattice monument the band six abreast will divide into two sections of three abreast and go around the 'dunny' then form up on the other side. All of the time playing a stirring tune and continuing to march in unison.

The command is barked out: 'Band, by the centre, quick march.' The reverberating sounds bouncing off the walls of the many high-rise buildings is enough to stir the hearts of all. I am in the centre of the front rank of the band members playing trombone and as the band approaches the elegant 'pissatorium' and begins to divide, I suddenly have a brain explosion. 'Hey, Lenny! Farewell, my friend.'

Lenny stops playing his instrument for a split second as he glances in my direction. The look of astonishment on his face I can still see after all of these years. I march straight ahead, walking into the open doorway of this lavatory, down ten circular iron steps, continue marching across the tiled floor of this abomination then head up the ten steps on the exit side. But I am horrified when I realise I have miscalculated. Instead of joining the rear band members I find myself twenty-five yards behind them. I am just in front of the honour guard of one hundred and twenty infantry soldiers with their rifles sloped on the left shoulder and with gleaming bayonets affixed. Fearful sanity returns as I hurry through the rear ranks of the band back to my rightful position at the front row. Fortunately for me, the bandmaster, who always marches at the back of the band, probably thought that I had dropped my card of music and had hurried back to retrieve it. Nothing was ever mentioned about this lunatic display. When I sober up my mates try to warn me about the consequences if I am ever caught doing these stunts again. I fail to take heed of yet another warning.

Mid-January, 1947—a night to remember. The band was on a four-day break. On the last day I make my way over to Victoria Barracks with the intention of having lunch and a drink with some of the band guys who lived in the band room, where ten rooms were available for their accommodation.

The day passes quickly; our time is consumed by playing jazz and drinking. Some time around 8 p.m. we call off our entertainment. I say my farewells then walk out into the darkness.

My mind is restless and ready for more excitement. Not content with seven hours of laughter, drinking and adrenaline rush, I wander the streets of Paddington rather than go home. After aimlessly walking, occasionally stumbling and having a conversation with myself for maybe two hours, I find myself standing outside a nightclub on King Street in the heart of Sydney—the Ziegfeld Café.

Standing at the entrance are two beefy bouncers. Behind them is a circular set of steps leading down to this basement club. My hazy mind wonders what I know about this place. I remember that a brother of one of the army band members plays clarinet with a group here at this club—Don Parry, brother of Jack. Donny and I have socialised many times.

'Where do you think you're going?' Mr Boofhead the bouncer says, his giant hand up against my chest. 'You look as though you have had enough booze for one night.'

'I'm okay, mister,' I reply. 'My brother plays in the band downstairs and I have to see him and pass on an important message from our older brother Jack.'

Boofhead turns to his mate and asks him to go downstairs and check it out. 'What's your name?' he asks me.

'Cliff Parry.'

Finally the other bouncer returns and says it's all right. I take a deep breath and am grateful that Donny knows it is me.

Upon entering the club, I find that the boys in the small band are having a break. Donny walks toward me. 'Hi Cliffy. What are you doing in this part of town?'

'At a loose end, mate, and I really need a drink.' Now comfortably seated on a sofa-like seat tucked away in a dark corner alongside the bandstand, I survey the room. On each table are small gold jars with a candle flickering away in each, giving off a yellow light that illuminates the faces of the many patrons. Even in my semi-intoxicated state the faces are clear and sinister. Scars, tattoos, dead marble eyes and curled-up lips speaking from the side of the mouth; most of them seem to be in whispered conversation. Some look up every so often, their eyes surveying the room.

Some years later I find out that of all the clubs and cafés in the inner-city area, the Ziegfeld Café is known as the lowest of the low, a place where gangsters hang out. In 1951, a notorious standover man walks into Ziggy's late one night and calmly shoots dead a well-known boxer as he sits at his table. Ziegfeld's is declared a disorderly house and shut down in 1952. Luckily, the night I am there produces only a few minor scuffles and abusive behaviour.

Here I am, sitting in my corner slurping away on a cheap Scotch whisky, wondering if my fellow patrons had all arrived here straight from Long Bay Gaol, a brothel or an asylum, when a very tall buxom blonde dressed in a full length red dress stops at my table. Her crimson lipstick is slashed across her mouth and painted on her eyelids she seems to have three coats of charcoal. A large tattoo adorns her shoulder. 'Do you mind if I sit here with you, sir?' she asks.

'By all means,' responds Sir Galahad.

My companion is charming and extremely sociable. My admiration for her is helped by the fact that she insists on paying for each round of drinks.

'Care to dance, cutie?' As we cruise or stumble around the dance floor I realise just how tall she is as I, at five feet seven inches tall, sing into her navel.

The band has a 'take ten'. Donny joins me. 'Cliffy, you're getting very drunk. Ease up, pal.'

'Donny, I'm in love,' I say. My lady friend has gone to the toilet.

A roar of laughter comes from my clarinet-playing mate. 'Cliffy, do you realise that for four or five hours you have been holding hands and dancing with a guy?'

My eyes seem to open an extra half an inch, and my back goes from a slumping position to almost upright. 'What, you're putting me on, aren't you?'

'No, son. He calls himself Thelma but his real name is Ivan. He works as a hairdresser a few doors up the street from here. He's a regular.'

This news almost sobers me up. 'Don, she's heading back to our table. Tell her I'm your brother and we're going to stay at your dad's house tonight because he is not in good health.'

Thelma accepts the news gracefully and sympathises with our situation. My mind is playing leapfrog, thinking that in a short while Thelma had been going to take me back to her place for early morning supper. I shudder when I think what she had planned for 'supper'.

The Proposal

The following day I am on my best behaviour at a lunchtime engagement in Hyde Park. During the performance I glance at the crowd and see a small, trim woman standing just a few feet away from me. She is dressed in a smart, navy business suit and seems to be looking in my direction. I am fascinated by the platinum-blonde colour of her shoulder-length hair. It reminds me of the American movie actress Jean Harlow, who caused a sensation with the male population of this planet, myself included, in the 1930s. It is the first time I have seen this colour hair off screen. After completing the performance I saunter over and introduce myself.

'Hello. My name is Cliff,' I blurt out as my suave approach deserts me.

'Hello, I'm Daphne,' she smiles, and my heart rate skyrockets.

I feel awkward and unsure as I ask, 'Did you enjoy the band performance?' Daphne seems very friendly and informs me that she loved the performance. Suddenly there is five long seconds of terrifying silence. I tell myself, 'Say something you fool.'

I am very nervous yet eventually summon the courage to ask Daphne out for dinner. She is such a lovely person and my greatest fear is her answering with a no.

'That sounds lovely, Cliff,' she replies. I am so shocked I don't know what to do next. There is silence again. Finally I ask for her phone number and we continue chatting as my confidence returns.

Three days later I go out of my way to impress Daphne. I take her to an up-market hotel, order an expensive seafood dinner and ask her to select a top-class wine. I enjoy her company and sense that she is attracted to me. It turns out that the feeling is mutual, and after our first date we socialise several times a week, going to movies, dinners, dances and the occasional picnic.

Eventually, I learn that Daphne is fascinated by my devil-may-care attitude to life and my ability to make her laugh. For her to be entertained in a humorous way is a refreshing change after the very dull, suburban existence she lives with her family. My confidence is boosted by having Daphne by my side but she does not realise how much alcohol contributes to my devil-may-care attitude.

During the first three months of courting Daphne I manage to control my drinking. When I am not with her I drink to excess and a few drinks soon escalates to daily drinking. I am not even aware that I drink much more than normal drinkers. One evening, however, I overdo it and become very drunk. The following morning

Daphne telephones me at the military camp and asks, 'Did you mean what you said last night?'

'About what?' I ask.

'When you asked me to marry you?'

I am surprised and have no recollection of the event. For a while I am speechless, and then say, 'Let me think about it. I'll call you tomorrow.' I do not tell her I have no recollection of my proposal.

Bewildered by this unexpected situation I hurry back to the barrack room to find my friend, Charlie. I feel I need the guidance of an older, more experienced person. When I explain my circumstances his first response is, 'Does she come from a good family?'

'Yes, she does.'

'Do you have a picture of her?'

'Hang on, I'll get it for you. It's in my wallet.'

Charlie studies the photo. 'She seems to have a nice face. I'd take her up on her offer.' Problem solved!

Charlie's advice aside, I'm afraid of offending Daphne. I feel I should be of good principle and keep my word. I phone her the next day and tell her, 'Yes, I did mean what I said the other night.'

Daphne accepts my odd proposal and makes the wedding arrangements very quickly because I've just got a posting to Japan. I have been stationed at Liverpool Barracks for some time awaiting a posting with the Occupational Forces.

I think it is a wonderful compliment that this attractive young woman from a good family wants to marry me. After our whirlwind courtship we marry on September 4,

1947. It is a small affair at a little chapel in Castlereagh Street, Sydney. A school day pal of mine, Lloyd Jansson, acts as the best man and Daphne's aunt is the other witness. Our short honeymoon is spent in a private hotel in Sydney. At twenty years old marriage is just another adventure for me. I do not have the faintest idea what love is all about.

Within three days I return to camp at Liverpool and await orders for my posting. September 11, 1947, I board the troopship HMAS *Manoora* and sail for Japan with the Occupation Forces.

My new home is at Morsehead Barracks, Hiro, Japan. The excitement of being in a foreign country for the first time is a wonderful thrill. At no stage do I become more preoccupied with this new experience than thinking of my wife. In fact I write to Daphne every day and even compose a song for her. I am now a member of the Australian 66th Infantry Battalion Band, which is stationed only a short distance from Hiroshima. This city is still a scene of devastation after the dropping of the atomic bomb in 1945. In November, the battalion band and one hundred infantry soldiers are selected for a tour of duty in Tokyo, which is quite a long distance north of our base, where we will be required to be part of the changing of the guard ceremony at the Palace of Emperor Hirohito. The riflemen plus the thirty band members move into the Tokyo Barracks called Ebisu.

The guard change outside the Palace is carried out twice a week. The infantry soldiers look quite impressive dressed in their khaki battle dress with snow-white web belt and gaiters, shiny black boots and a brown slouch hat with white hat band. The hat is turned up on the left hand side to reveal the highly polished, golden rising sun badge. Against each left-hand shoulder of the troops sits a large .303 Lee Enfield rifle with a chrome-plated bayonet affixed. The band is dressed in a ceremonial uniform, navy-blue tunic with gold buttons up to the neck, navy-blue trousers with a red stripe running vertically down the outer leg, and a white pith helmet.

One night before the guard change I am off duty and out with two of my friends from the band. Their names are Dudley 'Irish' Callahan and Roy Le'Minn. We find ourselves drinking in a small, off-limits beer house. Suddenly, our host informs us he has run out of beer. This is devastating news. He tries to compensate for having no beer, asking, 'You boys rike whisky?' Then like magic our host produces a large bottle of liquid labelled 'Red Horn Whisky'. Despite the ominous dark-brown colour of this whisky, I try some. The first mouthful goes down my throat and it feels as though my windpipe has been severed. It takes five seconds before I can let out the words, 'Whooah! Shooh! Geeze! Haarr! God almighty, this stuff will fly a plane!' We only consume about one third of the potent brew—luckily. A few days later we realise how fortunate we are when we read a bulletin pinned on the regimental notice board, warning against illegal whisky and advising that its potency has already caused blindness in some troops. We discover that the nerve endings and cells in the retina can be starved of oxygen and nutrients thus causing irreversible eye damage. We breathe a sigh of relief that we can still see.

The following day, the guard change is a nightmare. My nerves are in shreds and double vision makes it difficult for me to march behind the leading bandsman. The day seems never ending. I am grateful when it does.

Friday, glorious Friday. This is a rest day. Late afternoon, Roy and I decide to take a trip down to the Ginza, a well-known shopping area of Tokyo. We stop at many drinking establishments and do very little shopping. Nightfall is closing in and the twinkling lights of the numerous stalls gradually begin to light up the place until the Ginza is bathed in a brilliant glow. We continue our wanderings unaware that our footsteps take us a long way from the Ginza. Finally, in semi-darkness, Roy and I find ourselves standing outside the Palace of Emperor Hirohito. Roy asks me if I am hungry, and I realise that neither of us has eaten for six hours.

'I'm bloody starving, Cliff!' he says.

I could do with a good feed myself, I tell him, but there are no eating houses around here. The closest one would be in town and that's over a mile away.

'Do you like duck?' Roy says, his voice a strange whisper.

'Never tried it.'

He points to the Emperor's moat which surrounds the Palace. 'Look, there's plenty in there.'

My mouth falls open in astonishment. I grab him by one arm. 'You must be joking. Those ducks are the Emperor's bloody sacred royal ducks.' Even I know this small part of Japanese history. A member of an occupying force should never tamper with the Emperor's ducks. 'Be sensible, Roy. Even if we catch one, how in the name of hell can we cook it?'

Sanity flies out of the window for Roy. He jumps into the moat with water up to his waist, looks back at me and whispers, 'We can figure that out later.'

There is a stream of curses from Roy and loud royal quacks from the ducks. 'Come here, you bastard!' Roy's hand flashes out as he gets a hold of one of the sacred birds. In a furious flurry its wings thrash the water. Roy tries to hold his footing. Water is flying in all directions. I offer my outstretched hand, telling him to pass the bloody thing to me. I fall in then and get drenched from my slouch hat down to my size-six boots, only to hear my fellow hunter informing me, 'The bloody mongrel got away.'

Suddenly, search lights pierce the darkness. Japanese voices echo all around. A siren wails loudly and Palace guards appear in the distance, running towards us. We soon forget about our appetites. The shock sobers our drunken minds and we know it is important to run. Boy, do we run! Two very breathless soldiers finally arrive back in the Ginza to be swallowed up by the crowds. After hailing a taxi, we head for home to Ebisu Barracks. Thankfully, no more is heard of the incident.

My twenty-first birthday is celebrated in 1948, with the boys in the band organising a party at the barracks. In the band room the celebrations get into full swing.

My thoughts are of Australia. I miss Daphne and feel so far from home because none of my family are here. I feel a sudden sense of loss and begin to plummet into feelings of worthlessness and loss. Why can't my twenty-first be celebrated like most other young people's? They have wives, mothers, fathers, brothers, sisters and old school friends at their birthday parties. Why can't I? I do not realise that the other guys here in Japan are in the same boat. All I know is that the blackness that descends upon me spirals very quickly and blots out my ability to see beyond myself and my pain. The emptiness I felt as a child comes back. I once again feel different to others and long for a loving family to give me a sense of belonging. Deep down I know that even if I had been back home this dream would never have eventuated. I need to fill this void inside me and proceed to get drunk. Booze gives me temporary relief from the pain of living as I silently apologise to the world for being born. I spend the rest of the night in oblivion. I do not stay in this state of depression for long.

Five months later my tour of duty in Japan comes to an end in July, and I board the small naval destroyer HMAS *Quickmatch* with four other soldiers, to travel back home. The Pacific Ocean becomes quite violent after two days at sea when the warship runs into the tail end of a cyclone. Feeling that my life is going to end, I sleep on the upper deck within the 'A' gun turret set on the bow of the ship. Surrounded by my steel cabin, I tie myself to the inner part of the turret with a length of rope from my kit bag to make sure I am not washed overboard. If the ship goes down I can swim for it, I think. The noise of the ocean forces me to pull the canvas curtain back from the rear of my hideout. I crane my neck around the side of the steel coffin and look to the front of the ship. Each time I am horrified at what I see. One moment there is an enormous wall of water that literally blots out the sky. The front of the ship is pointing down as if it's going to stand straight up on its nose and disappear into a watery grave. Suddenly, the sky comes into view. This time the bow of the ship is pointing skyward as if on top of a roller coaster. The ship then rolls to the right as if it is going to turn over, then it slowly comes back to an upright position. Next, it slowly lurches way over to the left before becoming upright again. Repetition of the wall of water and disappearing sky continues and I'm wondering if I shall ever see home again. This horror ride strikes so much fear into me that I cannot remember how to pray. For another two hours I question if this nightmare is ever going to end.

Twenty days later I arrive in Sydney Harbour on a bright, calm, sunny day, grateful I am still alive after my terrifying experience on the destroyer. Finally, I am reunited with my wife, and when ten days' leave is granted, Daphne and I rent a holiday cottage near the ocean and relax. There is great joy and excitement because we are together once more. Daphne cannot help but notice the increase in my daily consumption of alcohol, but she assumes I am drinking so much because I am excited to be home. She hopes I will settle down soon. I, however, am aware of my need to escape into alcohol when I cannot cope with life. I am unable to talk to Daphne about my feelings and continue drinking.

After a wonderful break it is time to return to Eastern Command Band at Victoria Barracks. Nothing seems to have changed. I see the same old faces, scarlet tunics and band room. But my closest friends notice how much I have changed. Even the bandmaster is aware of the manner in which I consume alcohol and he gives me a stern warning about it. I ignore his advice. One night the band is giving a recital on the veranda of the officers' mess. After playing for half an hour we are given a ten-minute break. A steward in a white jacket, red bowtie and dark trousers stands before the band with a large tray of alcoholic refreshments. I consume two beers rather hastily. These two drinks, coupled with the six I drank prior to the concert, are enough to stoke the fire within my addled brain.

Five minutes before the second half of the recital, I wander to the rear of the officers' mess. Here I observe a full nine-gallon keg of beer sitting on the ground outside the back door. My first thought is: I'll take this keg so the band can have a nightcap later on. I start to roll the keg along the ground towards a friend's car. I open the back door and almost have the keg into the vehicle when a thunderous voice booms out, 'What the hell do you think you're doing soldier?' I drop the keg and quickly turn around. Confronting me is a very rigid regimental sergeant major. Just visible underneath the peak of his cap are marble-like eyes, which are wide open and glaring at me. The lights of the carpark are bright enough for me to see his ginger, waxed moustache, pointed on either end and twitching rapidly. Noticing a baton firmly wedged underneath the arm of this very efficient man, I become terrified. I know he will not hesitate to throw me into the barracks' gaol, and indeed I am arrested and thrown into gaol overnight.

The following day my world collapses. I am heavily fined and can't understand why the powers that be are dismissing me from the band. The army band has been my home and family for nearly two years. Now even that is taken away. Later in the afternoon I learn that I am being transferred to ground staff. This section is made up of elderly soldiers awaiting discharge, and those who are considered medically or mentally unfit to perform regular army duties. Ground staff members occupy a large barrack room, which is situated five hundred yards from the band room.

My new team mates and myself perform such exciting tasks as cleaning toilets, weeding gardens, pushing wheelbarrows, picking up litter from the parade ground and slapping paint on fences and rooftops, whether they need painting or not. This new career is far removed from the glamorous life in the band.

My first 'contract' is to paint the sixty-foot long corrugated roof of a barrack room, which is situated near the rear gates of Victoria Barracks. Having to paint the roof doesn't worry me, but being fifteen feet above the ground and exposed to everyone's gaze does. Each morning at 8.55 a.m. the band marches from the back gates of the barracks along a winding roadway that leads to the main parade ground. I am on top of the roof slopping paint onto this unfriendly surface when my ears suddenly hear a faint, familiar sound. It is the tap of a drum. I prepare myself for the band to come marching past. Wearing old khaki overalls and floppy giggle hat I have a large six-inch paint brush in my right hand and a can of dark-green paint alongside me. The moment the band comes marching past I stand up and play out a charade. I do my comedy routine, holding the paint brush under my nose with one hand and with my other arm and fingers outstretched, I give the Nazi salute. I also pretend to throw the can of paint all over them as they pass by. My comedy is an attempt to convince them that I'm all right. I pretend it does not really bother me that I am no longer with my friends or a member of the band.

Tears form in my eyes when witty comments come from some of the bandsmen as they pass: 'Don't drink the turps, Nicko!' and 'Painting the town green this time, Nick!' This is my first experience of total humiliation. My two best friends, Bob Rowan and Len Evans, look up without saying a word and give me a slow, warm wave. They seem to be silently saying, 'We're sorry, Cliff. We know how you feel.'

When the band disappears out of sight, deep feelings of loneliness and grief overwhelm me. I have no need to pretend any longer because nobody is in sight. Everything around me seems to be so quiet. I stand here alone, lost and beyond all hope. I wipe my eyes with the sleeve of my overalls and contemplate throwing myself off the roof head first. Instead, deep hurt goes straight to my soul. Once more the boy from the balcony of Jarocin Avenue, Glebe, is alone.

Second Chance

Daphne and I have been living with her parents at Concord since I returned from Japan. Fred and Nell are not aware of my return to Australia, nor my whereabouts. Fred has a nomadic existence and I cannot find him and Nell is in an alcoholic world.

My relationship with Daphne is on rocky ground because of my increased drinking and erratic behaviour. I feel unsettled being married yet when Daphne informs me that she is pregnant I feel elated. I hope that fatherhood will help me be a better husband and good father.

Our first child, Christine Judith, is born October 6, 1949. We, the proud parents, become quickly aware that she is the cutest and prettiest child ever born. It takes me a month to locate Fred and Nell to tell them they are grandparents. Both receive the news joyfully. A few days later a very strong rumour circulates about another regular army band being formed in Brisbane. Wanting to be a good father and to get away from painting rooftops and picking up litter, I make further enquiries. The rumour is true and the band is to be stationed at Enoggera, an inner suburb of Brisbane.

A letter to Mr Bob Rignold, the bandmaster of this new band, is written to outline the better side of my qualifications. Accommodation at reasonable rent for my wife and child is also requested. I then arrange an appointment with Bill Pearson, the bandmaster of Eastern Command Band, to obtain a reference. Gaining this will be essential if I'm to have any chance of obtaining a position with this new band. Entering Mr Pearson's office I feel a little sheepish, but he makes me welcome. 'Sit down, Cliffy. What can I do for you?'

I take a quick breath and address him with the only title I've ever known him to have: 'Boss, I have written to Northern Command hoping I can become a member of the new band that's being formed. I know my chances will be better if you can give me a reasonable reference.'

The boss leans back in his chair, pushes his peaked cap to the rear of his head, fixes his eyes on me and speaks: 'Cliffy, what's wrong with you, son? Why do you carry on the way that you do? Don't you know that your father is worried sick about you? You are aware that your dad and I played in a few bands together as young men. My respect for him is of the highest order. Not only are you blessed with a wonderful father but there is also your lovely wife Daphne and your beautiful little daughter. You have everything to live and work for.'

I sit up straight in my chair and look Bill in the eyes. 'Boss, I have finished with booze forever. Alcohol is out for me. No more, I've learnt my lesson.' He stares at me for a few seconds, then I blurt out, 'All I'm asking for, boss, is one more chance!'

Silence, dreadful, fearful silence. He seems to be looking into my mind. Why doesn't he say something?

Slowly, he rises from his chair, turns his back on me and at the same time speaks. 'Son, I believe that everyone deserves a second chance.' My heart nearly leaps out of my chest. His words are slow and precise: 'Do you really mean what you say? Are you finished with alcohol for good?'

'Boss, I have never been more sincere about anything in my life.'

Bandmaster Pearson's words ring in my ears as I prepare to leave his office. He promises to put in a good word for me with Bob Rignold in Brisbane, and his final comments as we shake hands are, 'We will all miss your vaudeville performances and comedy routines with the band. To be honest with you, even I had a hearty, inner laugh many times when you were putting on your little act on top of that roof. I know you were bleeding to death inside because you were no longer a member of our band. Good luck, son.' I walk out of the office floating on a cloud.

My application for transfer is granted. Daphne and the baby leave for Brisbane in advance to set up house in the suburb of Mitchelton, while I await my departure date from the Department of Army. It's three weeks before I travel north for my second chance.

On a Wednesday afternoon the large steam train wheezes, screeches and grinds to a halt at South Brisbane railway station. I feel tired after my long journey from Sydney, yet excited—it's a time for celebration. Just one or two drinks is all I need. I make enquiries, and an elderly railway guard tells me where to find a nice little hotel. What happens to the wonderful promise I made to Bill Pearson? I promised him so sincerely that I was finished with alcohol for life. All of my promises are soluble in alcohol.

At 6 p.m. I stagger out of the pub, find my way back to the station, and wait for the train to take me to Mitchelton, where Daphne and Christine are waiting in the new little home. It is dark and raining heavily when I alight from the train, the streets are deserted and there is nobody on duty at Mitchelton station. I start staggering in a direction which I hope will lead home. People often wonder how I am able to pinpoint time when under the influence of alcohol. I can do it because I have a strange obsession for time. I don't mean I am a responsible, punctual citizen. I just have a compulsive need to know what time it is. At least twenty times in a given day I ask or observe the time. I still have this obsession.

A shadowy figure with a flickering, big red eye appears in the distance. Through the darkness of the night and the misty rain I am aware of it heading towards me. The red eye seems to grow larger as it zigzags from one side of the street to the other. My fuzzy mind tells me it is some strange being from another planet. I feel like I am about to be attacked. When it is just a few feet away from me, I realise it is only a man on a bicycle.

'Do you know where Hicks Street is, mate?' I ask.

'Yer goin' the wrong way. Go back the way you came. Go over the railway line, turn right, then it's the third street on ya left,' the phantom rider replies.

Following his directions, I soon find Hicks Street. It is an unsealed street covered in ankle-deep slimy mud with many deep puddles of water. I fall face down several times, floundering through this quagmire, before knocking on the front door of my future home. After reassuring Daphne of my identity, she opens the door. My wife discovers her mud-spattered, drunken Prince Charming on the front step. I do not receive a warm welcome. Daphne is furious upon seeing me in such a drunken state. She was expecting a sober husband home three hours ago. Immediately, she retires to her bedroom and tells me I can sleep on the kitchen floor.

The next morning I apologise to her for my broken promises. We eat breakfast in a very strained manner and few words are spoken. And I continue drinking despite my promise to Daphne. Most times I am oblivious to her pleading, anger and frustration; I just wonder what all the fuss is about. I do not spend much time with Christine because I am caught up in my own selfish world.

After settling in with the new band, I hear that my friend, Bob Rowan, is transferring from Sydney to join our band. Bob is a man of solid build, six feet tall, with fair, sandy hair and shaggy blond eyebrows. He is a man with a sensitive nature; he has no malice in his make-up, a wonderful sense of humour and is a brilliant musician.

On Christmas Day 1949, Bob and a few of the boys from the band play carols on our front lawn prior to Christmas dinner. For some unknown reason I only have two or three small drinks of alcohol all day. I am quite sober. Daphne and I are not fighting. There is no hurrying, no racing of the mind or anxieties. I feel safe and have a sense of belonging. My feelings and emotions are at peace. I feel loved and needed and enjoy spending time with my wife, child and friends. Maybe for the first time in my life I am tasting freedom, peace and contentment. I feel warm and clean inside. The sense of not belonging to anyone, anywhere, has been with me for years despite my father's love and my musical talents. Fear and isolation have also been my constant companions since my mother gave birth to a large, raw, exposed nerve with blue booties attached to its ends. Not a normal baby with head, arms and legs. No! Just a raw, quivering nerve, named Cliff. Somehow, a few moments after birth, this shaking pathetic nerve was set adrift from planet Earth. Some unseen force cut the nerve's lifeline and it was destined to float for eternity in space. Lost out there in the galaxy never to return. Alone, never to belong. Cliff, the nerve clown, always looked for approval as a child and continues to do so as an adult. I not only want to be liked, but always seek to fulfil a strong desire to be loved and needed. This Christmas is the first time I can ever remember feeling loved, needed and having a sense of belonging. I feel good inside. Unfortunately, these feelings of contentment are only fleeting.

By 1952, my marriage to Daphne is on very shaky grounds. She is at her wits' end trying to cope with two children, one in the pram with the bottle of milk and the other on the floor with his bottle of alcohol. To prevent the inevitable happening, an attempt is made to get my life back in order. I figure that if I can get out of the band and away from temptation, then my marriage will survive these troubled times.

The bulletin on the notice board reads: 'Members of the Regular Australian Army, who have experience in Cipher and wish to apply for a refresher course in March, may apply in writing to above address. Successful applicants who complete the course will then be assigned to Corps of Signals.' Having completed the full cipher decoding course when I was a member of the Royal Australian Air Force, I see this as my chance to get out of the band. Within the walls of a signal office there is no limelight, booze or excitement. I can now have a nice, quiet, responsible way of living without the temptations. The stage is set to save my marriage, get off the demon drink and be a responsible person.

The refresher course is completed within eight weeks and I await transfer to a signal regiment. Meanwhile, my attention is once more drawn to a bulletin which reads: 'Members fully trained as Cipher Operators may apply for service with British Commonwealth Occupation

Forces stationed at Australian Signal Regiment, Kure, Japan.'

'Daphne,' I yell into the phone, 'what do you think?' I explain the possibility of an overseas posting to Japan. She is reassured that this can be my chance for promotion as well as saving lots of money. Though she agrees quietly with everything I am saying, she seems totally disinterested. Perhaps she has heard too many broken promises. There is no emotion in her voice as she replies, 'Yes, dear. No, dear. If you think so, Cliff.'

Within three days I am accepted, receive my departure date and prepare for my trip to Japan. Daphne arranges for a removalist to transfer our belongings back to Sydney, where she will stay with her mother.

There are fifteen other soldiers on board a civilian Qantas flight from Sydney to Japan. As the plane settles above the clouds and seat belts come off, the pretty stewardess asks me a sociable question: 'Can I offer you a drink of alcohol or otherwise, sir?' Realising that the offer is free of charge, how can I be unsociable? I proceed to get drunk.

Mid-morning we land at Kowloon Airport, near Hong Kong. We are informed that a bus will take us to the Seven Seas Hotel for our night's accommodation. After arriving, I convert my Australian currency to the local money and do my usual wanderings after lunch. By evening I am very intoxicated. Unfortunately, this member of the party does not taste the joy of a luxury stay at a grand hotel. I end up exploring Kowloon and its backstreets, finding myself in a very sleazy and dangerous part of this city.

Darkness closes in, but I soon have several new friends. Chinese men, women and children are all sitting or lying on large wooden platforms strewn along the sidewalk. These are their beds for the night. In my pockets I am carrying a large quantity of local currency, Hong Kong dollars; money I share generously with my new comrades. In no time we have a wonderful party going with booze flowing, grinning faces, laughter and loud chatter. Sign language is used for communication. If the signal is to be 'more booze', I half close my hand and move it towards my mouth in a drinking motion. At the same time, I produce a fist full of dollar bills and bingo—instant refreshments! My moment of recognition has arrived. Standing up, I clap my hands a few times to get their attention. As the chatter dies down to a quiet murmur I make my announcement: 'Ladies and gentle-man, I give you the star of Bridge Road, Glebe—me! The first part of the night's entertainment will include my singing the popular old song, "Carolina in the Morning". At the same time, my flashing feet shall tapdance with such grace that even the great Fred Astaire would be proud of my routine.' The first part of the show is met with great applause and cheering. There are many garbled words in their foreign tongue, and laughter. It's a sidewalk asylum. 'Friends,' I call out. 'Your attention, please. You are about to hear my rendition of that wonderful poem, "The Highwayman", by Alfred Noyes. Quiet please!' I put my forefinger to my lips.

The chattering and laughter subsides and a hush comes over my audience. I continue:

'The wind was a torrent of darkness
upon the gusty trees,
The moon was a ghostly galleon
tossed upon cloudy seas,
The road was a ribbon of moonlight
looping the purple moor,
And the highwayman came riding—
Riding—riding—
The highwayman came riding,
up to the old inn door . . .'

As I conclude there is silence. The faces of my audience have a confused look. Small dark eyes are squinting, puzzled. Mouths are wide open with astonishment. Being the egotistical drunken star performer, all I can see is that at last my talents are appreciated. This audience is spellbound by the magnificent entertainer and poet. I have them in the palm of my hand. I can feel the tremendous impact that I am having on my captive audience. While they are probably thinking, 'What in the name of hell is this bloody lunatic talking about?'

I keep producing money to buy the booze I need to have a great night with my newfound friends, and I keep my audience entertained for hours. Eventually, tiredness creeps in and my energy level begins to drop rapidly. My audience also tire and begin falling asleep. I slide down onto one of the hard wooden planks. Silently, a quiet darkness descends within me. It is only then that the star of the show retires and finally passes out into a deep drunken sleep.

The smell of rotting cabbage tingles my nostrils as I come out of my unconscious state. Sitting up, I am not sure if it is a grey night or murky dawn. All around me are sleeping bodies strewn about like heaps of discarded clothing. I begin talking to myself. 'This must be the end of the world. Perhaps sometime during the night everyone on earth has died and right now it is Judgement Day. I must be the first one out of bed. Surely I can't be that bad!'

'We go, you hully,' a voice rasps in my ear. I slowly ease myself up onto my feet. It's the little Chinese rickshaw driver who taxied me here the night before. Looking at him I realise he has celebrated as much as I did. Gingerly, I climb into the rickshaw. My taxi driver picks up the long shafts of the vehicle, adjusts a leather harness over his shoulders and turns to give me a sickly smile. 'You okay?'

Still a little under the influence, I put my slouch hat on his small head, throw my arms up in the air and give the command: 'Let's go, General. Find the enemy. Charge!'

Back at the hotel I shower, change my clothes and make my way into the dining room for breakfast. I am confronted by a few of my soldier, travelling companions. 'Where did you get to last night?' they ask.

'Had a party in downtown Kowloon.'

A British army officer sitting at a nearby table suddenly turns and addresses me. 'Did you say you were in downtown Kowloon last night on your own?'

'Yes. I slept down there all night. Why?'

The officer frowns and says, 'Good God, young man. I'm stationed here and I would not go down there after dark with a platoon of twenty men. Don't you realise they are anti-British and would slit your throat for ten dollars?'

This news seems to bring a charge of new life into my weary body. All I can think is thank goodness I gave them all of my money. Maybe they were so amused by the uniformed lunatic jumping around that they did not wish to terminate the entertainment.

Finally, I arrive at Britcom Base Signal Regiment at Kure, a seaport on the southern tip of Japan. This is to be my place of residence for some time. Several weeks pass and I find the signal office boring; the monotonous tasks of sending and receiving messages is only broken by frequent pauses for cups of coffee. Doing shift work is a drain on my mind and body. My need for stimulation and excitement grows stronger as each day passes. On the regimental notice board, I read an ad for a clearance sale of tools, typewriters, heating appliances and musical instruments. The listing of musical instruments grabs my attention. I discover that some of these items have come from the American PX store in Tokyo. Immediately, I head for the store where the sale is being conducted. I am the only customer in attendance.

Searching through the many items for sale, I suddenly come upon two magnificent treasures. One is a gleaming gold-plated Selma trumpet and the other is a gold-plated Selma saxophone. My hands grasp both items and

I hurry downstairs to where the clerk in charge of the sale is sitting. 'Are these for sale?' I ask.

The clerk gives me the impression that he is bored with the temporary duty thrust upon him and the sooner it is finished, the better. Looking through his stock sheet he replies, 'Yeah, Selma sax and trumpet.' He then checks the square cardboard price tags hanging by string on each instrument case. His eyes wander back to the stock sheet. 'That's funny. On my stock sheet it says each of these instruments are forty-five pounds, yet on the price tags they only show twelve pounds each.'

'That's easy to explain. You see, these two instruments are out-of-date models,' is my ridiculous reply. I hope this will influence our negotiation, and I fail to tell him that I swapped price tags while he wasn't looking. But this guy is in the mood to clear the stock as quickly as possible and get back to his unit's routine duties, so we agree on the cheaper price and I am happy to pay. Walking from the building a feeling of levitation is with me and I'm sure my feet lift well off the ground. My decision to avoid the musical scene, booze and trouble is forgotten. Here I am just a few months in Japan and already planning to form a jazz band.

I track down Ted Trigg, a remarkable jazz pianist. I find him one evening playing piano in a beer hall. He is a British lad stationed within the same signal regiment as I am at Kure. Another Australian soldier, named Johnny Booth, also plays trumpet and agrees to join. Bobby Welsh is a drummer, who has played professionally prior to joining the army; he also becomes a member.

Les Rassmussen, a friend of Johnny Booth, brings his saxophone and clarinet along; he plays very well. Finally, a Canadian soldier, who plays trombone, joins after discussions between his commanding officer and our boss, Colonel Croft. Both officers are right behind us forming this jazz band.

Our group collects a good library of musical arrangements and rehearses regularly. Colonel Croft has me immediately transferred to his administration building for daytime office duties instead of shift work in the signal office. Finally, the 'Magnificent Six' are ready and engagements come thick and fast from the British nursing officers, Canadian officers' mess, Australian officers' clubs, New Zealand groups and American organisations. We are in great demand, sometimes working six or seven nights a week. The individual payment to each member of the band is almost on a par with a general's weekly pay. My drinking becomes consistent and heavy. The only bonus is that I can lick my wounds from the night before while wandering around the administration building doing absolutely nothing. I plan my recovery drink at lunchtime in the camp canteen and spend the day trying to settle my nervous system. I virtually have a free reign because of Colonel Croft's love for the musical group within his command. He affectionately refers to the group as 'his boys'.

Colonel Basil St Clair Croft, our beloved leader, comes up with an idea one day that leaves us almost speechless. 'Cliff, what do you think about putting on a show? A full musical production performed by our own signal regiment with dancing, comedy skits, solo performers and musical routines. Perhaps a comedy sketch with an all-male ballet, similar to live theatre back home. We have the Kure Theatre across the road, which seats about five hundred people. Other military personnel can operate curtains, spotlights and act as stage hands. Costumes and props can be prepared by the Japanese work force within the signal regiment.' I stand there speechless with my mouth wide open looking at Basil in wonderment. 'Well, what do you say?' he asks.

'The idea sounds really great, sir. Can I give you an answer after I have had time to think this through?' I add.

That night I confer with three of my friends, who have had theatrical experience prior to joining the army. 'Choc' Moran worked with the great comedian George Wallace Senior back in Australia. Barry White had been connected with amateur theatre in Melbourne. Freddie 'Buggsie' Elliot knows song and dance routines very well. Buggsie is a very comical man—he has protruding upper teeth and claims he is the only man in the world who can eat a carrot through a venetian blind. The four of us agree that we have nothing to lose by giving this our best shot. It means hard work for three or four months as we put the show together and rehearse, but we like the fact we will not have to do any regular military duties.

Amazingly, 'Folies Berserk', opens after twelve weeks of constant rehearsals. People come from near and far to see our opening night. The unanimous opinion of all is stated when an American military journalist writes, 'The musical variety show, namely "Folies Berserk", presented by members of the Royal Australian Signal Regiment at Kure last night, was an outstanding success. The show moved with smooth precision and provided wonderful entertainment to a capacity house. My congratulations to all people connected with its production. It was a truly professional performance.' The show runs for five consecutive nights.

Life after the show moves along in an irresponsible way. I experience heavy drinking bouts, yet still manage to play regularly with the jazz band. There are many times when I completely forget that I am a member of the Australian Regular Army. But I know this lifestyle will have to end at some stage. And my assumption proves correct.

Colonel Croft is suddenly posted back to mainland Australia. The new commanding officer, whom I call Colonel 'Hit 'em Hard', is a dour little man, a cross between a gospel preacher and prison warder. He is intent on turning this regiment into a full-time military machine. He immediately disbands the jazz band. The only music I reckon he can tolerate is the 'Funeral March'! This new officer applies pressure, discipline and military law. I apply for a compassionate posting back to Australia. He most likely knows my track record because my transfer is approved within one month of his arrival. I board a medical evacuation plane, stop for one night at Guam American Naval Base in the South Pacific, then fly home.

Farewell to Khaki

For a brief time Daphne and I go through the motions of being a married couple with a child. It is hopeless. I know nothing about my family's needs or feelings and continuous drinking prevents me from bonding with them. Even Fred comments on how I have changed. He tells me that my attitudes towards life cause me to be full of resentment and anger. I know he is right but I cannot admit the truth. My life consists of living from one crisis to the next. I do not care about people, places or things. My fear of the unknown creates great anxiety, which constantly eats away at my soul. Many times my fear becomes stark terror. I am slowly reaching the point of being too frightened to live, yet too scared to die. Stationed back at Victoria Barracks' signal office, I am even admonished by my old friend, Warrant Officer Ray Warren. We have been friends since early days at the signal regiment in Japan. He is in charge and warns me of forthcoming disaster if I do not pull myself together.

I become so dependent on alcohol that I always carry two small bottles of brandy in the pockets of my military jacket for emergencies.

'I cannot go on like this any longer, Cliff. I'm sick of your promises. I won't put up with this insane way of living. I'm leaving you, Cliff, and may God help you!' are Daphne's final words. They mean very little to me because of my befuddled brain. She doesn't mean it, is my only thought as I lie back on the bed and act like nothing is going to happen. I fall into a deep intoxicated sleep. The following morning I awake with the sun streaming into the bedroom. There is no response to my call. The room suddenly feels bare. Climbing from the bed, I open the wardrobe. It's empty except for a few of my clothes. I'm shocked and say, 'Hell, she's done it. She really has gone!' Throwing my few belongings into a suitcase, there is only one course I can take. I leave the rented house, go to Victoria Barracks and report my situation. I am assigned to living quarters, not knowing that I would never see Daphne again.

By June 15, 1954, my six-year term of enlistment has expired. I receive my discharge papers and walk through the large gates of Marrickville Barracks. By mid-afternoon I am a civilian. A free man in the heart of Sydney. Part of me wants to run back through those gates to rejoin my military family. For roughly eight years the army has been the only place where I have experienced family, discipline, security and meaning. I feel a sense of both panic and freedom. Suddenly, I am on my own. At twenty-seven, I am attempting to stand on my own two feet and there is no path to follow. I'm in the city of my birth but where is home? Where do I belong?

Many people after completing their service in the armed forces return home, but I don't have such a place to go. My mother's wealthy sister, Aunt Ethyl, has purchased my old home at 2 Jarocin Avenue. She is a deeply religious person and regularly entertains important church dignitaries. I called her a hypocrite one day because Nell, who is still drinking and causes no trouble, is only a tolerated resident, provided she does all the household chores and leaves or enters the house via the rear door. Aunt Ethyl was furious with me and told me not to enter her home again. Fred and I are like ships in the night and are unable to locate each other. I have no idea where to find him.

The Department of Army has deposited large amounts of operational service and accumulated leave payments into my bank account. There is only one place to go.

'Taxi,' I yell. 'Take me down to the Central Railway Hotel.'

The foyer and reception area of the hotel is deserted. The large clock reads 3 p.m. I slap the small bell on the counter and a tall, pimply faced youth appears. 'Yeah, what is it?' Taken back a little by his warm welcome, I book a room for one week. 'That's fine. Sign here. The rent is in advance,' says the spotted clerk. I then walk up the circular stairway to the first floor, find room number fourteen and enter.

Sitting on the hard single bed, my eyes wander around the room. A drab, dark-brown dressing table, with a broken brass handle hanging from one of its two drawers, stands in the far corner of the room. On the top is a lonely, large bottle of water with a clean beer glass draped upside down over its neck. My glance turns to the other corner of the room. I see a small porcelain sink, which is attached to the wall. It is chipped on the rim and within the sink bowl is a rusty water mark stretching from the tap down into the plug hole. I believe this stain could never be removed no matter how hard one scrubbed. Near the sink is a straight-backed, solid, hard wooden chair, which looks to offer far more pain than comfort. The carpet is almost paper-thin and stained in many places by former tenants. They probably abused this room with lonely, insane behaviour. There is one solitary window that opens to reveal a view of a brick wall belonging to the premises next door. The curtains are flimsy and a wishy-washy grey. They perform a time-worn flutter dance as the winter breeze floats through. I close the window quickly. There is no sign of a heater. I know by looking at the thread-bare blankets that I am going to be in for a long, cold night.

After convincing myself that I have made the right decision, I close the door behind me and walk downstairs into a small back parlour to order a beer. The only other customer in the parlour is a little old lady, maybe in her seventies. Her bony fingers wrap around a small glass of deep-red wine as she looks into space. I doubt if she has even seen me enter the room.

'Hello, love. Do you mind if I sit with you?' I ask.

She gives me a warm smile and very quietly replies, 'Not at all. That will be all right.'

The compulsive clock-watcher has to know the time of day. It is 4 p.m. After a few drinks, I start to tell her about the marriage breakdown, my little daughter Christine and my hope for the future. She has lost her grandson in the war and her husband deserted her. Living in poverty, she can only live in a small guest house on the fringe of the city. She just struggles through each day. Two lost souls seek comfort by giving each other precious time to talk of our deepest feelings and emotions. After six or seven drinks we both feel as though we have reached a new plateau of joyous wellbeing. There is laughter and songs to sing. Sadly, it is finally time for departure. My dear, old, new friend rises out of her chair, informs me that it is now close to 6 p.m. and she has to leave for home. I walk with her to the front door and hail a taxi cab. I also put some money into her hand. She is embarrassed to accept it, but I insist. Prior to stepping into the vehicle, she turns and says, 'Thank you for a wonderful time, Cliff. Thank you for listening. You take good care of yourself, son.' The taxi speeds off and the last I see of this wonderful old lady is her waving hand from the back seat of the cab.

I purchase a bottle of wine from the bottle department and walk upstairs to room fourteen. Once inside, I sit on the bed. After pouring a drink from my sole companion, the bottle of red, I slowly sip the wine and contemplate my future. No answer is forthcoming, so I start to softly sing, 'Nothing would be finer than to be with Carolina in the morning . . .' As the night drags on, my state of drunkenness increases, along with the isolation and feelings of abandonment. Just prior to falling asleep, I once more feel the powerful emotion I experienced as a small boy. For the second time in my life the walls are weeping.

Over the next few days I go from pub to pub in the Haymarket area. Skid row is only a few hundred yards from where I am staying. My intention is to find Fred, who is well known for busking in this area. I enter the bar of the Palace Hotel and think, What a joke naming this dive the Palace. I'll bet a member of the Royal family never got within six blocks of this place! Fred's face lights up when he sees me. There is a mixture of love and excitement as he speaks. 'When did you get home? How's Daphne and Christine? Where are you living?' Fred is not aware of what has transpired in my life. After hearing all the sad news, he just lowers his head and wipes his face with a handkerchief. I wonder if he is brushing away a tear or two. He quietly asks, 'Would you like a beer?'

'Would I ever,' is my response, as I begin to feel the pain of the marriage breakup and my leaving the army. We chat for a while then Fred heads to another hotel to busk. I proceed to get drunk to drown my troubles. Both Fred and I are wanderers.

I continue to hang around the Mad Mile area, frequently drinking at local watering holes like the Palace, the Capitol and the Stadiums. Desperate forms of humanity, the least and the lost, gather here to console each other. The main conversation is what life could have been like . . . if only? Drinking and gambling on race-horses shrinks my bank account. In a space of three months, I squander over three hundred pounds of my military pay. By September, my bank balance is two pounds and I become homeless. Unfortunately, my need for the demon drink and compulsive gambling are ever present. Both escapes are impatient and do not allow time for me to organise things or think. I pawn the Selma trumpet and saxophone for a mere fraction of their worth to feed my drinking and gambling addictions. If I had been patient and advertised, I would have received at least ten times as much for these two wonderful instruments.

Often I am found drinking in the back parlour of the Palace Hotel at 7 a.m. This area is unofficially reserved for Aboriginal men and women. I don't understand how they tolerate me. Many times I am up dancing on the table singing 'Old Man River' or the ever faithful 'Carolina in the Morning'. For a change of pace, I start protesting about the injustice handed out by the current government toward Aboriginal people. 'What about the rights of Aborigines? Are they always to be regarded as second-rate citizens? It's time for action!' One particular Aboriginal man, Jim, a former champion boxer, is very kind toward the crazy, tap-dancing drunkard. There are times when he gently lifts me off the table and he softly says, 'Come on, Cliffy. I've bought you a drink. Stop sounding off. You are putting Aboriginal rights back ten years with your antics.'

Sleeping arrangements are wherever I can find a bed for the night. Drinking partners sometimes make an offer for me to sleep on a couch or spare bed at their home. Other times a railway station or a park under the stars is my night's accommodation.

One balmy September evening, after another day of heavy drinking, I walk through Belmore Park in the inner city. Looking up I see the dark-blue, velvet sky parading a galaxy of its brightest stars. My feelings are those of a man on a mission. I want to walk right up to the moon and perhaps stay there for just one precious night. Oh to get away from hell on earth. Maybe there I can find peace and freedom. A heavy hand is suddenly on my shoulder. Startled, I turn around to hear a burly, stern-faced policeman say, 'You're drunk!' He grasps my upper arm and guides me towards the patrol vehicle. My park associates call this means of transport either the 'Black Maria' or the 'Hurry-up Wagon'. I laugh to myself as I remember one of my funny drinking companions, who is often arrested for being drunk. He tells me that he must be the 'Son of God' because every time he is arrested the police officers greet him in the same way, 'Jesus Christ, not you again!' I experience my first time being in the 'Snake Pit' or the 'Drunks' Tank'. I manage to sleep for a few hours.

When I wake up, the overpowering stench of human excrement in the police cell attacks my senses. There are a dozen bodies sprawled and writhing in a putrid mass of humanity. I close my eyes, hoping everything and everyone will disappear. I hear a policeman call my name, and follow him out into the charge room of the police station. Relief washes over me as I see Fred standing there paying my ten-shilling fine. He tells me that one of my drinking mates, who saw me arrested and taken to Central police cells, sought him out and informed him of my plight. Good old Fred once more to my rescue.

'Where are you living?' he asks.

'Nowhere!'

Fred has recently moved into an old, two-storey house with six other male tenants. The house is in Foveaux Street, Surry Hills, right in the heart of the city. I join Fred and take up residence in my new home.

One tenant, Alf, digs trenches and lays pipes. When he digs the earth he stirs up the fleas living there. They jump onto his legs and clothes, making him a two-legged means of transport for a mass emigration of fleas into the house at Surry Hills. The 'Flea Trap Inn' is therefore the name the tenants bestow on this flop house. During long, suffocating summer nights, the fleas attack me. Even while drunk on cheap wine they still disturb my sleep. Often I stagger from filthy bedding in the early hours of the morning, walk downstairs, sit on the front veranda and await the sunrise.

Some mornings, around 5 a.m., I leave the house and stroll around the inner-city streets. Cockroaches scurry across my path, the odd grey rat slithers down an open drain. Every now and then a slight breeze causes sheets of newspaper to flutter along the gutter. The deserted streets and eerie silence of the grey, concrete jungle make me think. Perhaps today is really our last day on earth. Is this the day of Armageddon? Suddenly, the silence is shattered by a whirring sound. The spell is broken. The invader of my silence is the circular brush feet of the street-sweeping machine kicking up puffs of dust. Perched on top of this mechanical monster is another human being who waves an early morning greeting to the only soul in sight—me. I realise it is not the end of the world. Instead, all I have left is another day of painful living. After watching the glaring, gold ball of sunrise appear between tall office buildings, I aimlessly wander back to the house. Life seems to have lost all meaning and I wonder why I exist.

Manure, Music and Love

My twenty-eighth birthday is no different to any other day. Most people celebrate their birthdays in style. Mine comes and goes in a blur of alcohol. Four days later I journey from Surry Hills to the British Lion Hotel in Glebe. I often come here for the nightly entertainment performed in the beer garden. I find myself a seat directly in front of the stage, and am about to order a drink when a waiter suddenly appears before me. He points towards the area where the band is to perform and says, 'You will have to move, sir. This table is reserved for the band.' I start to rise out of my seat, when a voice from the stage says, 'He'll be all right there.' I nod my thanks to the banjo player and instantly like this slim-built man with a distinguished look. He has fair hair, a blond, neatly trimmed moustache and is dressed in a well-cut, grey, business suit. He looks to be about fifty years of age. I thank him once more and resume my seat.

There are three people on stage, the banjo player, a middle-aged woman playing piano and a young man on drums. I settle in and order a drink. Suddenly, I hear a familiar voice ring out. There, to my surprise, is Fred. I point to an empty chair at my table and beckon my dad to join me. Fortunately for me, Fred has had a good week busking. He has plenty of money to ensure a good night's entertainment. Fred buys me a few drinks and coaxes me to get up and sing. He is naturally concerned about how much I have been drinking of late yet most times he keeps his thoughts to himself. Fred is always in control of his drinking and only has a few drinks. When he sees me out of control he usually tells me to get off the spirits and drink beer because spirits send me off my head. When I eventually get up on the stage to sing a few songs it is received favourably, probably because I am still reasonably sober.

Later my attention is drawn towards a tall man walking in a peculiar way through the crowd. He is swaying from hip to hip, carrying a large, black piano accordion case. He gingerly approaches and then places one foot tentatively on the stage. It is then I see the steel callipers attached to his boots. 'Can I give you a hand up there, mate?' I ask pointing to the high step.

He gives me a beautiful, warm smile, accepts my assistance and says, 'You're a good man!'

'I know!' We both look at each other and laugh loudly. The bond between us is instant. A mentally handicapped person helping a physically handicapped person is somehow understood between us.

When the band takes its first break, Fred generously invites them to join us at their own table. We learn that the piano accordion player is known as Jock. He is thirty-five years old and lives on his own in an old weatherboard house at Naremburn, on the northern side of Sydney. Three years ago he had a motorbike accident, which crippled him, and shortly after this tragic accident his wife left him. The evening festivities continue and the band joins us once again during their ten-minute break. By this time we are all in high, friendly spirits. Bruce on banjo, Rona on piano, Keith on drums, Fred, Jock and myself all enjoying each other's company.

Fred starts to boast about his son's talent as a comedian and musician. 'He started his career with the Glebe Band when he was seven and when he was ten he studied and played the piano accordion with another talented young musician, called Enzo. You know, Enzo Toppano, the world-class musician.' Fred's promotion of my talents causes the band members to insist that I join them on stage. After singing and telling a few jokes, I play Jock's piano accordion. I even have a turn on the drums. Several free drinks later, I unofficially become the band's star. It is a case of an instant miniature floorshow without rehearsals. Our audience is too pissed to recognise any mistakes.

The publican approaches me at the end of the night. He suggests that I join the band. He is prepared to offer a small fee, free drinks and my evening meal on Friday and Saturday nights. I am excited at the prospect and accept. I mention to Jock about my living conditions at the Flea Trap Inn, and he immediately offers me accommodation at his house. He adds, 'I don't expect you to pay any rent, Cliff. Just chip in for food.' This seems to be my lucky night. Fred informs Jock that he, too, is residing at Itchy House and would appreciate the chance to evacuate. Within minutes the three of us climb into Jock's old, chugging truck, drive to Surry Hills to retrieve our belongings and then drive towards our new home. As we drive over the Sydney Harbour Bridge, Fred and I gaze at the night lights surrounding the harbour. We feel like kings. What an odd assortment of lost souls! Fred, a sixty-three-year-old World War I veteran, his twenty-eight-year-old alcoholic son and Jock, a thirty-five-year old cripple left alone by his wife. We don't feel sad, because we all have renewed hope for the future.

Jock informs us that he works part-time for himself as a 'compostologist'. This 'profession' involves picking up horse manure and delivering it to vegetable farmers and householders for their gardens. Jock recently lost his assistant and he is delighted when Fred and I offer our services. We are thrilled when we are promised a weekly wage.

Monday morning Fred and I climb aboard the truck. Jock hauls his semi-useless legs into the cabin. But his disability seems to vanish as he gives two quick movements on the gear stick and the truck roars out of the driveway. Our heads are jerked back during take-off and we see the magic transformation of Jock the cripple into an Indianapolis speed king. The vehicle tears down the highway at frightening speed, while Fred and I wonder how he manages to do this with his crippled legs.

On arrival at the first racing stable, horses heads peer at us. Jock hands me a large, five-pronged pitchfork and says, 'Here take this, Cliff.' I follow him for a short distance as he hops along on his crutches. Finally, he stops in front of a square, six-foot-high, brick structure. Jock points and gives the order: 'Jump in.'

I climb up to see what's inside and discover steaming horse manure piled at least five feet high. 'What do I do?' is my fearful question as the stench takes my breath away.

Jock gives a cheeky grin and laughs, 'You hop in and fork the manure into a chaff bag, which Fred will hold.' My stomach churns at the thought. He then turns and addresses Fred. 'You stand on the ledge that surrounds the bottom of the manure pit. Hold the bag open for Cliff to fill.'

Fred and I hesitate at the edge of the pit. We give each other a horrified look and both wonder how the hell we got ourselves into this situation. Neither of us wants to return to the Flea Trap Inn so we both begin our day's labour. This activity is not recommended for anybody suffering from a hangover.

I become drenched with perspiration because I am not used to such hard physical activity. The heat is suffocating. Fred's task is less stressful but by the end of the day he is exhausted, too. That evening at the local pub we are barely able to pick up the first glass of refreshing beer. While we are drinking and laughing about the day's long torture in the manure pit, Jock breaks the news that a young chap is starting work the following day. He is to get into the pit of horror, I am to hold the bags and Fred is to stay at home to take telephone enquiries. My father and I are relieved, and Jock sits there grinning with a glass of beer in his hand. His eyes twinkle in a devilish way as he reflects on the comedy of the 'father and son show' in the pit today.

My good fortune continues. Three days later Jock informs me that he has hired another young man to hold the bags in the 'No Mercy' pit. He then explains my new position. 'Henceforth, you will be known as the company's Manure Sales Representative!'

I am relieved to get out of the pit and excited to be promoted. 'What do you want me to do?'

'You just need to knock on the doors of wealthy, prospective buyers, who live in large homes, and convince them that our bags of horse manure are of premium quality. You can work three days of the week, starting at 1 p.m. each day.'

Knowing that I have the gift of the gab, I reply, 'This will be easy, Jock.' I drink more beers to celebrate my promotion.

The week begins with Jock and the newly hired hands leaving home at 7 a.m. to do the daily rounds for the vegetable farmers. At noon they return home for lunch. When the truck is reloaded with large chaff bags full of manure, I'm ready for my afternoon shift. Around 1 p.m. Jock and I start to deliver the phone orders taken by Fred. Some additional bags of manure have been added to the load so that I can do my door-to-door sales.

The old truck slithers into the kerb outside a large white mansion. Jock has that big grin on his face and points to the large, double oak door. 'Off you go, Cliff. Let's see you strut your stuff!'

After my hesitant knock, the door slowly opens. A middle-aged woman dressed in a scarlet satin dress stands before me. She has six diamond rings on her left hand and a ruby ring the size of a strawberry on the other. Sitting obscenely above one breast is a giant, emerald-green brooch surrounded by small diamonds. The weight of this ornament would make me round shouldered. Around her neck hangs a glistening, three-strand set of cultured pearls, and matching, large, pearl earrings glare at me from droopy earlobes. She has tight, pursed, scarlet lips and a nose that is upturned, sniffing the air. This woman is endowed with wealth and my first impression is: bloody hell, is this how these people dress for lunch? I am not impressed by her ornamental appearance or her I'm-better-than-you aura, but I immediately start to feel self-conscious about my own appearance.

'Yes, what is it?' comes the question from Her Highness.

Panic grips me and I blurt out, 'How are ya fixed for horse shit, lady?'

The door slams shut in my face with a large bang.

My first point of sale is disastrous, and Jock informs me that I am never to refer to our product in that manner again. The correct term, I learn, is compost. After receiving more of Jock's sound instruction, I change tactics. From that moment on I never have another door slammed shut in my face. I assure people that our product does not come from underprivileged horses or the common cart horse. No, sir! Our manure comes from the finest thoroughbreds that grace the racetracks of Sydney. My sales pitch works. I am amazed that it actually impresses some upper-class people. They only want the best in life, even horse manure for their gardens! As my confidence grows my line of sales improves. My favourite sales pitch is, 'Thoroughbred manure is quality compost. It is far superior to that of the common horse. Yes, madam, it's the breeding, you know!' To my surprise my sales figures are very good. Both Jock and Fred are impressed and I start to feel like I belong somehow to the human race.

These are happy carefree times for all of us. On Tuesdays and Thursdays we drink at the local hotel and become an instant hit with the local patrons. Fred plays guitar while Jock and I take it in turn to play the piano accordion. Fred is very popular among the older patrons with his solo renditions of the First World War old favourites like 'Keep the Home Fires Burning', 'The Rose of No Man's Land' and 'Tipperary'.

Friday and Saturday nights are our big nights, though. We scrub up after our working week and drive to Glebe for our regular musical gig at the British Lion. We become enormously popular and I christen our little group the 'Oughta-be-Shots'.

One Saturday night after playing a bracket of numbers a woman walks up to the stage and bellows out like an army sergeant major, 'Jock, you old bastard! Where in the name of hell have you been?' She is short, about thirty years old, has a lovely, warm, open face and a nice compact figure.

Jock instantly recognises this dark-haired dynamo and replies, 'Well, I'll be damned! Is it really you, Ella?'

Jock and Ella were dance partners in their teenage years. They have not seen each other for a long time and there is much hugging and laughter. Ella notices the callipers on Jock's legs. He tells her about the accident and his wife leaving, and she is shocked into silence for a few moments, probably thinking about what a great dance partner Jock was and how he will never dance again. She then looks up at him and says in her usual loud voice, 'Look, when the pub closes why don't you and your friends come around to my house. I'm going to have a party.' She then turns to face the audience and announces, 'I'm having a Saturday night bash to welcome the return of my old mate, Jock. Everyone is welcome.' The intoxicated crowd cheers at the thought of more entertainment after the pub closes. Ella makes it quite clear to everyone that each person is to bring at least one bottle of alcohol, only the band is excused from this requirement.

The small, two-storey house is packed with about forty people by the time we arrive. Ella has a heart of gold and warmly greets her guests. Suddenly, with her auctioneer's voice she says, 'Now I want everyone to have a good time. I don't want any punch-ups or anyone puttin' the 'ard word on the women. If ya feel crook, then don't have a technicolour yawn in the house. Get down the backyard and bring it up. Okay?' A few of the crowd respond with grunts and others say, 'All right, Ella.' She resumes her instruction, 'Now we can all have a good party and sing along if everyone behaves. We can . . .' She stops speaking. Her gaze is now on the dining room table where one lonely bottle of cheap wine stands. She then continues, 'Right, you slimy pack of bastards. Go and get your grog from wherever you have hidden it. I'll check every one of you bloody mongrels to make sure you all bring a bottle of booze back. Now move it!'

Whenever Ella puts on a party, we learn, the guests try to conserve their own booze by hiding it and drinking the grog left out on the table by the 'mugs'. They stash their grog in Ella's garbage bin, the garden, the bottom of her stove or under her house. After consuming someone else's grog, they later retrieve their own bottles to take home.

Slowly, the hidden supplies start to appear and the party takes off in full swing. As the night progresses some of the guests find their voices. One bloke is sitting under a table singing into a shoe that he is holding to his mouth like a microphone. A young woman feels the desire to be the queen of strippers. Inspired by the urging cheers of the crowd, she strips down to her bra and black lace panties. Her husband grabs her by the scruff of her neck and drags her into the kitchen. He has a bundle of her clothes under his arm. A romantic couple stand in the middle of the room with their eyes locked together. They have their arms around each other's necks and are singing 'The Indian Love Call', loudly—their voices are totally out of tune. The room is filled with cigarette smoke, wild singing, insanity, screaming and laughter. The clatter of glasses is intermingled with people crying and shouting. It's bedlam at Ella's house.

A banging sound is heard at the front door and a voice booms out above the noise: 'Open up! Police here. Open up, Ella!' When the door is opened it reveals a large sergeant with his equally big partner.

'Hello, Donk!' Ella says in greeting.

'Don't call me that, Ella!' snaps the sergeant. Donk is the nickname given to him by the locals from Glebe. 'Listen to me, Ella. There have been several complaints about the noise coming from here.' He steps inside the house. 'God almighty, Ella, you must have half the population of Glebe in here!'

The dishevelled hostess is in tipsyland and replies, 'Awww, sorry about the noise, Donk, er, I mean, sergeant. We're having a musical evening. Come in and have a beer. I'll quieten things down for you.'

Within half an hour Donk and his partner are singing louder than anybody in the room. Ella has the policeman's cap and jacket on and begins to threaten everybody with the possibility of arrest. We, the Oughta-be-Shots, continue our mad antics and should have been shot! Eventually, the merrymakers start to collapse onto the floor, chairs, beds and even the front lawn. As rays of sunshine filter through the large lounge room window around 5 a.m., Jock suggests to Fred and I that we end our festivities and go. He wants to leave before the coppers sober up, change their minds and arrest the lot of us. We give our farewell hugs and kisses to Ella, file out the front door and get into the good old truck that will take us back home.

A few days later, I do something very rare; I decide to go to the movies at the Lyric Theatre in the Haymarket. A strange feeling of normalcy begins to occur as I do what the rest of my fellow human beings do—stand in the queue to buy a ticket. Unaware of who is standing behind me, I hear a voice say, 'Cliffy?'

I turn around and before me is a fantastic-looking brunette, who is the image of the actress Jane Russell. Her face is very familiar and eventually I realise who it is. 'Shirley? Shirley Ogden?' is my shocked response. 'God you were about twelve the last time I saw you.' I am so thrilled to see her. I give her a big hug and say, 'Let's buy our tickets, have a coffee before the show and do some catching up.'

'I'd love to, Cliff,' she smiles.

We buy our tickets, find a cosy spot and begin reminiscing. We have known each other since 1936 when Shirley was seven and I was nine. It is now 1956. As children we played together and celebrated our birthdays on the same day. Shirley would always come and watch when I played in the Glebe band at Rest Park. She was my childhood sweetheart and number one fan. There is much to reminisce about our school days and the antics we used to get up to, and we laugh about those happy times. Shirley also explains that she has just walked away from a failed marriage. We both have a sympathetic ear for each other.

Over the next few months we see each other frequently and old feelings are rekindled. Our relationship takes on a new meaning and we finally decide to move in together. I have been living with Jock for over twelve months and in April I say my farewells. I inform both Jock and Fred that I will no longer be a member of the British Lion Hotel band because I am moving in with Shirley and want to make something of my life. I tell them that I want to get away from the booze and my irresponsible lifestyle. Fred approves of my decision to try and get myself together, and Jock is very understanding, yet both are disappointed to see me leave.

Shirley and I rent a two-bedroom furnished flat away from Glebe and the temptation to drink. I really want this relationship to work, so I begin to look for suitable employment. Within a few days I am successful in applying for work as a tram conductor—but no-one informs me about the dangers associated with the job. Being a conductor entails walking on a very narrow, twelve-inch footboard which runs along the outside of the tram, and trying to walk along this ledge I am hampered by a large, leather money bag hanging over my right shoulder. A fifteen-inch-long ticket book is held in my left hand and my other hand is used to slide the compartment doors open. The lack of a third arm makes the job extremely perilous, especially when the tram is moving at high speed. Here I am issuing tickets and change from my bag while unable to hold onto anything. The risk factor is normally high, but dramatically increases when I am continually pissed on the job.

After four weeks at work, I am summoned to appear before the depot master. I wonder if he is going to promote me. His opening question as he puffs himself up and squares his shoulders is, 'Number 9975, do you have a problem working out finance?' After seeing the confused look on my face, he continues, 'Is it 'ard for you to work out 'ow much change to give when you collect a fare?'

'Not at all, boss,' I reply.

The depot master squirms in his chair. He slowly leans to one side as if he is about to pass wind, lowers his head and peers at me from above his rimless glasses. He has a flushed face and looks similar to someone with acute constipation. Suddenly, he lifts his head and yells, 'You have the worst money shortages I have encountered. The first two weeks your shortages totalled ten pounds, seven shillings. The third and fourth weeks, six pounds, nine shillings. What do you have to say?'

I reply with confidence, 'Don't worry about it, boss. I know about the shortages. I've been a bit short of funds at home. Treat the money as a sub, you know, an advance on my wages. Just take it out of my pay each fortnight.'

He gives me a look as if I have insulted him. His face turns as red as a beetroot. I am still explaining the situation when I notice strange hissing sounds coming from within him. My concern is that the poor man may have a fit. He finally speaks and spittle flies out of his mouth.

His voice is thunderous as he beckons his assistant into his office. 'Come and take this man's bag, uniform, cap, ticket book and anything else that belongs to the Tramways Department. Get him out of my sight and this depot before he sends the State Government bankrupt!'

This display of anger shakes my self-esteem and sense of reality. Even at the age of thirty I still have a kind of boyish lack of understanding about how the 'real' world works. I cannot understand why I can't expect generosity from the boss. Other bosses had always given me a sub. I'm confused about why this man is in such a fluster over a few pounds. His actions interrupt my good intentions to get my life in order and once more I am unemployed. I begin to wander from job to job, managing to obtain work on building sites as a labourer or working in factories. Unfortunately, my drinking increases and I am unable to maintain steady employment. Shirley works in a sandwich bar to make ends meet and eventually becomes the sole breadwinner. She is annoyed that I cannot manage to keep a job and often pleads with me to cut back on my drinking.

Despite Shirley becoming very disillusioned regarding our relationship, she decides that having a child might make me a responsible person, give me something to work for and curtail my drinking. In October, she informs me that she is pregnant. The news thrills me and once more I promise that I will reduce my intake of alcohol and settle down. Although I manage to control my drinking for almost nine months I am very irritable and discontented. All my emotions are trapped inside and I have no way to escape them. I feel very restless.

On the evening of June 18, 1957, our destination is King George V Maternity Hospital in Camperdown. After I assist Shirley into the building, the staff immediately take control. I am left alone to sit in the waiting room. Several hours later, a nurse walks towards me and tells me that I am the father of a seven-pound girl. I feel a tingle race through my body. The same nurse reappears later with a small bundle in her arms. I gaze at the baby with admiration. Is she really my daughter? She is so tiny. Her mouth opens and closes gently and her eyes are shut. In her soft blonde hair is a small pink bow, a decoration courtesy of the medical staff. The nurse looks at me and asks, 'What do you think of Miss Australia 1977?'

'She's so beautiful!'

We name our daughter Helen Anne.

Home for the three of us is a rundown, semi-detached cottage in Glebe. This is all we can afford to rent and Shirley is not impressed. The house is set only a few paces back from a very busy highway, and trams, commercial vehicles and cars roar past our front door continuously. The brick walls of our house are unpainted and have many small gaps, because the solid white cement which once existed between the bricks is deteriorating. When it is quiet, late at night, I can hear the loose, sandy cement cascade onto the bedroom's linoleum floor, usually when a tram rattles past and vibrates the house. The backyard is forty feet long and twenty-five feet wide, and covered in knee-high grass. The small outside laundry is attached to the house and has loose rusted iron on its roof. Inside are two well-worn cement tubs with an old, rusty, tin bathtub. It is not inviting at any time, especially now that winter is here. The outside toilet is something straight out of a horror movie. The door hangs by one hinge. The wooden seat is partially buckled on one side, and there is a wide, one-inch gap at the front of it—whenever I squat on this seat, precaution is in order to prevent giving myself the 'pinch test'.

I have not seen Nell for a long time. She has become a person I can neither love nor hate. I feel sad that she cannot be part of my new family. She has become another lost soul.

It is well over a year since I have seen my good old dad. I guess he is enjoying the break from the stress of having to be responsible for me. I had not contacted him because I did not need his support. He hears through the grapevine that I am living in Glebe and he visits just before Christmas. He decides to rent a small room in Glebe and becomes a regular visitor. Shirley and I appreciate having Fred around. He is great company, often assists with the household chores and tries to keep me off the booze. His devotion to Helen is obvious when he teaches her songs, plays shops or takes her for long walks in the pram. We all become very close companions.

On March 8, 1959, Helen's sister, Kim Therese, is born at the same hospital. She is a dark-haired beauty, who motivates me to really want to take responsibility for my life. I manage once again to refrain from overindulging in alcohol. I now work at a factory in Glebe and love being in charge of the steel store. Only on the odd occasion do I step over the line into a wild binge. Without alcohol-induced dramas in my life, I start to believe that life is finally in order. But nothing ever prepares a person for the unexpected.

Heartache

It is a warm January day in 1961. Around 6 p.m. Shirley goes to the corner shop to purchase milk. I keep an eye on the girls, who are engrossed in Mickey Mouse on TV. Fortunately, I am sober. I turn around to speak to Helen, who is seated in her highchair. 'Do you like Mickey Mouse, love?' I notice there is something odd about the way her head is hanging down, her chin on her chest. Her body suddenly twitches and stops. Again it happens, a short, sharp burst.

Jumping to my feet I ask, 'What's up, love?' There is no reply. Lifting her chin with my hand, a cold chill sends shockwaves through my body. What confronts me is two vacant eyes with only the whites visible. Her mouth is opening and shutting with so much force that I can hear the clicking of her little teeth. Her whole body is convulsing. I grab a blanket, wrap it around her and am about to open the front door when Shirley arrives home. 'No time to explain,'

I tell her, 'I have to get Helen to the Children's Hospital.'

I am suddenly on the busy street, clutching Helen. My little finger is in her mouth to stop her from biting her tongue. My head is spinning. A large truck is heading straight for me as I stand in the middle of the road. I keep nodding my head up and down in a plea for the driver to stop. The large Coca-Cola truck screeches to a halt and the driver jumps out cursing, 'What in the hell do you think you're bloody doing?' He sees the child's condition and without hesitating guides me up into the cabin of the truck. 'I'll get you straight to the Children's Hospital, mate.'

I look back to where Shirley is standing and yell out, 'She's convulsing, Shirley. Follow me over to the hospital at Camperdown.'

The engine of the truck roars into life as we speed off in the direction of the hospital. My only concern is that my little girl may die. I am unaware of the pain or trickle of blood that is coming from my little finger. My saviour in the Coca-Cola truck assists us into the casualty department. After seeing Helen's condition, the nursing staff quickly take her behind closed doors. My new friend waits with me for quite some time. Eventually, I thank him from the bottom of my heart for all he has done. I convince him that I will be okay now and that I do not want to hold him up any longer. 'Hell, I don't even know your name!' I say. 'I feel embarrassed I haven't asked you before now.'

'People call me Popeye. I used to be in the navy,' he says as he stands up. When he reaches the door he turns and gives me a reassuring farewell wave. Popeye will always be my hero.

A nurse interrupts my thoughts. 'Helen is resting comfortably and will be kept here overnight for tests. Now let me look at that finger of yours.' She takes me into a small room and bandages my little finger; only now do I become aware of the painful throbbing.

When Shirley arrives she is very flustered and fires questions at me. 'What's happening? How's Helen? Where is she now?'

'She's in behind those closed doors. The doctors are examining her,' is all I can say.

We both sit speechless and afraid of the unknown. After an hour a medical officer advises us: 'Helen is resting quietly at the moment. We have managed to stop the convulsions but will need to do further tests tonight. Hopefully we will have the results for you both tomorrow morning. There is nothing more you can do tonight. Why don't you both go home, get a good night's rest and come back first thing in the morning.'

I ask the doctor, 'Are you sure she will be all right tonight?'

'Yes, she will be fine.' There is nothing else we can do but go home.

Fred kindly offers to look after little Kim while Shirley and I return to the hospital the following day. After four hours we still have no answers. Suddenly, a tall, grey-haired, senior medical officer appears. He introduces himself and his first words are, 'It is not good news.

Examinations reveal that your little girl has what is commonly known as a hole in the heart.'

The blood drains from my body. Shirley and I look at each other. Her face is the colour of chalk.

'What happens now?' I ask.

'It is imperative that the child be operated on, otherwise, in later life, this type of abnormality can be very destructive.'

We both contemplate what he has said and give approval for the operation to take place as soon as possible. Arrangements are made and the date is set. Our little girl is to undergo an operation which is virtually in its pioneer stages.

It is a worrying time sitting beside Helen's bed the day after the operation. She is a sorry sight, encased in a type of plastic tent. There are different kinds of monitoring equipment above her bed, leads are connected to her chest and neck, and tubes are attached to her small frame. She looks so tiny and helpless as she sleeps. Whispered conversations intermingle with the continuous bleep, bleep, bleep coming from one of the machines. Time seems to have stopped. We feel trapped in this never-ending moment. 'Please God bring my child back,' is my unspoken prayer.

Miraculously, we hear a soft voice say, 'Daddy. Mummy. Why are you crying?'

I cannot speak with this lump in my throat. I hold Helen's hand and comfort her. Thank you, God.

Mr Cohen, the surgeon who operated on Helen, greets us and says, 'The operation has been successful. After a seven-day precautionary stay in hospital, I see no reason why Miss Helen can't return home.'

Shirley and I hug each other with relief.

By March, Helen has been home for two months and is progressing well. But another drama is about to unfold. One day after breakfast, I go to our bedroom, and am shocked to find Shirley doubled up in pain on the floor. She begs me to call for a doctor. His diagnosis is severe kidney disorder.

Immediate arrangements are made to take Shirley to Royal Prince Alfred Hospital. Thankfully, Fred arrives after the ambulance departs and suggests that I go to the hospital, while he looks after Helen and Kim. At the hospital Shirley explains that she has a kidney infection and will be in hospital for four or five days. She then drops a bombshell: 'Cliff, I have phoned my mum. She will come over tomorrow and look after you and the girls while I am in hospital.'

I nearly fall off my chair. This woman, known by the name of Toddy is abrupt, intolerant and seems to have a great need to dominate my life. On the rare occasions that we have met it always seems to be a silent war. She is very antisocial and resents a lot of people. I happen to be one of them. She does not just have a chip on her shoulder, she has a railway sleeper. Toddy is a walking disaster. All I can say to Shirley, though, is, 'That's nice.'

Fred sits there with his mouth wide open when I tell him the good news. 'Toddy. Coming here tomorrow? Son, you don't want her to be here with you, do you?'

'No way. Does an Eskimo need ice water?'

The ogre arrives. Toddy is short with a large bosom and an equally large rump. She has flaming red, shoulder-length, curly hair and green eyes full of fire. Questions and criticisms fly out of her mouth as she struggles through the front door with two large suitcases. 'This place is a mess. Where are the kids? Have they been fed? Why haven't the beds been made?' I mention that I will be taking the children over to the hospital to see their mother. The tyrant yells, 'No you bloody well won't!' Helen cries because she can't come with me. 'Shut up, you bloody little whinger,' says Grandma.

I try to console Helen, tell her to be a good girl and I promise to bring her back a nice surprise. Fred has evac-uated the house and waits for me on the footpath, having decided to come to the hospital with me. After crossing the road we hear loud screaming accompanied by Toddy's voice yelling abuse. We both turn around and see to our horror Toddy holding Helen by one arm. Helen's feet are unable to touch the ground as Toddy belts the daylights out of her. 'God almighty,' I hear Fred call out, 'the child is not that long out of hospital.'

I run across the road. 'I'll fix that bitch!' I push the tyrant out of the way, grab Helen and pass her to Fred, who is now alongside me. There is an angry exchange of words between Toddy and myself.

'The child is still on medication after her operation.'

'She's a whingin' little bastard,' fires back the 'Enforcer', walking towards me with raised fists.

I give her a solid shove. She lands on the footpath and bounces after landing on her large rump. She curses as she gets to her feet. 'I'll get the coppers onto you. You rotten mongrel. I'll have you put away for assault.'

'Do what you like but you won't touch Helen again.'

She throws Kim into the stroller and storms off towards the Glebe Police Station.

Fred is very concerned and he says, 'Son, she is serious about having you charged. Go down to the police station now with Helen. Show them the welts on her legs. Tell them about her recent operation. I'll go with you as a witness.'

Ignoring Fred's wise advice I reply, 'No. I doubt that she will even go to the police station. All I did was give her a shove.' Lifting Helen up, I give her a kiss on the cheek and say. 'Let's all go and see Mummy.' Naturally, we don't mention the incident to Shirley—she's ill, and doesn't need the upset.

After returning home from the hospital there is heavy thumping on the front door. I open it to see two large men dressed in police uniform.

'Clifford John Nichols?'

'Yes,' I reply.

'We would like you to accompany us to Glebe Police Station. There has been a charge of assault laid against you.'

I turn to Fred. 'Take care of Helen. I'll see if I can straighten this mess out.' I leave in the police car expecting to get this matter over and done with in a short time, only to end up spending the night in the cold, dreary cell of the police station.

Next morning I am informed by a young officer that I will be going before the magistrate within two hours to answer the charge of assault. I have to enter a plea of guilty or not guilty. I tell him that my plea will be not guilty, because it is such a trivial matter and I have to get home to look after my little daughter. One hour later the same young police officer asks me, 'Have you changed your mind about pleading not guilty?'

'No. Why?'

'Please yourself. This case can drag on for days and that's probably the last thing you want to happen. If you plead guilty, the judge will give you a good talking to, then let you go. You can then pick up your little girl from the children's shelter and take her home.'

His words hit me as if I have been punched. 'Shelter? What are you talking about? My father is looking after my daughter.'

The policeman moves his head from side to side. 'No, mate. After you were taken into custody we notified the Child Welfare Department. They put your child into the children's shelter.'

I almost faint. 'My child is on special medication, which she has to have on a regular basis. She recently had a heart operation.'

The copper has control of my emotions and knows it. 'That's all the more reason to plead guilty. Take your dressing down from the judge. Your case will be dismissed and you can pick up your little girl. I'll even drive you there in a police car, then run both of you home.'

128

'Okay. I'll plead guilty.' I am so worried about Helen.

Outside the courtroom I hear Fred's voice call out from the street, 'Plead, not guilty.' Inside, the judge is wearing a moth-eaten, grey wig and a black gown. He peers over his glasses from an elevated position seated behind a dark-brown bench. 'How do you plead?'

'I plead guilty, Your Worship.'

The judge has read the evidence of what transpired and does not expect this plea. He actually encourages me to plead not guilty by emphasising that I have never had a civilian police charge before.

My devoted mother-in-law is insensitive to her surroundings. She stands up in the courtroom and shouts, 'Give the bastard ten years. He's so stupid he'd get lost in a telephone box!'

'Madam, enough of that type of behaviour.'

Toddy has no idea what the judge means. Toddy wants blood, mine. Fired up, she gives me another character reference. 'If you mention work to the little arsehole, he'll vomit!'

The judge looks at the raging woman and informs her that if she continues with this behaviour, she will be held in contempt of court. He turns his attention to me. 'I hereby place you on a good behaviour bond for a period of two years with a surety of two hundred pounds cash.'

Fred is led into my cell at the Glebe Police Station. 'Cliff, you bloody fool. Why in the name of hell did you plead guilty? Whatever possessed you to do such a stupid thing?' I relate the advice given by the young copper and Helen being in a children's shelter. His shocked response is, 'Helen is with your Aunt Sarah. I took her there straight after the police drove you down to the station. She is getting her medication and being spoilt with kindness. She is doing fine. Toddy has taken little Kim back to her home. Son, you have been conned!'

For the next minute or so we are both silent. I reflect on how naive I have been, and then I ask, 'How long do you think it'll be before they release me from here?'

Fred's brow furrows. 'Son, don't you understand what the judge meant when he said two hundred pounds cash surety? Until this amount of money is presented to the court as a guarantee that you won't break the law within the next two years, then you will be detained out at Long Bay Gaol.'

Now my mind is in turmoil. 'Two hundred pounds! That's a fortune. How am I going to get that kind of money?'

'Leave it to me, son. The sooner I get going and try to raise this money, the better. Keep your spirits up.'

I watch Fred leave and trust that he will get me out of here. Unfortunately, a policeman informs me later that day that my surety has not been presented and it is now time for me to take my ride out to Sydney's main gaol, Long Bay. I am frightened and don't know what to expect.

Three burly prison warders are my welcoming committee. The sombre, grey atmosphere within these prison walls is similar to walking slowly through a murky dream. There is no sunshine, only high walls. The harsh concrete yards are surrounded by numerous twelve-feet-high wire cages. These, I am to learn, are the exercise yards, where men walk around in a seemingly never-ending circle. Suddenly, I feel very cold and numb.

'Conviction and sentence?' is the gruff question coming from one of the warders. Looking at his face, I see black, currant eyes set above a large, boneless, flat nose. These beady little eyes bore into my head. Above his eyes are two thick strips of shaggy, tar-coloured eyebrows. His peaked cap sits squarely on a box-shaped head.

'Assault. Two years, er . . . sir.' My fearful thought is, What in God's name am I doing here?

'Strip off. Go over there and shower. Come back to this point and you will be issued with regulation prison uniform and shoes.'

Prison gear, I discover, is not to be recommended for the fashion-conscious male. The waistband of the trousers tucks comfortably underneath my armpits. The shirt is a miniature tent hanging loosely from my frame. My left foot is dressed in a size-seven shoe and my right foot in a size-nine. Both shoes are minus laces. I know there will be no performance of 'Carolina in the Morning' at this venue.

I am now a crim of absolute novice standard. I could have saved myself this procedure and stayed in my street clothes if, after being asked the initial question of conviction and sentence, I had said, 'I am awaiting surety of two hundred pounds and on a two-year good behaviour bond.' My time would have also been spent in the area known as the remand yard, rather than in one of the cells designated for people sentenced to serve time. The following seven days seem like an eternity. I wonder if Fred has forgotten about me.

My new home is known as No. 3 Range. It is a very confined space, which I share with two other people and a latrine bucket. We are locked away in here at 4 p.m. each day and let out again at 7 a.m. the following morning. The days drag by very slowly. The food is not my idea of high standard. The inmates have a name for the mush that is served; they call it 'grey death'. I therefore live on a diet of bread and water for the length of my stay, though I must admit the bread is of excellent standard, having been freshly baked in the prison bakery.

On the seventh day, Fred succeeds in getting the two hundred pounds from one of his wealthy sisters. It is freedom day for Public Enemy No. 1.

My father gives me the despairing news, however, that Shirley has finally had enough of my drinking and behaviour. My going to gaol marks the end of our relationship. Tired of the lifestyle and misery she has been living in, she has moved with the kids, to take up residence with her mother. Our old home is now occupied by new tenants. I suddenly feel empty inside and ponder over what the future holds for me. Will there be a future? I feel robbed. I didn't get much chance to bond with Christine but I have with Kimmy and Helen so the pain is even greater. My insides feel like they have been ripped out. I am bewildered and numb as I wonder if I will ever see them again. I am trapped once again with my emotions and begin to look for alcohol to blot out the pain.

Fred understands my plight and gives me some money for a drink and to rent a small room in Glebe. I am afraid to move away from this area of Sydney because it is the only way of life I know. I somehow feel safe here.

Hitting Rock Bottom

April, May and June pass slowly. I have had no contact with my young daughters and I miss them very much. I had been trying to be a good husband but had great difficulty fully developing my sense of responsibility. I did however, love my children and tried to be a devoted father. Grief fills my soul. My will to live is waning away and time has little meaning. At the age of thirty-four, I once again wander Sydney's skid row in the Haymarket area. I drift from one pub to the next, walking through the doors of wine bars searching for a familiar face. All I need is a friend and a drink. I run into Vera, my mother's drinking companion. 'Hello, Vera?'

'Well fancy bumping into you. Are you looking for Nell?'

I haven't seen Nell for some years. Nell's drinking has swallowed her up and there has been no real relationship to be had with her. Her short-term and long-term memory are both in a sad state. A sense of duty causes

me to want to see Nell and I reply, 'Is she here?'
'No, love, but you can find her at the Rocket Range.
She's usually there most weekdays.'

'I haven't seen her for a while. How's she been?'

Vera laughs and says, 'The same old Nell. She will
never change. She's still living at Jarocin Avenue and her
sister is still treating her like a second-class citizen. Can
I buy you a beer?'

'Thanks, Vera.'

Even though I do not have any great emotion of love
or hate towards Nell, I decide to visit her at the Rocket
Range. Its correct title is the Orlando Wine Saloon, and
to be a patron a person has to be at rock bottom on
the social scale. Nell is a regular customer at this rubbish
tip of unloved souls and manages to find companionship
here among the lost and the least.

Inside this place of desperation the lighting is very
poor. Even in the middle of the day it is shrouded in semi-
darkness. The people within act out their insane
fantasies. One pathetic individual is sitting at a table
having a conversation with himself. After chattering
away for a while, he bursts out in obscene laughter; he
is obviously amused by some funny story he has just
related to himself. In another area, a woman in a zombie-
like state is just sitting, staring at the wall. Her hand is
clutching a glass of cheap red wine as though it is her
life blood. She begins urinating and is not even aware
that this degrading thing is happening to her. A small
puddle forms on the floor alongside where she is sitting.
I feel shame and disgust for all alcoholics. There's an

ex-boxer shadow sparring with himself. Every now and then he stops. He looks around the room to see if any poor devil is interested enough to watch his performance. When he sees his captive audience of one, the boxer raises his arms in a victory motion and starts again for the next round.

I listen to the drone of voices and the clinking of glasses. The air is thick with cigarette smoke. I smell the aroma of unwashed bodies. I feel like I belong in this asylum because I am an alcoholic drifter looking for love and acceptance like the rest of them. Occasionally, there is an outburst of anger. A patron jumps to his feet, trying to engage in fisticuffs with anyone willing to oblige. Then there is a scuffle of push and shove. The manager hurriedly frogmarches someone through the front door and out onto the street. Others are totally intoxicated, sleeping face down on the tables. The tops of these tables are sticky with streaks of spilt wine and cigarette ash from overflowing ashtrays.

These are hard times and to survive I have to either work, thieve or borrow money. Any self-respect, dignity or courage I may have once had is gone. I am now at a stage where I am too sick to work and too frightened to thieve. I survive by borrowing money. My body begins to tremble and fear overwhelms me. I know I need a drink to settle my nerves.

I am relieved when I see Nell in her usual seat at the rear of the wine bar. Little Nell, the perfect lady. Her hat covers her grey hair and is perched at a cocky angle on top of her head. The handbag is safely draped over her arm.

Her dark-navy coat is well worn, yet presentable. On the lapel of her coat is her pride and joy, a shiny, imitation, jewelled brooch. It depicts a vase full of colourful blue, pink, green and silver flowers. These are her 'diamonds and emeralds'. She is always clean and well mannered.

Her companion today is a very heavy woman with large, flabby, puffy hands. Her wrinkled face looks as though she has slept facedown on a washboard. She has no teeth, at least not in her mouth, and is dressed in a wrinkled garment that hangs off her enormous frame. I have never laid eyes on her before. Unfortunately, this woman overhears me asking Nell for the loan of some money from her aged pension. Out of the corner of my eye I see the woman's hand. It is clutching a large handbag, which is moving in a wide arc. Suddenly, it's too late to move. The heavy handbag crashes forcefully into the side of my head. The impact is so hard it lifts me off my stool and I land a few feet away on my back.

Stunned by the event, I hear her yell, 'You dirty little bludger! Fancy asking a poor, old-age pensioner for money. Get out of here, you worthless bum!'

Nell jumps quickly to my rescue and tells King Kong this is her one and only son. The Wrinkled Warrior apologises and buys me a large glass of red plonk. While she is not looking, Nell's hand wanders to the top of her stocking. This is where she keeps her finance. She produces two one pound notes and says, 'Now you look after yourself and don't waste the money.'

I kiss her on the cheek and leave before something else happens. Even though I am carrying a large lump on the side of my head, I feel the day has turned out all right.

I decide to search for Fred. Grizza, his best mate, tells me that Fred has gone to Cooma with Aunt Sarah. Sarah is Fred's sister. She is comfortably off, has a nervous, paranoid disposition and is a religious fanatic. She would have talked Fred into going to Cooma to see all our relatives. Fred is a very patient man and would have been able to tolerate her. I have great difficulty coping with her religious domination. I feel uneasy. How will I survive without my Saviour being around?

Saturday morning and a more pathetic sight is hard to find. I am a lost, trembling soul waiting outside a pawnshop in the Haymarket. There is an eternity of ten minutes more to wait before the large, steel front doors will clang open. I am a frightened, bedraggled figure. Under my left arm I hold a bundle wrapped in layers of newspaper. People seem to be everywhere and I feel as if they are all looking at me as they pass. I am terrified of them. They are all in different shapes and sizes. People off to play sport have tennis racquets and golf clubs. Others have binoculars hanging around their necks and are clutching race papers. There are women shouting at children as they hurry across the road. The street sweeper with his long-handled broom is gliding it in smooth strokes along the gutter. The stationary fruit and vegetable carts have owners calling out in a morbid tone, 'Get ya nice ripe tomatas, fresh strawberries and luvly granny smith apples.' The aroma of food cooking is coming from the open doorways of restaurants and cafés. The smell of fresh vegetables set out on the peddlers' stalls at nearby Paddy's Markets also fills the air. A tram grinds to a screeching halt, disgorging people to join the happy rat race. Everyone seems to have a purpose to fill this morning. Mine is to get into the pawnshop, obtain some money and get drunk. As each tram passes, I move away from the front of the pawnshop. I am afraid somebody will recognise me and know that I am about to enter this shop of desperation.

Suddenly, a loud voice from a man walking by calls out, 'Hey mate, the leg of your trousers is hanging out of your bundle.' I look down and find this to be true. Sure enough the trouser leg of the only good suit I possess is dangling down below my waist. The jacket sleeve is also limply hanging. I try to hide it in the loosened newspaper. I feel a hot flush of embarrassment flood into my being. My immediate thought is that every living person within five hundred yards from where I am standing will now know that I'm about to enter the pawnshop and pledge my suit. I start to shake and become paranoid. Fearfully, I expect another call to come from another person out there. 'Look at the freak! The "one and only" after ten years. There he is pawning his suit for money! He can't make it any other way!' Thankfully the sound of a clang and a screech penetrates my ears as the gates of the shop slide open. I scurry inside and at last I am a man with a purpose!

The Piano Player, the Movie Star and Me

Sometime, somewhere, in everybody's lifetime we meet a few people who leave us with an everlasting impression and fond memories. In my case, two of these people are Keith Gleeson and Nicky.

While Fred is away in Cooma, I do my morning patrol of the early opening hotels, searching for a drink and a 'Captain'. A 'Captain' is a person with money in their pocket willing to shout drinks for a person whose company they enjoy. One morning, at seven-thirty, I walk into the Prince of Wales Hotel on the fringe of the Haymarket. There are about twenty customers standing around the bar drinking. In one corner a man is sitting on a stool, thumping away on a well-tuned piano. He is of thin build, dressed in a dark suit, which has seen better days, and his fair hair is brushed back and slicked down with hair oil. The shirt he is wearing is mauve and adorned with a black and white bowtie as a finishing touch. He appears to be around fifty years of age. What impresses me is the brilliant manner in which he plays. After watching and listening for a while, I realise he is playing for the occasional drink. This seems to be the only reward he is receiving. The music brings me out of the fog of despair. I introduce myself and ask, 'Do you mind if I sing a few songs to accompany you?'

'Be my guest,' he says.

I know singing is something that not everyone can do, and when I hear Keith's reply I begin to feel worthwhile. I feel a warm glow inside. I am no longer a nobody. I am now a somebody.

After a bracket of numbers, I am surprised at the ovation from the early morning patrons. Not letting a chance go by, I borrow a customer's hat, turn to Keith and tell him to keep playing. Bugger entertaining this mob for nothing, I'm thinking. Hat in hand, I proceed to take up a collection. 'Come on men, don't let the artists die of thirst or starvation. Any requests will be played gladly. All you have to do is drop a coin into the hat.'

At about 9 a.m. Keith and I depart and go to the nearest café for a much needed feed. Over breakfast Keith suggests, 'Let's do our same routine tomorrow morning. The publican doesn't mind us putting on a bit of a show. He has been a friend of mine for ages.' I feel excited about the prospect.

Next day's show is better than yesterday's. There are over fifty people in the crowd. The early-start workers really enjoy our little cabaret performance. Keith plays so beautifully while I sing and tell some rather risque jokes. I discover that Keith has been a well-sought-after pianist. He has played at top venues in Sydney and Melbourne and also spent two years in London playing at many high-class restaurants and clubs. I am shocked to discover Keith is only thirty-two. This deception in age is the result of eight years of drinking coupled with grief. He never did get over his wife walking out on him after being married for a short time.

After one week of doing our little act at the Prince, Keith calls me aside and speaks to me in a very quiet voice. 'I have been offered a part-time job playing piano at the Bourke Hotel.'

'That's great news, Keith.' I wonder why all the secrecy.

He almost whispers, saying, 'Cliff, I can fit you in as well.'

I'm bewildered. 'Doing what, Keith?'

Excitement is mounting in Keith's voice. 'Listen! They've got a kit of drums. What do you say?'

'I am more than interested.'

'Great!' says Keith. 'We will both be paid a reasonably good fee. We can also have one of the hotel's twin rooms free of charge on a permanent, weekly basis. Our nights of engagement will be Thursday, Friday and Saturday from 7 p.m. until midnight.' Keith gives a great big smile that could light up the world and adds, 'How about this? On Friday and Saturday nights we get our evening meal in the restaurant absolutely free. Once we are on stage all of our grog will be supplied free of charge!'

I feel as though I should fall down on my knees right now and cry out Hallelujah, because at this very moment I know, at last, there must be a God. I realise now why Keith is being so secretive, too. If some of the patrons at the Prince of Wales overheard our plans there would be more than a trickle of freeloaders wandering into the Bourke Hotel expecting us to shout them drinks.

The lounge area of the Bourke Hotel is situated on the first floor, a few steps up the social ladder from the street-level bars we usually frequent. The clientele are a little better dressed than the regulars of the Rocket Range, or the Prince of Wales. There is no need to give notice of departure from the room I am living in at Glebe. When it's time to leave I just pack my bag and go. When the rent is overdue a moonlight flit is normal practice for me.

Friday is opening night. Keith and I have finished our evening meal. We head back to our room and prepare to dress for the big occasion. Keith dresses in his well-worn, oyster-grey dinner jacket with satin lapels. The jacket is slightly crumpled and on one sleeve is a cigarette burn. One lapel of his jacket carries a visible brown stain. His black trousers are shiny and well worn. Any resemblance of a crease down the front of each leg has long since departed. On the clean lapel of his jacket he wears a small red imitation carnation. It looks more like a faded blotch of red ink than a flower. His grey-white shirt, starved of the love of an iron, gives support to the bent red bowtie around his neck. Keith's drummer is a picture of elegance as well. A laughing barmaid affixes a large safety pin to hold the back of my black pants together.

They are a few sizes too big because I borrow them from the publican, who has a rather large waist. Keith loans me a yellowish, once-white shirt with cuffs that come halfway over my hands. Around my neck is a droopy red bowtie. Keith is definitely wearing the better of the two bowties. The battered black shoes on my size-six feet, however, belong to me.

By 6.55 p.m. we are on the stage in the lounge bar. The miracle of the moment is that I am still sitting up straight instead of being horizontal. By this time of evening I am always so intoxicated that I can hardly scratch myself. After playing our first bracket of popular numbers, we feel very pleased with ourselves. The wonderful applause from about seventy patrons means that they are happy with the entertainment.

We soon learn that punchups are not unusual and brawls erupt easily among these weekend drinkers—and that the manager, Bob, is often the instigator. He is a very heavy drinker, who can suddenly erupt in a display of violence and go right off his crumpet. One moment he is moving among the tables as the perfect host, smiling and greeting one and all. Then next minute, something does not meet with his approval or someone says a word out of place and in a flash he starts hurling abuse, prior to delivering a knuckle sandwich to the unfortunate patron. Whenever this situation occurs, Keith knows to play Bob's favourite song to pacify him, signalling to me with a yell, 'Cliffy—"It's a Sin!"'

The first time I hear Keith's signal, I turn around and see Bob with one beefy hand around somebody's neck, his other arm drawn back with a large clenched fist about to deliver some unfortunate patron a physical sleeping draught. Knowing that 'It's a Sin to Tell a Lie' enthrals Bob every time he hears it, we begin singing his song loudly over the microphone. The effect is like a shot from a tranquilliser gun. The second he hears his song he stops as if frozen in time, looks in the direction of the stage, releases his grip on the intended victim and gives us a great big smile. His face splits open to reveal a set of healthy, pink gums and he then bursts forth in the most shocking voice, completely out of tune, 'Be sure it's true, when you say I love you . . . It's a sin to tell a lie.' Three minutes after his rendition of torture, the patrons give a thunderous round of applause. The lounge is restored to order and everybody once again thoroughly enjoys themselves. The conviviality and good spirits continue until the next upset.

Sometimes in the lounge bar of the Bourke, a ray of sunshine appears among this jumble of seedy humanity. At around seven-thirty one evening she enters. The eyes of the patrons swing in her direction. Keith and I almost stop playing as she stands in the middle of the room. She and her friend are looking for a vacant table. This petite blonde is about five feet, two inches tall. Her platinum blonde hair reaches halfway down her back and her skin is beautifully sun-tanned. Her magnificent green eyes survey the room. She is dressed in a tightfitting skirt with a pastel-pink sleeveless top revealing large breasts. Mother Nature has been very kind to her. On her tiny feet are white high-heeled shoes that accentuate the curves of her well-formed legs. She looks towards the stage and smiles, revealing perfect white teeth. I nearly fall off the stool I'm sitting on.

When we have our first break I ask Keith, 'What do you think?' as I nod towards the blonde.

Keith casually looks in her direction and suggests, 'Probably a movie star or stage actress out on the town absorbing some atmosphere for her next role. She could be one of those society dames wanting to see how the other half lives. Maybe that's how she gets her kicks in life.'

Later in the night, I summon up enough courage to go over to the table where The Goddess is sitting. Her male companion has gone and she is alone.

'Can I buy you a drink?' she asks in a soft, well-modulated voice. 'I'm really enjoying your show.'

I sit down and thank her. We introduce ourselves. Her name is Nicky and the man, with whom she arrived, is her brother, Tiggy. Apparently the two of them have been living up in Brisbane for five years working with a land developer. They had invested a tidy sum of money into a business, but unfortunately it did not turn out the way they had hoped. The final blow came just a month ago when they lost all of their money. The accountant fleeced them of all finances and fled the country. She adds, 'Thank goodness I had a small savings account put aside, otherwise we would have had to walk back to Sydney.'

I tell her that when she first came into the lounge I thought she was either a movie star or a theatre actress. Moving her head slightly to one side she laughs out loud and says, 'Believe me, Cliff. I am a star of neither stage nor screen. To be quite frank, I've been a knockabout for most of my life. I don't feel uneasy in a place like this.' She points towards the stage. 'I think your friend on piano is calling for you to start again.'

Thanking Nicky for the drink and her company I ask, 'Do you think you will ever come back here again?'

She smiles and says, 'Cliff, you can bet on it.'

Over the next few weeks Nicky is a regular hotel visitor on Friday and Saturday nights. One Saturday night, after I finish playing, I walk over to her and ask if I can escort her home.

'That would be lovely, Cliff.'

'Great! Where do you live?'

'Glebe,' she replies. 'Do you know where it is?'

It is now my turn to laugh. 'Yes, Nicky, I know it very well.'

Neither of us own a motorcar and Nicky suggests we walk rather than take a cab. Walking down the main street in the early hours of the morning we spot a small coffee shop in an arcade.

'This place looks friendly and warm. What do you say, Nicky?'

'You must be reading my mind.'

We talk and consume numerous cups of coffee. Nicky relates to me how, at the age of five, her mother abandoned her. Tiggy and Nicky were left with their father, who could not cope with the two of them. He put nine-year-old Tiggy into Gosford Boys' Home. But Nicky's dad was also a cruel person. He had beaten her many times and often stayed out all night, leaving her at home alone. Twelve months later he, too, abandoned her and she was put into an orphanage. She recalls how Tiggy was released from Gosford when he was sixteen. He went back to his old home only to find that his father had departed some years before. Fortunately, the elderly next door neighbour informed Tiggy that his father had been unable to look after Nicky and had put her into an orphanage. She even remembered its name and told Tiggy where to go to find his sister. He finally found Nicky and visited her regularly over the next four years, and he was there for her on the day of her release from the orphanage when she turned sixteen.

After many hours of chatting, we finally stroll towards Nicky's home. 'Well, here we are. Home sweet home,' says my beautiful friend. We thank each other for a wonderful evening. As I open her front gate, Nicky leans over and kisses me on the cheek. She softly says, 'Life can be good, Cliff. Thank you once more.'

While waiting for a tram to take me back to the Bourke Hotel I feel wonderful as I watch the sun begin to appear over the horizon. Nicky gives me a wonderful feeling of belonging. She is the sister I always longed for. The weeks that follow show me the fulfilment of having a true friend. There is no intimacy of a sexual nature between us because we are two friends too busy laughing at life and drinking.

A few months after starting our gig at the Bourke, I realise that we have not seen Nicky for three weeks. She is always a regular on Friday nights, so I wonder if she and her brother have returned to Queensland. I do not want to go to her residence in Glebe. If she has formed a relationship with some guy I do not want to put my nose in where it doesn't belong. I feel a great sense of loss but adopt my usual attitude—oh well, that's life—to hide my real feelings.

It is now October, 1961. Four months have passed since Keith and I began living at the Bourke. Both of us are tired of working such regulated hours and neither of us wishes to be tied down in one place for too long. For the last time Keith plays my favourite number from his magic fingertips, 'Canadian Sunset'. Then we both agree to move on. I never see Keith again. In 1967 my friend is to finish up as a six line paragraph in the middle section of a Sydney newspaper.

> *A derelict, aged 38 years was found dead in a back lane in the suburb of Surry Hills. Empty methylated spirit bottles were found alongside the body. There were no suspicious circumstances. The deceased was identified as Mr Keith Gleeson, a former musician. He was of no fixed abode.*

Satan's merry-go-round would finally stop for Keith. God would come to take his talented child home. But for now we are just two lost souls wishing each other good luck and farewell.

Without any income or shelter from the elements, I am once more exposed to the night. Now with the loss of my music and structure in my life I nose dive very quickly. I begin to miss Keith's company and laughter. For a paltry few shillings, I know I am able to get nightly accommodation at a central city hostel run by the Salvation Army. It is known by the desperate as the 'House of Bricks'. At this place in Foster Street, you can get a single bed in a crowded dormitory. The vile aroma of stinking breaths, urine-soaked garments, buzz-saw snoring and unwashed bodies is a form of slow suffocation. It makes sleeping in this putrid gas chamber almost impossible. To stay overnight in this place I have to sleep fully clothed, tie my shoes together with their shoelaces and drape them around my neck. If anyone has false dentures, they wrap them in a handkerchief and put them safely in a trouser pocket. If this procedure is not followed, then by morning they will be gone and there is a good chance they will be on their way to the nearest pawnshop. Yes, two shillings for a set of teeth is enough to buy a family-sized bottle of methylated spirits! One night in this place is enough for me. I never return. No matter how desperate my situation, I feel it would be much better to spend the night down in the police cells at Regent Street or Central. I am grateful when prostitutes, criminals and friends in the Haymarket area offer me a bed and shelter for the night. Other times I sleep in parks or railway stations.

Late November and I am grateful to see a familiar face in the crowd. There, leaning on the bar at the Prince of Wales Hotel, is my dad, Freddie. Boy, am I glad to see him! After a good meal, Fred informs me that he has

I played the triangle then tenor horn in the Glebe District Silver Band. I am the tiny seven-year-old sitting to the right of the bass drum in this 1934 photo.

My oldest friend, Mick Lamrock (left), and me in 1942 in our Depression-era clothes. I always thought the coat lapels looked like they'd been pressed with a waffle iron.

TOP LEFT
My buddy 'Tich' Cooper (left) and me in the Australian 66th Infantry Battalion Band, Ebisu Camp, Tokyo, October 1947.

TOP RIGHT
Posing with a Japanese girl during my tour of duty in Tokyo, 1948.

RIGHT
The program cover from 'Folies Berserk', the musical variety show I produced, arranged and starred in while stationed in Japan in 1952.

All dressed up for a night out with my first wife, Daphne, in 1947. Sick of my constant drinking, Daphne left me in 1954, taking our four-year-old daughter, Christine.

On-stage at the British Lion Hotel with my second wife, Shirley, to show off our new baby, Helen, in 1957. Helen's sister, Kim, was born in 1959. Even after Shirley gave me a second chance in 1962, I could not control my drinking, and she went to live with her mother and Kim, leaving Helen with me.

Helen, aged seven, at a school ball in 1964. Helen was living at St Joseph's Home for Children during the week and staying with me on the weekends. When I married Kath in May 1964 I finally had a home fit for Helen to live in.

Helen's seventh birthday party in our backyard at Croydon in 1964.

My girls, Kim and Helen, posing with 'Santa' in 1969. Kim was still living with Shirley's mother, Toddy, and Helen and I rarely saw her.

My dad, Fred, with his dog, Bob, in a wine bar in 1955. Bob was blind, but he could still manage to follow Dad's scent from home to the local bar.

With my mum, Nell, in 1972. Nell spent the final years of her life in Vaucluse House, a rest home for the aged. Nell died a few months after this photo was taken.

Helen with my third wife, Kath, in 1970. Kath and I were married from 1964 to 1970, and I will always be grateful to her for her kindness to Helen and me during my drinking days. With Kath's support I joined A.A. and finally managed to overcome my addiction to alcohol.

Getting married to Sue (centre) in 1977. The stress of running our Brisbane-based business while raising a family proved too great, and we separated in 1986. The company collapsed and Sue moved back to Sydney with our two young daughters, Jody and Kelly.

With Helen and Kim, my beautiful girls all grown up, and Kelly and Jody, aged four and five, in 1982.

My eldest daughter Christine, me, Kelly and Jody in 1999. After not seeing Christine for forty-three years, we finally found each other again in 1998.

Helen with her children Katie and Jamie in 2000.

It is my five-year-old granddaughter Nicky's turn to sing an old favourite, 'Carolina in the Morning', in 1997.

My boyhood friend Enzo Toppano (right) and his wife Peggy, who inspired me to write my story, 1995.

With my soul mate Dian in 1996.

crossed paths with Shirley, who asked about my whereabouts and how I was getting on in life. Apparently
Shirley and Helen are living in a new home. Kim,
however, is still living with Toddy, her grandmother.
Helen is doing really well after her operation. I wonder
what on earth is going on for poor Kim. I can't understand why she is not living with Shirley. I feel powerless to change the situation.

Fred suddenly becomes very serious. 'Son, you will
have to pull yourself together otherwise a mental institution or a long gaol sentence is awaiting you. It could
be even worse. You may end up on a slab in the morgue!'
His tone then softens. 'Shirley is prepared to give you
another chance for the sake of the children. She is only
interested if you make the effort to stay off the booze.'

My initial reaction is excitement because I so desperately want to belong and feel normal. The possibility
of being with my children again brings tears to my eyes.
I suddenly become conscious of the state I am in and
wonder if I am dreaming. My need to belong is temporarily greater than my need for booze. I want to make
the supreme effort to straighten myself out and be
reunited with my small family.

Fred organises for me to share his guesthouse room
for a period of two months—we figure it will take two
months for me to show some form of rehabilitation. Fred
has me walking daily and insists I drink milkshakes. One
day I say to him, 'If you pump any more of these bloody
milkshakes into me I'll have more calcium in my body
than blood!' He just laughs quietly as he hears my

complaints. The exercise and fresh air improves my appetite tenfold. My nervous system is almost at peace. I am now clean-shaven, walk upright and dress nicely. I have an all round feeling of wellbeing. Christmas Day, 1961, is a quiet, sober day for Fred and me. We go to a small, downtown café, have a simple meal, take a long walk and return home to retire early.

I have mixed feelings as Fred and I walk up the pathway to Shirley's small cottage, mid-January, 1962. I am surprised that Shirley's new home is only one hundred yards from where we used to live. Both mother and child look well. Helen runs straight towards my open arms and there are lots of kisses, cuddles and questions from her. When I discover that Kimmy is not here I feel very sad. Our little family is not complete without her. I cannot make too many waves about her still being with Toddy. I hope that she will rejoin the family soon.

Shirley's first comment is, 'Well, I must say, this is the best I've seen you look in a very long time.' We discuss plans for the future. She agrees that I can move in with her and Helen provided I keep myself on the sobriety path. A few days later I return with my belongings and once more our little family is reunited.

I gain employment as a storeman with a medical company and soon my life is progressing along quite happily. I become a hard-working husband and father, who is a responsible, sober citizen. But after nine months of being 'so good' my life seems to lack action and adventure. I am bored again and the novelty of this nice life starts to wane.

In October, Fred greatly appreciates being able to move into our spare bedroom. Having Fred under the same roof gives me a great feeling of security and now I feel I may be able to cope better with my restlessness and boredom. Shirley appreciates his help with the household chores; her favourite time is when Fred takes his little mate, Helen, for long walks in her stroller, giving Shirley many hours of peaceful freedom each day. I speak to Shirley about bringing Kim home from Toddy's, and she informs me that Kim seems to be contented there, that for the time being she has decided to allow Kim to stay on as company for Toddy. I feel very uneasy about this arrangement because I know what Toddy is like. I hate the thought of my daughter growing up without her parents being there for her. Over the next few weeks my anger begins to mount. When I ask Shirley how much longer Kim has to stay with Toddy, Shirley always says, 'When everything settles down I'll bring her home.' I suppress my anger to try and keep the peace because I know Shirley has trouble with Toddy's dominance.

Eventually, my thinking turns negative. I tell myself, 'Surely after working hard all day I can reward myself with just one beer. Other men do.' I feel trapped in a revolving door syndrome and continue telling myself, 'If I'm sensible, surely a couple of drinks will not be the end of the world. Anyhow I have been off the booze for so long I feel like I can now have control.' Mid-October I pick up my first drink after many months of abstinence. It is my lunchtime break at work and I walk the short distance to the local hotel and order a beer.

I only have three and feel quite proud of myself being able to stop after just three beers. I then return to work.

Within three weeks I am back on the merry-go-round again. Monday, prior to the running of the November Melbourne Cup, I am sacked from my position as storeman for the medical company for being drunk on the job. I arrive home and sense Shirley's disgust in me when she says, 'This time I really mean it, Cliff. Pull yourself together and stop drinking for good or I will leave. I promise you, this will be the end if you keep this up!'

I start to shake and beg forgiveness. 'I will stop. Please believe me.' I am grateful for my reprieve. Mr Booze is patient, however, and will wait for another time.

Short of Breath

Early January, 1963, that time comes without warning and for no reason at all. I am a cleaner and one morning, after receiving my weekly salary, I forget about my job, walk straight to the nearest hotel and start drinking. I have no idea what transpires over the next two days. I am in a blackout.

On the third day I wake early with my body aching from head to toe. The usual dry mouth and sandpaper tongue are back again. At first I have double vision as I try to take in my surroundings, then I realise that I have slept the night in one of Sydney's electric trains, which is now standing empty at its depot. Checking the contents of my pocket, I find enough coins to get me back home again. My only thought is, 'What am I going to tell Shirley?'

'She's gone,' says Fred when I return.

'Where to?'

Fred's eyes open wider. 'God, son. Look at you! Your

clothes are torn and filthy. Your right eyebrow is covered in congealed blood.'

I ignore his comments. 'What do you mean she has gone? Where is she?'

Fred looks away and mutters, 'She has gone for good. She has left you. The poor woman is on the verge of a nervous breakdown.'

Little Helen peeps out from behind her grandfather's leg and gives me a curious look. My father takes a deep breath and beckons me inside the house. 'Cliff, the woman has very little money and nowhere to go. She was forced to contact her mother, who agreed to take her into her small flat. Toddy only let her stay with her on the condition she leave Helen with you and me.'

I am angry and reply, 'To hell with her! The three of us can manage on our own.' A boiling anger like a volcano churns within me. How could Toddy reject a beautiful child like Helen? How could a grandmother separate two sisters? My own childhood isolation and rejection allows me to understand how Helen might be feeling.

After showering and changing my clothes, I tell Fred that I am going out to look for work. Fortunately for me, a position of handyman has become vacant at a private hospital near where we live and I am successful in gaining the position. My early days at the hospital go along reasonably well. But just as well the chores are simple. I polish floors with a machine, sweep the yards and driveways, clean the toilet areas and wheel patients from one point to another. The best duty of all, however, is joining the matron in her office for a couple of brandies. I believe this lady has a worse problem with booze than I have. Most days Matron calls for me, hands me money and a large canvas carry bag, and gives a direct order: 'Cliff, go up to the local hotel and get the usual, two large bottles of brandy. Have a beer for yourself while you're there.' With the contraband wrapped in brown paper and nestled inside the canvas bag, I return to Matron's office. After closing the door, we settle down for a few social gulps. I tell 'My Fair Lady' some rather rude jokes, which she loves. This becomes our morning and afternoon ritual, which lasts for about fifteen minutes.

Home life for the three of us proceeds along reasonably well, too. Fred makes arrangements for Helen to attend kindergarten three days a week. But I am still drinking in a fashion that can only be described as 'controlled drinking'.

It's Saturday morning near the end of January and my father has taken Helen out for the day to see my Aunt Sarah. I am having a few beers at the local hotel. Suddenly, I feel as though all of the air has been squeezed out of my body. Struggling for breath, I turn to my drinking companion and ask, 'Do I look all right? I can hardly breathe.'

His quick response is, 'You look bloody dreadful! You've gone grey in the face.'

Instinctively I know that my right lung has collapsed. As I slowly walk out of the hotel, my companion calls out, 'Do you want me to call a doctor or an ambulance or something?' I just wave my arm and move my head from side to side, indicating I want neither. I head for home, terrified all the way that the 'Hurry-Up Wagon' will come along. If the police see me they will think I'm under the influence, arrest me and shove me into their wagon. I will probably die. How will they know my lung has collapsed?

Intense terror fills my being as I shuffle sideways in a crab-like manner. I hang onto people's front fences to prevent myself from falling or appearing drunk. The journey home seems to go on forever; each slow, painful pace is not more than six inches at a time. Breathing comes in terrifying short gasps. I am shaking uncontrollably as I walk through my front gate. On entering the house I realise that Fred is out, at his sister's place. We do not have the luxury of a telephone, so all I can do is slowly lower myself onto my bed, wait and pray.

The first sound I hear is the front door being opened. I am relieved when I hear Helen's voice, 'Look what I've got, Daddy.' Then Fred enters the room. 'My God! What's wrong?' he cries.

The ambulance duly arrives. I am painfully placed on a stretcher and carried out of the house. The next six long weeks are spent in the Page Chest Ward at Royal Prince Alfred Hospital. I have been operated on for cysts on the right lung, which are probably the result of smoking cigarettes, and physiotherapy is necessary following the operation. My right arm has become semi-paralysed during the procedure. The ribs on my right side had to be bent almost to breaking point with a small vice to form a tunnel for the surgeon to work in. It is some time before I can raise my arm more than twelve inches. It takes even longer before I can raise it above my head.

Another patient in the bed alongside mine is a man called Les, who was admitted two days ago. I sense a lot of anxiety and fear in Les as we get to know each other. His operation is for a small cancer spot on his lungs. It was detected very early and the doctor stated that his operation would not be as dramatic as mine. After my surgery I see tremendous fear in Les's eyes as he watches the tubes draining my wound and the pain I go through trying to lift my arm. He always asks, 'Does it hurt much, Cliff?' He stares at the saline drip, the plasma tubes attached to my body and the thick rubber drainage tubes inserted into my lungs. I attempt to put Les at ease by telling him that the pain is not too bad. I also try to reassure the man that his forthcoming operation is of minor consequence compared to mine. The poor guy is a picture of extreme fear, stress and anxiety. The mind of a human being, if allowed to run riot, can become very destructive. In some cases it can be tragic. Les's case is one.

The second day after my operation, Les is hovering around my bed again asking me the same questions. He is overwhelmed with anxiety. The head nursing sister of the ward asks Les how he is feeling. He replies, 'Good thank you, nurse.' She then departs. Les hurries over to my bed, almost in tears when he informs me that he has addressed the sister by the incorrect title of nurse. 'What should I do, Cliff?' By now my patience is almost drained. 'Les, for God's sake! I'm sure you won't be put in gaol for such a small oversight!' I give him my best smile, hoping this will pacify him.

It is the start of visiting hours and the day prior to Les having his operation. Late in the afternoon I learn just how damaging negative thoughts can be. A piercing scream splits the air at 5.30 p.m. People run everywhere, shouting, doors are slammed. It's pandemonium. A voice from afar shrieks out, 'Stand back!' I am frantic with curiosity.

A young person on the nursing staff rushes past my open doorway, and I call to her as loud as I can, 'Nurse!' She comes hurriedly into my room. 'What's happening out there?' I ask.

Leaning over she speaks in a whispered tone close to my ear, 'It's poor Les. He has thrown himself over the balcony!'

Even though I am still chronically ill, I am shocked when I am told that Les is dead. I understand Les's anxiety and how anxiety can cause everything to grow out of all proportion. I too have had fears that have climbed to the highest peak, stark terror. Unfortunately Les's fears took him to the point of no return. Around the Haymarket I have seen people whose minds have snapped and they, like Les, seem to enter that dimension where the will to live is gone and the light of the soul is extinguished. All that seems to remain is the shell of a human being that is compelled to run and run, finally taking flight into eternity. Cold shivers go down my spine as I wonder whether I could have done more to help him. No answer is forthcoming.

Fred and Helen are constant visitors. Fred reassures me that everything at home is going along well. Aunt Sarah is helping out and Fred has been to see the matron I work for. I am pleased that my job is still safe. She has hired an elderly pensioner to do the duties for the period that I will be hospitalised. Eventually, I recover, wave my farewell to the staff and walk out into the beautiful mid-March morning, grateful that I can take deep breaths into my lungs. One week later I am back on the job with Matron and the floor polisher, and my home life with Fred and Helen is comfortable.

But disaster strikes again. In the middle of April, Fred complains of nasty pains in his back. By nightfall he is in agony. I organise an ambulance and he is admitted into Concord Repatriation Military Hospital. I am informed that he has spondylitis and will most likely need to undergo an operation, which will mean he will be in hospital for some time. On the return journey from Concord Hospital, Helen and I stop off at Aunt Sarah's home. She lives at Leichhardt, which is four miles from Glebe. I ask her to come to my home each day to look after Helen while I attend work.

'No!' is her emphatic reply. 'Firstly, it is too far for me to travel at such an early hour each morning. Secondly, I do not wish to become involved in your messed-up life. It's time you did something about your drinking problem. Your poor father is worn out. If you want my opinion that little girl would be better off in a foster home.'

I am stunned by her response. How can a woman who spends most of her time on her knees praying in the local church be so uncharitable? How can she turn her back on me so coldly and slam the door in my face when for the first time in my life I am being responsible? I am thinking of Fred and Helen this time and I want to keep my job. I begin to feel very angry and deeply hurt. Nell's words come back to me: 'Don't go near relations, they'll give you nothing.' Helen and I catch the tram and return home.

When I explain my situation to the matron at the hospital she shakes her head and speaks with sympathy. 'Cliff, I can't hold your job indefinitely. I need someone for all the day-to-day jobs that have to be done. The old chap who filled in for you while you were in hospital has moved out of the district. We will have to employ someone in your place.'

I feel powerless. Over the next seven days I sit around the house smoking cigarettes, drinking cheap wine and having the odd meal. Helen entertains herself and her doll in her own little world in the backyard. She asks me at least three times each day, 'When will Pa Pa come home?'

Ten days after Fred's admission to hospital, there is heavy pounding on the front door early Saturday morning. I wonder who is calling as I open the door. Standing before me is the owner of the property. He comes straight to the point: 'I want your rent, plus the week that you are in arrears.'

My mental and physical condition is in very poor shape. I plead with the rent collector, 'My father is in hospital. When he returns in a few weeks I will start back at work and . . .'

He cuts me off. 'Listen! I don't run a benevolent society. I'll be back here at six o'clock this evening. If you don't have the money for two weeks rent, then you are out. Do you understand?'

'Yes,' is my feeble reply.

On the Streets

Half an hour to go before the deadline for eviction. I pick up the large, solitary suitcase that has been packed for some hours. It is Saturday just before Anzac Day. At 5.30 p.m. Helen clutches my free hand and we walk out of the house. I feel the chill of night creeping in as we reach the main highway, Parramatta Road. The evening shadows are growing longer as darkness closes in. Traffic is hurtling by and lights are coming on in some of the small cafés, hamburger joints and fish and chip shops. The tantalising aromas go straight to my stomach. I have not seen food today. I look down at my small child, her blue eyes are pleading with me to tell her what is happening. This curly headed, blonde angel is dressed in a small, well-worn overcoat and rather scuffed shoes. She has a tiny handbag hanging on her arm and her tired little doll is clutched under her armpit.

Suddenly, it hits me like a ten-tonne truck. She depends on me! I'm all that she's got. My God, I'm not even capable of looking after myself. I stand with her on the corner of the highway, frantically looking both ways. I try to decide what to do next. The traffic lights high on their poles turn green and make the decision for me. I'm holding Helen's hand tightly as we quickly cross the busy street and enter a hamburger shop.

Inside the little shop is warm and I can smell the sizzling onions on the hotplate. Funny little sounds are coming from my stomach, similar to water going down a drain. Miraculously, I have some money in my pocket. A jockey-sized man of Italian origin calls out, 'Watcha wanna order, mister?' I order our meal. Sitting in the little shop I feel safe and warm. The smell of the food cooking on the hotplate gives me a feeling of security. Our waiter returns and in each hand he holds a large plate of brown hamburger and French fries settled on two halves of a toasted bun.

Helen's eyes widen to twice their size. Her mouth is open with surprise, then she laughs excitedly and asks, 'Can I have a milkshake, too, Daddy?' I look at our waiter and order her a milkshake, and a coffee for myself.

'You like da hamburger, darlin'?' the man asks Helen, who shyly nods and continues to bite into her meal. 'You movin' on, mister?' he adds, pointing to my suitcase.

'Yes, mate. My wife ran away with a sailor.' This feeble attempt at a joke falls flat.

He asks me, 'You in some sorta trouble, mister?'

'Just a little,' I reply. Then I tell him a fictional story that comes into my mind, 'We are on our way to my mother's house, which is up at Gosford, sixty miles away.

She returns from holidays tomorrow. I'll phone her in the morning and she will then drive down to Sydney and pick us up.' The little guy is listening intently. I continue my story, 'My worry is that I forgot to go to the bank yesterday and draw out some money. Unfortunately, I don't know anybody here in Sydney. I'm getting worried about where my little girl and I can spend the night. Do you sleep here at the shop?'

My host straightens up and tells me, 'You musta be jokin', mister.'

I take a deep breath and feel there is nothing to lose. 'I'm wondering if it would be possible for us to sleep here for just one night?'

A frown comes over the face of my newfound saviour. 'I don't know if dis is gonna be any good, mister.'

I quickly speak over his doubts, 'By the way, my name is Cliff and my little daughter is called Helen. What's your name?'

'My nameza Frank.'

'Frank, we won't touch anything in your shop. Everything will be quite safe. It would be terrible if my little girl had to sleep all night in a cold park.'

He ponders my desperate situation. Finally, he relents. 'Okay, mister. I gotta da blanket out back of my shop. Udder ting I got is . . . how you say . . . marteres? You know, sleep ona da bed.'

'A mattress?'

'Yes, datsa da ting.'

It is now 6.30 p.m. and Frank does not close his business for another three hours. Rather than sit around waiting, Frank suggests that I take Helen for a bus ride into town and return in a couple of hours, which we do.

The last customer wanders out of Frank's shop just before 9.45 p.m. I help him close the steel mesh doors and clean up the shop. Frank bids us both farewell and assures us that he will be back about 8 a.m. the following day.

It's a cold night. Helen and I huddle together on the old kapok mattress. We cover our bodies with two well-worn blankets. Sleep does not come easily. The continuous flow of highway traffic close by is disturbing. It's a busy Saturday night. I hear the roar and whine of trucks, cars, motorbikes and buses, flashing headlights shine through the café's front glass window and light up our sleeping area. Maybe two hours pass before the traffic settles down. Helen then stirs and sits up, 'I don't like it here, Daddy!' I settle her down, rub her back and she soon dozes off to sleep. I'm not too keen about spending the night here either, but it's better than being out in the cold.

In the early hours of the morning my eyes are still wide open. Helen is in a deep sleep. The closed, deserted café has a sickening odour of stale grease and onions, and a foul stench of nearby rotting garbage. It is nauseating. Horrible sounds come from various corners of the café. I hear scratching and fluttering emanating from empty cardboard boxes. Cockroaches are darting everywhere and I hear the continual flurry of night critters scurrying across the floor. I shudder when I hear the loud munching, gnawing sound of what can only be a rat from behind the refrigerator. These sounds are accentuated by the early morning silence. As each car passes outside on the highway, the room is lit up so brightly that I can actually see small mice and cockroaches hunting for food. I am too terrified to sleep. My fear of the night is that some rodent will start eating at my baby's face. It is close to sunrise before I doze off.

Clang! The sound from the front door wakes me. I hear a screech as the mesh grille is slid back. I sit up and in the morning light see Frank rugged up in a big overcoat. On his head is a black beanie. 'Hello, Cliff. You sleep all right?'

I rub my eyes, which feel like grit has been thrown into them, stretch my aching joints and lie, 'Very well thanks, Frank.'

Helen is still sound asleep, and Frank and I whisper in conversation over hot black coffee.

'Mister, you not havin' mucha luck hey! You broke? You no gotta no money?'

Gazing into the black steaming fluid in my cup, I cannot bring myself to look at Frank. He stands up and asks what I would like for breakfast, but my appetite has deserted me, so all I ask for is another cup of black coffee. It's a different story for little Miss Helen, who has finally come to life. She is now standing alongside where Frank and I are seated. She asks for scrambled eggs and toast. Frank gives her a warm smile and says, 'For you, my littla darlin', Frank make'a you da nice scramble eggs.'

Steady rain has settled in on this overcast Sunday morning. The three of us stand at the front door of the café. Picking up my suitcase, I shake Frank's hand. I thank him for everything that he has done for us. This compassionate man has not charged me one penny for the food we have consumed.

He bends down and gives Helen a kiss on the cheek, then turns towards me for the last time and says, 'Hey mister, you keepa your chins uppa high.' He then presses a five-pound note into my hand. This is a considerable amount of money and will keep me going for a few days. After being so coldly rejected by Aunt Sarah, this stranger's kindness and compassion leaves me speechless. I can now understand the feelings of a convicted prisoner when he is about to go to the gallows and he receives a last moment's reprieve. Thank God I still have a chance because Frank took the time to care. I shake hands with Frank and express my gratitude. Helen grabs my hand and we walk out into the rain.

The double-decker bus is quite steamy inside. All of the windows are closed because of the sweeping rain. The lack of oxygen and abundance of cigarette smoke makes breathing uncomfortable. Helen and I travel along in silence. I wipe the mist from the glass and look out the window. The view is depressing. On the black glistening street motorcars throw up sprays of water from their front wheels; the drivers' faces show the usual impatience and frustration of wet weather travellers. Twenty minutes later, we alight from our bus at the Haymarket. The rain stops and the sun comes out. Aimlessly and for a long time, we walk the deserted streets. Finally, it is almost mid-afternoon. Helen and I consume a late lunch bought from a small fish and chip shop. I make sure that we have shelter for the night, booking us both into a small, private hotel. This place is anything but cosy. Despite the furnishings being the bare necessities and the two single beds only having thin blankets we sleep soundly. This place is like a palace after the floor of the hamburger shop.

Monday morning we awake refreshed. I take my suit-case up to the storage area at Central railway station, deposit our belongings into the safe hands of the railway cloakroom attendant and pay the daily storage fee. By 10 a.m. we are seated in a small back parlour inside the Stadiums Hotel, right in the heart of Chinatown, in the Haymarket. It has a large jukebox in one corner, and I sit Helen on a chair behind this musical machine, where it's near impossible to see her from the front bar. Our companions in this parlour are two ladies of the night, probably in their mid-forties, with lined and weather-beaten faces. They fire many questions at me. Where's her mother? Do you look after her on your own? What happens to her while you are at work through the day? How come you have her here at this time of day? The questions are endless. I have answers for every one of them but they are all lies. The two women fuss over the child, buying her potato crisps and lemonade. They take it in turn to nurse Helen and talk quietly to her. These unfortunate women have a story to tell, too. Their stories are filled with shame and heartache. Like so many others who finish up on the Mad Mile, they have also experienced a lifetime of suffering.

Late Monday afternoon, the money has dwindled to a meagre amount. That night we sleep in our hotel again, and next morning, having sobered up, I panic when I realise I am almost broke. We return to the Haymarket, and I'm greeted by former acquaintances on skid row with calls of, 'Where've you been, Cliffy?' and 'Who's the kid?' It's no big deal for these people to see the abnormal down here. It is not perceived as unusual when a man is dragging a five-year-old child around with him. Nothing can shock these people because they have already experienced the worst that can be handed out in life. When living on the Mad Mile a person is reduced to associating with fellow 'desperates', and here I am again. Broke as I am, though, I can still manage to get drunk. People rarely go without a drink of alcohol here, because there is always someone willing to buy a drink—the buyer usually needs company to erase loneliness.

Around 5 p.m. a compassionate prostitute tucks a ten shilling note into my pocket and orders me to give the kid a good feed. Helen and I leave the hotel and enter a Chinese restaurant. We are the only patrons. After eating soup and fried rice we head toward Central railway station. I am very intoxicated as I stand in front of the ticket seller. She is not impressed. A one-way ticket to the outer suburb of Liverpool is purchased with the last of my money. I have no idea why I choose this station as our destination.

I am grateful for the interior warmth of the electric train and sink down into the soft leather seat. Many people alight at Liverpool station; the crowd is mainly working people arriving back from their daily duties in the city. They disperse quickly and head for the comfort of their homes. Helen and I walk into the platform waiting room and sit down on the hard wooden seat. I doze off for an hour or so. When I awake I look up at the waiting room clock. It reads 8 p.m. Helen is in dreamland alongside me.

Suddenly, out of nowhere, a skinny little man dressed in a motley, old military overcoat appears. He is about seventy and on his hands are old woollen gloves with a few moth holes in each one. On his feet are well-worn shoes held together with fine copper wire. Sitting down next to me he whispers, 'Your little girl?'

I look at him more closely. He appears to be harmless and I answer in a civil way, 'Yes, she is.'

From his coat pocket he pulls out a large bottle of cheap red wine. 'Wanna drink?'

Eagerly I accept. It takes us about half an hour to drink the contents, then like magic, he pulls another one from the other coat pocket. Conversation is moving along in a very slurred manner.

He tells me that he has three daughters, but he has not seen them since their early childhood. His wife left him and returned to England with the children back in 1934. 'She was English you know,' he adds as an afterthought. He goes on with his story after another gulp of the red. 'In my younger days I had a very good position as chief accountant with a large Melbourne firm. The demon drink was always there to haunt me. By 1943, I was unemployed. It was a bad year. I also heard that my ex-wife and three daughters were killed in an air raid. The house in London where they were living took a direct hit.' He pauses as tears well up in his faded eyes. He looks at me for understanding. I, too, have tears in my eyes. Here we are, two lonely men, lost in the sea of life. There is not another soul in sight. It is like sitting in a tomb. He continues, 'After hearing that dreadful news my will to live just slipped away. I realised that I would never see my children again. My drinking went past the gutter level. I'm in the sewer of life now.' He rises to his feet and is off balance. Managing to quickly straighten himself up, he stands in front of me swaying back and forth and says, 'I'm going now, son. Got itchy feet. Can't hang around in the one place too long. Got me nightcap here.' He produces yet another bottle from the coat pocket. It is methylated spirits. Then he says, 'I'll give you some fatherly advice, if you're interested. Get off this rotten booze!' He points towards Helen, who is still sleeping. 'Straighten yourself out and find the real meaning of life through the eyes of your little girl. Goodbye, mate.' And he walks out into the dark night.

I am really drunk. Everything is so still and quiet as I sit in the lonely waiting room. Helen sleeps on. The railway clock on the wall of this tomb reads 10 p.m. I stand up and almost fall. I lurch towards my right-hand side in rapid paces, trying to regain my balance. Holding onto the far wall, I slowly walk back to where I was sitting, and gingerly lower myself down onto the hard seat. Not a sound to be heard. It is so fearfully quiet. Then, mysteriously, a faint sound comes to my ears. It is almost a whisper at first. The hushed voice is cursing as it grows louder and louder. I start to perspire. It is taunting as if coming from the devil himself. Over and over and over the voice repeats the same words: 'Sick lost. Sick LOST. SICK LOST. SICK LOST.' Looking up, I become aware that the voice is emanating from the object stuck on the far wall of this tomb. The object is framed in dark cedar wood and has round, polished glass on the front. Behind this thick glass are black numerals on top of faded yellow parchment, which form a complete circle within the glass. In the centre a long, wide, flat strip of gold metal is hanging downward. Attached to the bottom of this metal is a gold ball swaying back and forth. I hear it saying, 'SICK LOST. SICK LOST.' My God, it's the clock of the devil! I start to moan in fear.

This sudden outburst causes Helen to awaken and ask, 'Are you all right, Daddy?'

I am terrified. 'Come on, love, let's get out of here.'

Bumpers, Gunshots
and Beaten

We hurry away from the station. Ten minutes later we find ourselves in a large paddock on the outer fringe of Liverpool. We sit down and huddle together. I wrap Helen in my old coat and she quickly goes back to sleep. Surrounded by grass and paspalum I stare into the night. About one hundred yards away are several tall buildings, partially illuminated by lights coming from the office windows. The night cleaners are hard at work. Still very drunk, the strangest feeling starts to come over me. I begin to shake uncontrollably. Standing up I feel like my head has been blown off my shoulders. I madly run in circles trying to find my head. I keep yelling, 'Where's my head?' A big black hole then appears before me. It goes down to the core of the earth, all the way down to hell. Terrified, I tell myself I must not fall into that hole. My body is soaked in perspiration and I am scared of dying or going mad. Stark terror takes hold again as I wander through the long grass trying to find

Helen. I am terrified that my child may have fallen into that big black hole. I panic and run in all directions trying to find Helen. Exhausted, I stand still and finally get my bearings. Eventually, I find Helen still sound asleep in my jacket. I collapse on the ground and pass out. I do not awaken until sunrise. Helen begins to stir. She stands up, rubs her eyes and says, 'I'm hungry, Daddy.' All I am concerned about is survival.

The train journey back to the city causes great uneasiness, because I have no money for tickets. My mind is playing leapfrog with me as I try to reason a way of getting through the barriers at Central station. I know they are guarded by Railways Department staff. Anxiety increases as I alight from the train. When panic takes over, I lift Helen into my arms, race through the barriers and ignore the call of a burly attendant. 'Hey! You with the kid! Come back.'

Adrenalin enables me to run all the way down to the Haymarket area. Once I put Helen down and intermingle with the crowd, I feel a small degree of safety.

I have only a hazy recollection of the next five or six days. I stop people in the street and tell tales of needing money to get back home one hundred miles away. Sometimes I just tell people that the child and I have not eaten for two days. Most times I am rewarded with a coin or two. This degrading act of begging money leaves me with disgust and any feelings of pride, dignity or self-respect die within. I am filled with self-loathing. One morning Helen and I awake in a dilapidated, inner-city house. I have no memory of how we got here. This is the home of a very old woman, whom I often see walking around the city pushing her trademark, antiquated, cane pram. It is always loaded with an assortment of worn clothing, newspapers, pots and pans. She is always muttering to herself. I am in a state of shock at finding myself in this house of horrors. Helen tells me, 'Daddy, I don't like it here. There are monsters in this house!' I agree with her.

This event makes me realise that my drinking is causing blackouts. I also know it is possible for Helen and I to be easily separated when I consume too many drinks; I could wander off drunk at any time and totally forget about the child. A safety precaution is now put into operation and every day we practise this procedure. I instruct Helen to always grab hold of Daddy's side trouser pocket when he is coming out of a hotel or leaving somebody's place. I tell her she must hold on tight. We go over and over this procedure many times until it becomes second nature. She learns the lesson well. Time and again when I am unsteady of foot and my mind is befuddled I look down and through a haze of double vision there she is. Helen clinging to my trouser pocket with a vice-like grip and her eyes looking up at me as if to say, 'I'm a good girl, aren't I, Daddy?'

Some nights are spent sleeping in a railway station or at somebody's home, if we are invited to stay. One night we sleep in the spare room of an inner-city flat belonging to a kind-hearted prostitute. She takes pity on the child, not me. During this nightmare period Helen and I do not change our clothing for seven days.

Unable to afford cigarettes, I begin another degrading act—bumper shooting. Each day I am desperate to feed my cigarette addiction. In my seedy, shaky state, I search the gutters and footpaths for discarded cigarette butts. Once I collect enough, I go through the process of breaking them open and piling the tobacco in a heap. I then roll my smoke by using cigarette paper or pieces of torn newspaper. Quite often I make a joke of my predicament and tell people, 'I was downtown yesterday picking up my cigarette supply when some clumsy bastard trod on my fingers!' This is always good for a laugh and somehow gives me relief from the shame of what I am forced to do.

On rare occasions I cross paths with people who knew me prior to my degradation. The story and people's body language is always the same. 'Hello, Cliff. God you look dreadful! What's going on?' I am so lonely that all I want from these former friends is to sit down in a coffee shop and for them to talk to me. I also want to talk about my pain, but no, it's always the same. They reach for their wallet, withdraw a bank note, thrust it into my hand, then as if on cue, look at their wristwatch and say, 'Gee, I'm running late. Must go. You take care of yourself.' I stand there watching the backs of these well-dressed people slowly disappearing into the crowd. All I want is their time. What a pity they don't have time!

One Friday night outside the British Lion Hotel I cross paths with a mate from my school days at Glebe. Colin is coming out of the pub with his arms stacked with bottles of alcohol. When he sees me he stops and says,

'You look like death warmed up, Nicko! What are you doing with the kid?'

'This is Helen, my daughter. My wife left me a few days ago,' I tell him. 'I've been on a bender and I'm trying to straighten myself out. But I have nowhere to sleep.'

This man is well known as an habitual criminal, and many of his dubious associates frequent his home in Annandale, a suburb adjoining Glebe. He nods his head towards his car, which is parked a few feet from where we are standing, and says, 'Hop in. You can stay at my place until you dry out.'

After a five-minute drive we arrive at Colin's small cottage. He directs us into a spare room with two single beds, and tells me that there will be some noise tonight because he has invited two men and three women over for a party. Too exhausted to party, Helen and I collapse onto our beds and sleep.

Angry voices slowly awaken me. I look across at Helen, who is in a deep sleep. The voices grow louder. There are sounds of scuffling, bumping and glass breaking. When I open the bedroom door I see Colin and a burly guy shouting at each other. There is pushing and shoving. The third man in the room suggests that they go out onto the street and have it out with their fists. They both agree. The boxing match goes on for a good three minutes until Colin becomes the victor. The big guy is on the ground covered in blood. Colin helps him to his feet and suggests they all go back into the house and have a drink. Back inside the house the party gets into full swing. I decide to join them. I tell jokes and we all begin to sing. Everyone gets very intoxicated. I look at the lounge room clock and it reads 3 a.m.

Without warning, the big man, who had finished up on the ground after the punch-up, pulls out a .38 revolver from his coat pocket. He fires it into the ceiling. Everybody freezes. In his drunken stupor the big guy warns us all, 'If anybody tries to mess with me then the next bullet won't go into the ceiling. It will go into you.' He stares at Colin, then each one of us. I guess I must have the look of a Catholic nun on my face, because I warrant only a passing glance. No-one argues with him. Needless to say the party breaks up very quickly. Drunken partygoers shake each others' hands, cuddle and hug before they leave. The place is quiet once more. I return to my room and Helen is still in a deep sleep. I am very grateful that she has not heard or seen the fracas.

One night's stay at Colin's place is enough for me. I inform him early next morning that I have to go into Central railway station and pick up my suitcase. We both need fresh clothing. Colin agrees about the change of clothes, 'Those clothes you have on, Nicko, are stinkin'. The poor kid is no better off. Do you both want to have a shower before you go?'

'No thanks,' is my quick reply. I am more concerned about the big guy coming back with his pocket cannon and shooting us all dead. 'I'm going over to stay at my aunt's place after I get my suitcase.' Colin places a one-pound note in my hand as Helen and I depart. I am grateful for the money.

After retrieving my suitcase from the station locker

room, Helen and I aimlessly walk down George Street. I did not sleep for more than three hours the night before and I'm still under the influence. I am in a bad way. I have not shaved, bathed or changed clothes for a week. I am ready to collapse on the footpath. Little Helen's hygiene and clothing are in the same state but she is well rested and chats away, oblivious to everything. My fears are starting to mount again. I am paranoid that people are laughing at me. I start to shake violently.

'Cliffy, is that you?' I look up and just stare at the beautiful vision before me. The voice speaks once more. 'My God, what have you done to yourself? Who's the child?'

My emotions go haywire. I stand before this person shaking and sobbing. I know in my heart that I am defeated. There is no more fight or hope. If this person had not come along I feel that within the hour I would have laid down in the gutter and prayed for death. She puts her arms around me and holds me. I repeat her name over and over. 'Nicky! Oh, Nicky!' My beautiful blonde friend from the Bourke Hotel, who I have not seen for such a long time, has come back into my life just as I am about to give up my struggle. Between fearful sobs I explain, 'This is Helen, my daughter. We have been on our own for some time and I need help.'

Nicky bends down, picks Helen up, turns to me and says, 'You both smell as if you have been sleeping on a rubbish tip!' Screwing up her nose she adds, 'Follow me.' As we walk there is complete silence. Some five hundred yards down the road I question our destination. Nicky stops, turns towards me and says, 'The Burlington Hotel.' She points towards the large, circular, five-storey building. 'I work there as a housemaid.'

This hotel is an early opener and one that I have frequented in the past. As we enter the very large lounge area Nicky directs me towards a vacant table. There are no more than five or six people scattered throughout the lounge. Each one of these people is sitting alone at different tables. The atmosphere is cold and desolate. I feel desperation in the air. Nicky sits Helen down on a chair next to me and then walks in the direction of the bar. She returns with a pink lemonade for Helen and a large double brandy for me. We consume our drinks quickly. Nicky reorders another large brandy for me. She then takes Helen by the hand, picks up my large suitcase and walks towards the circular staircase leading up to the guest rooms. Looking over her shoulder she calls, 'I won't be too long. I'll give this child a bath and a change of clothing. You wait right there. Don't go away, because you're next!'

Me, go away? I certainly have no intention of going anywhere. There is nowhere to go.

Helen looks like a little angel as she now walks towards me. Her face is aglow. She has a pretty ribbon tied in a bow on top of her shiny, fair hair. Her red velvet dress is ironed and on her small feet are pure white socks with her best black shoes.

'On your feet, my boy, your turn,' says Nicky, pointing in the direction of the staircase.

'You're not going to bathe me are you, Nicky?'

She laughs loudly. 'You must be joking. Even if I had a tetanus shot, I reckon I'd still be contaminated after bathing you. Here, take this key. It's for a vacant room on the first floor, number seven.'

A snow-white towel is draped across the bed alongside a large cake of soap. The room is warm and safe. I sit down on the side of the bed wondering if I have the strength to strip off and get under the shower. The double brandies have helped to settle my nervous system but the fears are still with me. Slowly I remove my filthy clothing.

Like a cascade from a waterfall, the hot water flows over my back, down over my buttocks and caresses the muscles in my aching thighs. It runs right down to my feet, which tingle to the warm dance of splashing water. I raise my face under the shower head and the sudden impact of hot water gives me a feeling of purity. My hair rejoices when the foaming lather of soap washes the dirt away. There is a razor in the bathroom which I use to remove my seven-day growth of black whiskers. Looking into the mirror I realise that the real Cliff has been missing for some time. I then take clean clothing from my suitcase and dress. The light and exhilarating feeling of having clean, fresh clothing on my body gives me back a small measure of confidence and self-respect. I do my best to tidy up the room.

'Well! Well! The man is not eighty after all,' is Nicky's remark as I approach the table in the lounge. Helen gives me a wonderful big grin over the top of a huge glass of lemonade. Perhaps she is thinking, 'This is my real Daddy.' After a short discussion regarding my homeless state and fears, Nicky pushes a hand-written note across the table and states, 'I have written my address at Glebe on this piece of paper. Here is my front door key. I'll phone for a cab in a moment. Now, when you get there make yourselves a meal. There is plenty of food in the fridge. Put Helen in one of the single beds in the spare room and yourself in the other. Get a damn good rest. There is nobody else living with me, so you won't be disturbed.' As we depart from the Burlington Hotel, her final words are, 'I'm a little behind in my work at the moment but I should be back home by five this evening.' As I leave the hotel the relief I feel is over-whelming. Knowing that I will be safe within Nicky's home and saved from such a hopeless situation gives me a powerful feeling of salvation.

Chattering, whispering voices cause me to open my eyes. Through these tired slits I see Nicky and two other women in the doorway of the bedroom. Looking across at Helen, I see that she is still fast asleep. I quietly get out of bed and throw on some clothing. Nicky intro-duces me to her friends. The taller and much heavier built woman is called 'The Duchess', the second person is a smaller edition, known as 'Mad Molly'. I address the first woman as Duchess but I'm not sure what to call the smaller model. If I am to abbreviate her name it will have to be either Mad or Moll. I play it safe and call her Molly. I soon learn that both of these women work profes-sionally as companions for lonely men.

Nicky informs the two women about our circumstances and the Duchess comes straight to the point: 'What are your plans for the kid?' I shrug my shoulders because I don't have an answer. The three women agree that I have to straighten myself out, and suggest that for the time being Helen be put into the hands of the Child Welfare Department. My answer to this suggestion is firm: 'No!' My reasons are a mixture of selfishness and survival. If Helen is taken from me and I am left alone, there will be nothing to live for. I am aware that the future is bleak, yet I know the child must stay with me.

Molly comes to my rescue by saying, 'If you find a job and a place for Helen to live, then I will babysit free of charge while you work. I don't have to entertain my clients through the day.'

'I can help out of an evening,' Nicky chimes in.

'I wonder where I can find a job?' I say, my head whirling with the way these women are taking me in hand.

'By bloody well looking for one, stupid!' blurts out the Duchess.

'Hold on,' interrupts Molly, 'a client of mine has been complaining about how hard it is to get labourers for his transport company. Apparently the only people who start working there are drifters, alcoholics and bums. They only work for a few days to get some money together, then move on to greener pastures. I'll give the guy a call. After all, he is one of the big bosses down there.' It sounds ideal. My credentials are in order for the job.

I am an experienced, unreliable, incompetent drifter and bum. I'm a natural!

The night before I start work a plan is put in place. It's agreed that Helen and I can both stay at Nicky's home for a few weeks. After that I must be ready to move into my own residence. Nicky is to receive half my pay for a compulsory savings plan to ensure that there will be enough for rent and other necessities when we move out. Molly will come over early each morning to watch over Helen during the day.

At seven the next morning, I join the motley collection of unwashed dropouts gathered outside the main gate of the transport company. The yard boss bellows out, 'Any workers for the pig iron, get on the truck!' I just follow the rabble and climb aboard. Scattered in great heaps along the waterfront dock are many bars of raw pig iron. Each bar is roughly the size of a gold ingot, minus the smooth surface, and the flesh-tearing edges inflict many painful cuts and wounds before the day is out. This boring exercise involves bending down, picking up the bar, dumping it onto the truck, then repeating the process all over again. For anybody watching this pantomime, we must look like neurotic emus.

At the end of the day's work I head for home with my head feeling like an over-ripe watermelon. My eyes are swishing around inside my head and my legs are doing a quiver dance. My poor hands are more like the victim of a razor blade attack than that of a musician. I now know why the transport company has such a large turnover of personnel.

At 5 p.m. Nicky walks through the front door and sees me sprawled out on her couch. She asks, 'Well, how did it go?' Every bone and muscle in my body is begging for mercy as I try to sit up. I open my mouth to answer Nicky but nothing comes out. I just flop back down on the couch exhausted. 'Oh no!' squeals Nicky and laughs hysterically, 'I'm going to wet myself.' She trips over a cushion lying on the floor as she races to the bathroom. When she returns she is much more composed but still has a wide grin on her face. She bends down and kisses me on the cheek saying, 'Welcome to the real world, dear friend.'

By mid-June, I have been loading pig iron for about four weeks. I try to find Fred and phone Concord Hospital. I'm told that he was discharged earlier in the week. There is no reason for concern, Fred knows how to take care of himself. I miss him right now, but I know that I'll track him down eventually.

Molly finds Helen and me a little, two-bedroom, furnished flat in Glebe. Our new neighbour, Ethel, is an elderly pensioner, who is grateful for the opportunity to look after Helen while I work—it's a means for her to make some extra money. Helen warms to her new daily companion, who is a very caring and patient human being. She escorts Helen to preschool each day and picks her up when school is out.

Towards the end of June I leave the transport company and secure a much better job as a cleaner for the Gas Company. Life now consists of going to work, taking Helen out on weekends, eating and sleeping.

It is a mundane lifestyle because I am still 'on the wagon' after seven weeks. Once again I become restless; my life lacks excitement, drama and romance. I feel like I have no life. I keep telling myself that I am entitled to some sort of social life.

Eventually, I pick up a drink to relieve my boredom. It happens again! I get fired from the Gas Company for drinking on the job. Within one week there is no money in the house and Ethel's services are dispensed with. Helen is very disappointed. At the beginning of July there is little food in the house, the rent is due and the outlook is grim. This repetitive failure brings me to a stage where hope is almost gone. I sit slumped on a kitchen chair, almost mindless except for the nagging thought of final escape—suicide.

The lone bottle of cheap wine on the table in front of me is half empty. Looking out through my kitchen window I watch the yellow late afternoon sun start to sink below the horizon.

'Daddy,' Helen's tiny voice breaks the silence.

'Yes, love.'

'Daddy, you know what?'

'What, love?'

She smiles and says, 'Keep your chins up high!'

I am amazed she remembers the words of wonderful Frank, who let us sleep on his café floor for the night. I cuddle her. My guilt and fear of failing Nicky and the girls, after all their wonderful care and guidance, prevents me from searching them out for help. I can't expect them to give me any more assistance because I know

I have let them down. What can I do? After putting on my woollen jacket, I dress Helen in a warm dress and coat. We walk out through the front door and stand for a moment on the street. It is after 5.30 p.m.

The red phone box on the corner seems to have an answer but who can I call? Once inside the phone box I see two letters 'A.A.', and a phone number scribbled alongside. I remember running into a friend of mine from Glebe, Tommy, back in 1957. He had always been a chronic drinker, in trouble with the police and bookmakers just like I was. This day I saw him he was sober, clear-eyed and well-dressed. I was shocked and immediately asked, 'What's happened to you? You look so well.'

He told me, 'I am attending Alcoholics Anonymous and that's what has changed my life.'

'I wonder if I could come with you to one of these meetings?' I asked, wanting to look and feel as he did. I began to have great hope as I observed his example. He had been on the same social level as me—three steps down from the gutter in the sewer, and now I could see he was on his way up the social ladder. I wanted so much to have what he had.

After hearing a few speakers at my first A.A. meeting I had realised one thing. If these people with their 'limited intelligence' could dress well, be sober and wealthy, then I, the genius waiting to be discovered, could achieve so much more if they could show me how to control my drinking. Unfortunately my attitudes were all wrong and I did not continue to attend A.A. on a regular basis.

Over the last six years I only went to A.A. meetings when trouble came my way. I was unable to accept that I was an alcoholic. I thought an alcoholic was a weak person who could not stop drinking. I was trying to find a way to drink normally, not have trouble follow me and not be an alcoholic. I did not want to be perceived as weak. I could not stop drinking with or without A.A. during this time. I blamed all my problems on my mother and father, my wives, police officers and the army. I knew that if people got off my back I would have a chance. I was not ready to take responsibility for my own life.

Although I do not believe that I am an alcoholic, I recollect that they do help each other. Perhaps they may help me out with some money to tide me over. I dial the number. The voice on the other end of the line says, 'Alcoholics Anonymous here. Can I help you?'

'I'm in desperate trouble. Will you please send somebody out to see me. Ask them to come in about four hours' time because I won't be home until ten o'clock tonight.' I then give my name and address. In the back of my mind there are grave fears that I am about to end my life, yet I'm not certain. Confusion mixes with fear and has me in two minds. I do not want Helen to be left alone if I do take my life. What made me say not to come until ten tonight? What's my reason? Am I putting off the inevitable? Leaving the phone box we walk towards the British Lion Hotel.

There are very few patrons in the beer garden. A couple of housewives and several men who have finished their day's work are having a drink before returning

190

home. 'Hey! Cliffy,' comes a call from an elderly mate. He is sitting with his wife having a drink. He beckons me to join them. Avoiding suspicious questioning, I inform them that I am still working and that everything is all right. I tell them Helen's mother and I will be getting back together very soon; this seems to satisfy their curiosity. I borrow some money from my friend and after about an hour make my departure with the words, 'Helen and I need to eat dinner and retire early. I have to start work first thing in the morning. I'll see you later.' On my way out of the hotel I buy a large bottle of cheap brandy and a bottle of red wine. We cross the street and enter a small café for our evening meal. Around 8 p.m. I purchase lemonade, potato chips, a large chocolate block and a box of sweets. Helen thinks it is Christmas. For me it is the Last Supper.

Within the walls of our small flat there seems to be an eerie feeling of peace as I sit in the semi-darkness. Helen is finally tucked away in bed, fast asleep. My mind is still. By the time I consume half the brandy, sadness joins me as a farewell companion. I reassure myself with muttered, one-sided conversation. 'Everything will be okay. Helen will be better off. Please Fred, don't be angry at me. I'm so sorry. It would be nice to see the boys of Eastern Command Band once more.'

I open the old suitcase and feel relief when I find a container filled with around one hundred black and green capsules. I don't know what they are or remember where they came from. They have been in my suitcase for a very long time. I start to swallow them by the handful, washing them down with brandy. When the brandy bottle is empty I keep swallowing more capsules, flushing them down with the cheap red wine.

Within I am crying and my mind is saying at least there will be no more pain. I start to write my farewell note and my blurry vision makes it hard for me to read what I have written. 'I'm sorry everyone. Please take good care of my daughter, Helen. I can't live with alcohol and I can't live without it.'

Drowsiness takes over and my limbs are heavy. I am still awake and panic strikes. Why isn't it working? Nothing is happening. I might be brain damaged. I don't want to be a vegetable. I quickly take more capsules and red wine. I am unable to confront my grief and it causes a death inside my soul. My limbs become transformed into useless sticks of jelly-like substance and my eyes, the windows of my soul, become sightless, steel marbles. I am now part of the living dead, without hope and faith. I am now floating on a pillow of relief. Wonderful peace . . . drifting in time . . . gentle, so gentle . . . my eyes close. Before me is the comforting colour of deep blue. Someone has painted the sky. The richness of the deep, dark blue has covered all of planet Earth . . . then nothing. Finally, the soft hand of submission comes and I slowly slither off the chair onto the floor. For a brief moment my eyes open and in my delirious state I see planet Earth like a huge floor. In the centre of this floor is a drain hole into which many grief-stricken souls have sunk before me. I sense its pull on my own soul. It tries to suck everything real and worthwhile from my body into its endless darkness. I know if it succeeds it will take my soul, my spirit and my mind, then only dry, thirsty skin will remain. My insides try to scream. I don't want to be a nothing. God help me.

The Parting

'Walk you bastard! Keep walking! Come on, keep going!' A voice from a distance echoes in my head. My feet are treading on sponge, my vision is blurred and inside my head someone is hammering. The only thought I have is, Please let me lie down and die.

'Walk! Come on, walk!' That loud voice is echoing again. I am conscious that a firm arm is supporting me, but I'm unable to recognise to whom it belongs.

I remember the many pills I swallowed the previous night as my insides heave and I vomit. My thoughts keep racing: Who is this person? Can't he see I want to detach from planet Earth? Doesn't he know that I'm on a lone journey, which began when my soul and spirit died? Why can't he leave me alone?

Eventually, I come back into the land of the living. I feel a mixture of exhaustion, embarrassment and disgust towards myself. When I ask who he is, he introduces himself as, Jack from A.A. 'You called A.A. for help last night. Do you remember? You said you wanted help. The earliest I could get here was six this morning. Just as well I came early, otherwise I don't think you would have made it.'

'I can't take any more pain, Jack. I want to stop drinking but I can't. I don't want to be like this. Living is too confusing and too bloody hard!' Suddenly I remember my child and ask, 'Hey, where is little Helen?'

'Don't worry, she's okay. She let me into the flat but now she's playing outside.' He talks to me for a long while and tries to encourage me to drink coffee. Finally, he says, 'Come on, Cliff. You are not in a fit state to care for yourself or your daughter. Neither of you can live in these appalling conditions. Come home to my place. My wife and I can help you sort out this whole mess.' Tears form in my eyes as I sense his love and caring.

The hand of friendship from Jack and his wife is wonderful. The home comforts and their companionship make Helen and I feel like royalty. The reality of my inability to care for Helen confronts me when Jack speaks to me about taking responsibility for her future. I know that I am too sick to continue looking after her and I am afraid of what might happen to her. I am also afraid of being alone.

For three long days I agonise over what to do regarding Helen. Maybe I can stop drinking and look after her. Perhaps I can get another job and earn enough money to keep her. Finally, I get ruthlessly honest with myself. The truth confronts me. Unless I am on a path of continual sobriety Helen's life will never be free from the risk of disaster. I realise I must put Helen's wellbeing before my own. I make the decision to send her to St Joseph's Home for Children.

The day of Helen's departure arrives. It is August, and on our way to St Joseph's, we stop at a little Catholic church in Haberfield. Ellie and Jack have arranged for Helen to be baptised. Everyone is waiting for the ceremony to begin. There are three tiny babies all dressed in beautiful, lace-trimmed, christening robes. The church is peaceful except for the occasional cry from one of the infants. Near the altar is a large statue of the Virgin Mary. She is looking down on us and her face conveys love to all. On the other side of the altar is a large statue of Jesus crucified on the cross. It is now very quiet. I feel unworthy and believe I have no right to be in this house of God. First they baptise the three babies, followed by beautifully dressed twin girls aged about two. When their ceremony is over, most people leave the church. Helen and four adults are the only people remaining.

The priest in white and gold robes then steps down from the altar. He speaks to Ellie as he glances at Helen. 'So this is little Helen?'

Helen's big blue eyes are wide with wonderment. She turns to me with a questioning look as if to ask, 'Why are we here, Daddy?'

The priest takes Helen by the hand. I nod my head to Helen to reassure her that everything will be all right. She follows him up to the altar and her baptism ceremony begins.

What transpires before us can only be described as majestic in its purity. The little blonde-haired child has her head upturned, looking directly into the priest's face. She is dressed in her well-worn, red velvet dress. On her feet are her slightly scuffed, best black shoes. There is no luxury of christening clothes. She looks so small in the vast, luxurious surrounds of the church. A soft glow appears from nowhere, forming an aura around her head and face as she is baptised. This moment becomes so very special. It is as if God himself is supervising this particular baptism. Helen turns her head to look at me and she smiles. Tears of joy begin to run down my cheeks. Jack and Ellie also wipe tears from their eyes.

After the christening we all travel to St Joseph's. Jack eventually breaks the silence, saying, 'There it is, just ahead.' I freeze in the back seat. The car stops near the circular steps leading up to the massive wooden doors at the entrance to St Joseph's Home for Children. I look at Helen and she smiles in her trusting way. I feel sick. Jack is first to reach the front door. He pushes the brass-plated button, which rings the bell.

The door opens and we are greeted by a matronly lady. She is clad in pure white from her veiled head down to the ground. Peeping from underneath the hem of her gown are little black boots. A thick black belt is around her waist and a black crucifix hangs on a cord around her neck. 'This must be Helen. We've been expecting you,' says the nun.

I look down at Helen, who has a tight grip on my trouser pocket. She looks so small as she inches further behind my leg. She stares at the lady in white. She is wondering how the nun knew her name. She looks at me as if to ask, 'Why are we here?'

Mother Superior leads us all inside. I look at the white, cold, marble statues and the black and white square tiles on the floor. It all feels clinical and devoid of hospitality. A very wide, circular staircase with twenty marble steps leads upstairs to the sleeping quarters for these forgotten children. Jack and his wife assist me with the formalities.

The moment I have been dreading arrives after the papers are signed. As I walk through the large wooden door and out into the sunlight, I turn to see where Helen is. The nun is standing inside the doorway and has hold of her hand. Helen has a bewildered look on her face. She can't understand why her small hand is being gripped by the lady in white. Helen's eyes seem to be painfully calling out, 'Don't leave me here, Daddy,' yet no sound comes from her mouth. She just stands there very still, looking totally confused. I wonder if she thinks that I don't love or want her any more. Her eyes never waver from mine. She still makes no sound. There are no tears or fighting against the woman holding her hand. She is almost a statue. Her eyes send out their silent plea again, 'Daddy, don't leave me.'

I walk back through the open door towards her, squat down on my haunches, put both of my hands on her small shoulders and try desperately to make her understand. 'Sweetie, it's just for a little while. Daddy will come and see you all the time. Soon I will find a new house for you and I to live in. Okay? Do you understand?'

Her sad, blue eyes still stare into mine. I sense she wants to move her head from side to side to deny what I am saying. I know she wants to cry out, 'Daddy, I want to come with you.' It does not happen. She just stares into my face, frozen in shock. After an agonising silence, she whispers ever so quietly, 'Yes, Daddy.'

I pull her towards me and hold her for so long, kissing her face and telling her how much I love her. I do not want to let her go.

Jack's voice breaks the silence. 'We have to go now, Cliff.'

I walk back out through the large door, turn and wave to Helen as the door starts to close. I see the cold, marble stairs and statues as the door slowly continues on its journey. In the middle of this heartbreaking scene is my little daughter. She stands very still, with her eyes locked onto mine, until the large door eventually slams shut. I die inside. I feel as though my heart has been cut out of my chest. Jack and Elsie have to help me down the steps to the car. I am shaking uncontrollably and sobbing with grief. I feel that I have betrayed and abandoned my little friend.

The following day, Jack graciously gives me some money. I am then able to book myself into a guesthouse in Croydon close to where Helen resides. Within one day I find myself a position as a storeman for an electrical firm in Ashfield, one train stop down the line from Croydon. I have every intention of getting off the booze for the rest of my life. I do not like the taste of any type of alcohol, and only drink it because it eases my pain.

I am unable to handle life and certain situations completely baffle me. Leaving Helen is one of them. Alcohol is only a symptom of my real problem: I have no living skills and my attitudes are often wrong concerning people, places and things.

August is cold and windy. I am grateful that Helen is safe, warm and regularly fed. My highest priority now is to fulfil my promise to Helen and I need to rely on good old Fred's help to achieve it. I realise that I have been caught up in my own selfish problems and have not given much thought to my father's wellbeing. Saturday morning I go looking for my dad. After visiting five hotels I am finally greeted by his familiar voice and I am so happy to hear it. 'Cliff! Over here.' There he is in the corner of the pub with a few of his cronies. 'Where in the name of hell have you been? You didn't even visit me in hospital, you rotter. How's Helen?'

I pour out my sorry tale to Fred but cannot bring myself to admit to my suicide attempt. I am too ashamed. We finish our drinks and I explain how I want to move out of my temporary room at the boarding house and rent a small, fully furnished flat close to St Joseph's. 'I want to have somewhere for Helen to come and stay each weekend. How are you fixed for cash, Fred?'

He gives me a sly smile and confides, 'It just so happens that the manager of the Prince of Wales Hotel owes me. We put a pound each on a horse last Wednesday and it won. My old mate Jackie the Snoop gave me the tip. I'll guarantee the boss really bet more than one pound because he knows what good information Jackie gives. He said if the horse won he would sling me a ten pound tip.' Fred rubs his hands together. 'The horse won by three lengths at twenty-five to one. Good old Jackie! Anyhow, son, I have about thirty-six pounds to collect. Let's go and gather the loot.'

This is not the first time Fred Nichols saves me from going under, nor the last. Fred and I have a wonderful friendship. I do not take from people all of the time and never give in return; there are many times when I keep Fred and others afloat. I have little respect for money; it's a case of easy come, easy go, and I don't mind sharing with my friends.

Fred and I walk into Croydon Real Estate office and make enquiries. The salesman reads from a card: 'A comfortable bedsitter unit with furnishings and cooking facilities. Weekly rental is five pounds, ten shillings per week.' This seems ideal because it is situated no more than two hundred yards from St Joseph's. It is like a little bit of heaven.

Lady luck is on my side when I am reunited with an old army pal a few days later. He informs me that there is a cleaner's job going at a large chemical company. The dust and chemical powders on the floors in the mixing rooms make this a dusty, messy job. The wages, however, are extremely high. There seems to be a bright light shining at the end of the tunnel when I obtain the position. I believe I have a future after all.

I now work from 6 a.m. to around 2.30 p.m., five days a week, and arrange to collect Helen each Friday around 3 p.m. I stand in the vestibule and wait for my little mate. My eyes are glued to the top of the winding staircase in anticipation of her appearance. The excitement is always the same. Finally, Helen appears at the top of the stairway. As she descends I notice she is clutching the hand of a junior nun. She is all spic'n'span and her big grin almost covers her whole face. Not a word is spoken as she descends the staircase. My 'date' for the weekend is Miss Prim and Proper. I can feel the joy mounting within me. She is holding her excitement within, probably from the discipline she has learnt within these walls. Once the big front door slams shut behind us her words pour out in a torrent: 'Are we going to our little flat? Can I make the dinner? Where's Pa Pa? Can I have a milkshake? See my pretty dress, Sister gave it to me.' I pick her up, give her a big cuddle and assure her that we will be doing all of the wonderful things that she likes to do.

Fred is a constant visitor and sleeps overnight Sunday so he can return Helen to St Joseph's around 8 a.m. Monday. This gives her a good break from the orphanage. Sometimes the three of us spend the whole weekend together. Other times just Helen and I go out on the town. I am certainly trying to walk a straight path— sometimes I control the amount I drink, other days I don't touch a single drop.

One Saturday morning Helen and I board the electric train for a journey into the heart of Sydney. As usual, my little travelling companion is chattering away. I repeatedly say yes to whatever she is talking about, even when the noise inside the train prevents me from hearing her questions. Soon we are caught up in the hustle and bustle of the city. People are either coming in and out of department stores, heading for the racetrack or the movies, or waiting in queues at restaurants. The human race comes alive on Saturday. Car horns honk as traffic darts in and out along the street.

'Cliff. Hey, Cliff!' I turn around when I hear my name called.

'Hello, Lenny. How's the world treating you?' We are both delighted to see each other and warmly shake hands. I introduce Helen and explain that Lenny Evans, from Eastern Command Band, is my old pal. Soon Lenny and I are reliving and laughing about our band days over beers at an inner city hotel. Helen is firmly planted on the pub step just a few feet from where I am standing. She is within my sight and enjoys her lemonade and other goodies. 'What about when the band was rehearsing outside and the bandmaster told the trombone section to put some fire into their playing so you lit a small fire of papers and twigs.' Lenny roars with laughter as he remembers the event. The hours slip away and Lenny suggests an early dinner at the Chinese restaurant across the street. Around 5 p.m. we consume a wonderful meal and a large bottle of red wine, after which Lenny looks at his watch and exclaims, 'Hell, it's six o'clock. I must rush.' And he hurries out the door.

Arising from my chair I walk towards the front door of the restaurant. As sure as the sun rises there is my little mate with the vice-like grip on my side trouser pocket. The voice of this patient child asks me, 'Can we have a ride on the double-decker bus, Daddy? Can we go upstairs and in the front?'

This is one of Helen's favourite pastimes so I say, 'Of course, love.'

Seated on the front, upstairs seat of the bus we look down at the road stretching before us. Helen goes into her own brand of travel talk. She points out shops, people, cars, trees, buildings, dogs, clouds, 'we've been there, Daddy' pubs, trams, street lights and anything else that takes her fancy. It is a nonstop narration of the passing parade. This is Helen's way of releasing pent-up emotion and making up for lack of communication, after patiently sitting on a hotel doorstep for such long periods with only herself for company. By the time we leave the bus at Chippendale, one and a half hours have passed. I buy us both a hotdog from the man selling this delicious cuisine outside a pub. I intend to walk down to Central station from here, board a train and travel back to our flat in Croydon. However, fate steps in.

Curiosity causes me to walk up a small lane just a short distance from where I purchase the hotdogs. I recognise a large, double gate on the right hand side. It is the rear entrance to a large house. My immediate thought is that I've been here before. Then a deep voice startles me: 'What do you want?' An enormous man materialises through the huge double gates and walks out into the glow of the street light. His arms are visible under rolled up shirt sleeves and look like the legs of a bullock. He is over six feet tall and his nose is so flat it appears to be part of his cheeks.

Fear mounts within me as I reply, 'Nothin', mate.'

The giant informs me that there is a swy-game in progress in the house. It's not advisable to hang around, especially with the kid. My mind clicks into place. Of course, I have been here before. I quickly tell him that 'the Ferret' from Glebe has brought me here on a few occasions. He comes closer, squints, wrinkles up what is left of his nose and says, 'Yeah, I think I remember your dial.' He then looks down at Helen. 'You're not plannin' on takin' the kid in there, are you, mate?' His face begins to twitch.

In my mind I question, why I have finished up here of all places. Is this an omen? I make a decision. 'Look, my friend, I'm on a journey of fate. Lady Luck has planned my destiny on this night.'

He gives me a funny look and says, 'What in the bloody hell are ya' talkin' about? What's with this fate bullshit?'

I speak quickly, 'If you hold the kid for just twenty minutes while I nick into the game, I promise you I will come out in twenty minutes, win, lose or draw. Come on, boss, be a pal.' I thrust Helen into his big, beefy arms. 'Twenty minutes, no more,' says the big bouncer.

The air is heavy with cigarette smoke. There are three women and about fifteen men inside. Money is being thrown onto the green cloth stretched across the floor. 'Come in spinner,' the voice rings out. The pennies fly high then down they come with a flop. 'Pay the heads.'

I check out my finances. I have fifteen pounds. I tuck a five-pound note into my inside pocket for later emergencies, then place the ten-pound note on the green cloth.

'I'll back a head,' is my confident statement. Lady Luck or Madam Fate is rubbing my back because in the next ten or fifteen minutes the call, 'pay the head' comes so often that I start to wonder if they are using double-headed pennies. When my time is up I have eighty-five pounds in my hand. I'm rich!

The 'Hulk' is holding Helen in his arms and singing songs to her when I return. Helen is singing just as loud to her companion and seems to be having a great old time. He sees me and moves Helen into my arms. His advice is, 'You get her home to bed. It's too cold for her to be out. Hey, she knows lotsa songs.' I press a five-pound note into his large hand. He looks down at the money and says, 'Gee tanks! Hell, I don't get much more than this for standing at this bloody gate for six hours. Tanks, mister!'

I wink at him and say, 'Told you I was on a journey of fate!' I hail a cab and head for Wentworth Park Race-track at Glebe, where the greyhounds are racing.

Sometime after 8 p.m night seems to turn into day as the large, bright overhead lights shine down on the track. After moving through the turnstiles, we are confronted by a man with a silver, box-shaped oven, which stands on four metal legs. I buy two hotdogs smothered in red tomato sauce, then pay for a race book. I turn to Helen and say, 'Tell me a number.'

She looks up at me with her mouth covered in tomato sauce and asks, 'Why?'

Taking a deep breath I explain, 'Daddy's going to put money on a doggie.'

Not impressed, she has another bite on her hotdog. With a mouthful of food she asks, 'How do I do the number, Daddy?'

I feel my right eye starting to twitch. 'God almighty, Lady Luck won't wait all night! You know love, one, two, three, four . . .' My patience is fading and I'm thinking, bloody hell, the rotten race will be over by the time the kid spits out a number.

Suddenly, it happens. 'Four,' she shouts.

'Hooray! Good girl. Give me one more number, please.'

She then becomes overconfident with this game, the next numbers coming out like machine gun fire: 'Ten, fifteen, forty, twenty, one hundred.'

'No love, just one number.'

She puts her finger to the side of her temple in deep thought and looks down at the ground. I wait and wait. 'Helen, you're not going to sleep are you love?'

She looks up at me and laughingly shouts, 'Number one!'

I am on the verge of mental exhaustion as I hurry over to the totalisator window. 'Number four to win and also a quinella on numbers one and four.' I outlay twelve pounds, and the race begins. 'Helen, they're racing. See the dog in the blue rug, that's our doggie. So far he is winning. She starts to cheer and doesn't stop. The dogs flash past the winning post with number four in the lead. Guess who is second? Yes, number one. This means we have won money on the winner and also on the quinella. Hurrying over to collect our winnings, Helen asks me,

'Did I do good, Daddy?' I gently pat her on the head and tell her she is the 'bestest'.

I collect the princely sum of one hundred and sixty-five pounds. We are on a roll. 'Hurry, Helen, pick some more numbers.' Our new numbers are two and three. Once more a bet to win on number two and a quinella on numbers two and three is placed. I outlay another twelve pounds. Over the public address system comes the announcer's voice: 'The green light is showing. The power is on and away goes the bunny. They're racing.'

Did I say we are on a roll? Well, that's partially right. The number two dog is skittled at the first turn and rolls over about four times before regaining his feet. He chases the field again but comes in dead last. As for the number three dog, he decides halfway through the race to either challenge the dog beside him to a dual or ask him for a date. I'm uncertain whether it's an amorous act or a display of anger. Our number three dog finishes the race, with his teeth clamped on the other dog's muzzle, in fifth place.

'Do you want some more numbers, Daddy?' asks Helen, ready for some more action.

I sigh, knowing my journey of fate with Lady Luck has finished for tonight. 'No thanks, darling,' I reply as I pick up my tired little girl. We walk from the track, hail a cab and I instruct the driver to take us home to Croydon. Tonight we ride in style!

I awake to the sound of church bells ringing on Sunday morning, still feeling elated about my performance the previous night. I open the dressing table drawer, take out the roll of notes, and count two hundred and thirty pounds. I think I have made a mistake and count it again. The total is the same. My back straightens to an upright position with my shoulders squared to almost military precision. I feel like I can conquer the world. My newfound wealth gives temporary relief from struggling to find the next meal, worrying about being unable to pay the rent and having to plan like a fox to work out where the next handout of money is coming from. From now on it will be porterhouse steak instead of just French fries.

'Daddy, can I make the cups of tea?' Helen interrupts my moment of glory. She is very proud of the fact that she has learnt how to fill the kettle, turn on the electric stove, boil the kettle and make a pot of tea.

'Yes, but you be careful,' I say.

There is a knock at the door and Fred's voice calls out, 'Are you two sleepy heads out of bed?' He enters and enquires, 'Where were you two yesterday? I came by early in the evening to take you both out for dinner but you were not home.' Fred is excited as he speaks. 'Yesterday was my lucky day. I won twenty-five pounds on the horses.' He pulls a ten-pound note from his pocket and hands it to me. I turn away with a smile and produce my roll of notes and throw it down on the table. His eyes seem to enlarge to twice their normal size and his mouth gives a good imitation of the Grand Canyon. 'Have you done a robbery?'

I laugh loudly because I can see he is serious. 'No.

I went to a swy-game last night and had a win. We went down to Wentworth Park dogs after that. Lady Luck was with me all the way. Helen even picked the numbers for the big win.' I peel off one hundred pounds and hand it to him. He accepts it and thanks me in a soft voice.

'This is your cup of tea, Pa Pa,' Helen chimes in, 'and this is yours, Daddy.' She sets our beverages before us, adding, 'I was good at playing numbers at the doggies, wasn't I, Daddy?'

'You were the bestest, love.'

Fred lifts Helen up on his lap and tells her that they will be going shopping next Friday afternoon. 'We will buy you some brand new shoes, a pretty dress and go to the fun parlour with the pinball machines. After that we will all have dinner at your choice of restaurant.'

She smiles excitedly and asks, 'When is Friday, Pa Pa?'

Fred gently lifts Helen's hand and counts the days until shopping day.

Blackouts

The months of September and October slowly creep by and my attempts to drink less, stay out of trouble and try to be a responsible parent are going according to plan. There are no great upsets and I am in a fairly comfortable routine working my five-day week. After work I have the usual drinks at the local hotel between 3 p.m. and 8 p.m., then head home to get my semi-intoxicated sleep.

But one Friday afternoon, in late October, another moment of insanity strikes. After being paid, I collect Helen from St Joseph's, and we head home to shower and dress so we can go out for the evening. Around 5 p.m. I hail a cab to take us to the British Lion Hotel in Glebe. It seems like a good idea at the time.

The prodigal returns and familiar voices call out, 'Hi there, Cliffy' and 'Hey, Cliffy, are you gonna sing us a song later?' My old drinking companions and I have a few drinks. Around 6 p.m. Helen and I go to the café next door to eat. We then wander back into the hotel beer garden. Before me is the stage where the Oughta-be-Shots used to perform; Rona on piano, Bruce on banjo and the others. The memories of the happy times come flooding back; Jock, Fred and I travelling in the manure truck dreaming of our moment of stardom.

By 7 p.m. there is a solitary person on the stage setting up the microphone and adjusting the speakers. On a chair nearby lies a guitar. I ask, 'How many players do you have in the group, mate?'

He looks at me as if I have dropped in from outer space. 'How many? I'm it. Just me!'

I nod, walk away and find a seat in the far corner of the beer garden. How times have changed. I long for the happy nights when I had Fred and Jock for company.

Friday night is rage night at the British Lion and as the night progresses everything starts to come alive. I can hear the finish of a race from Harold Park Trots on the radio in the public bar. Many people in the beer garden are chattering away, laughing and shouting. Some volup-tuous beauty, who has apparently been pinched on the bum, squeals. There is the clinking of glasses and the lin-gering aroma of cheap perfume. Grey cigarette smoke fills the air. Bodies continually move to and fro between the bar, seats and toilets. The lone musician on the stage is strumming away on his guitar. He is singing a song that is hardly audible above the din. I am sad and iso-lated; the great majority of these patrons are complete strangers, and I feel a lack of identity here. I remain seated at the rear of the beer garden and continue to drink. Helen is strategically placed alongside me, out of sight behind a large, potted palm tree. She loves listening to the music and munching on potato chips. I drink myself into oblivion.

Saturday morning, Jock's friend Ella tells me what happened the night before. 'You were so drunk, you couldn't scratch yourself. I brought you both home here otherwise you would have been in serious trouble. You were getting quite nasty towards a group of people, Cliffy. I stepped in and assured them that I would get you out of there.'

I shake and complain of a dry throat. Dear Ella produces the only tonic that will tie my nerve ends together, a bottle of cheap red wine. The first mouthful is hard to keep down, I choke, gag and cough. My stomach rises rapidly almost up into my neck. Finally, the first glass of wine stays down. The second is easier to swallow and by the time I down the fourth my motor is once more running. I turn towards Ella and say, 'You have been a wonderful friend caring for Helen and I. Thank you for all your help.' We eventually bid her farewell and walk out into a sunny day.

All day Saturday I wander around Glebe talking to various mates that I have not seen for some time. Each time I stop for a chat there is the customary couple of beers at the nearest pub. Helen patiently waits on the hotel steps drinking lemonade and eating chips. Hotel patrons often stop to have a talk with her. By late afternoon I am unsteady of foot.

That night Helen and I eat our evening meal at a café before wandering up Bridge Road at the bottom end of Glebe. As we walk past a big church, a stream of light pours across our path from an open doorway. After pausing and looking in the direction of the doorway, I slowly stagger forward, following the beam of light.

Once inside the church a loud and clear voice from nowhere greets us. 'Hello there, I'm Lynton. Welcome.'

I blink and turn around to see who he is greeting. No-one is there. I eventually realise that we are the only people in the room. I am astounded that anyone would want to know me, because I am drunk and dishevelled. My first thoughts are that he must have mistaken me for some other person. Maybe he is really hard up for company. 'Er, I'm Cliff and this is my daughter, Helen.'

His glance travels from me to the child and he asks, 'Would you like a cup of coffee? How about your little one? What about a nice big glass of milk and a sandwich?' Helen nods her head.

Over the next thirty minutes other people start to enter the room. When many of these people come over to shake my hand and say hello to Helen, I am convinced that they have mistaken me for someone else. I think I might be able to put the bite on everyone in the room—if I can get one pound from each of them, I'll have a total of forty pounds. Helen and I sit in the last row of chairs at the back of the room. My mind is fuzzy and my vision blurred. I manage to see two large, white, calico sheets hanging on the wall at the front of the room. Written on one are the words 'The Twelve Steps of Alcoholics

Anonymous', and on the other 'The Twelve Traditions'. Then it hits me like a thunderbolt! I'm at an A.A. meeting! I remember some caring soul taking me to one of these meetings a long time ago. However, I was too drunk to remember much about it. I am in the same state now and cannot understand a thing that is going on. My mind enters a time warp and all it can understand is the present moment. It has no recollection of yesterday. All I can do is pull two chairs together for Helen so she can doze off.

Unexpectedly, the meeting finishes. I am in a sad state of bewilderment. I'm still very drunk and can't remember anything about today. I have no recollection of how I came to be in this room with these A.A. people. I am not even aware of what suburb I am in.

'Here, drink this,' says Lynton, as he places a cup of coffee into my hand. 'This is my wife, Jean.' His wife questions me in a very caring way, 'Son, do you have a home to go to? It's most unusual to see someone here with a little tot.'

I do not remember that we have our little home at Croydon or that Helen is a guest at St Joseph's Home, so I reply, 'No. We need somewhere to stay.'

Jean turns to her husband. 'We should take them home with us. We can't have them wandering the streets. Look at the condition he's in and God only knows what may happen to the child.'

We arrive at their one-bedroom flat in Glebe Road. After Jean makes Helen a bed on the floor of their bedroom and tucks her in for the night, she turns her attention to me. I am sitting in a dazed state on a chair in the kitchen. She goes to a cupboard and produces a bottle of whisky and a glass, pours me a large drink and hands it to me, saying, 'Drink this, Cliff, before you go into the horrors.' I down the contents of the tumbler in two painful gulps, spluttering and coughing both times. It burns the lining of my stomach.

My bedding for the night is some blankets and a pillow placed on the kitchen floor, and prior to my sliding into this bed, I ask Jean, 'Can I have one more belt of whisky before I go to sleep? I can feel the "electric fleas" still itching my skin. I'm scared that I might really go into the horrors, Jean. You know, "zoo night".'

Lynton's voice comes from another room. 'Jean, give him another charge. He needs it. If we don't give him one, he may have an alcoholic seizure.'

Ding, dong. Ding, dong. My eyes open slowly as I recognise the monotonous sound of church bells ringing. It must be Sunday.

'Come on, mate. Up you get. There's a hot cup of coffee waiting.' Lynton and his wife are sitting at the kitchen table. Alongside them, with a grinning face, is my little girl, eating a large bowl of cereal. Helen acts as if she has always lived here.

After finishing my coffee I wander around the small backyard. I am still in a confused state, my stomach is heaving and the fears are real. I seem to have completely lost my identity. I sit down for a short period, then I stand up and walk around in a circle like a trapped animal. I can hear Helen chattering away inside the house, telling Jean and Lynton all about nothing yet everything. I ask myself, Where do we go from here? Restless, I sit down again on the cold cement step and almost immediately stand up again and walk around. Sit down, stand up, walk around, sit down. It is impossible for me to stay in one place for more than a few minutes.

Helen comes to stand by my side. 'Daddy, can we go home now, to our flat?'

'Home?'

'Yes, Daddy, to our flat in Croydon.'

Suddenly everything becomes crystal clear. I remember I live in Croydon near St Joseph's. I hurry back inside. 'Lynton, Jean. How did you people find me and where?'

They look at each other and smile. Lynton explains the night before and how I walked in off the street to the A.A. meeting.

I have absolutely no recollection of last night and it startles me. 'Jean, do you think I might be losing my mind and my sanity?'

They both laugh out loud. 'No,' says Lynton. 'What happened to you is what we A.A. people recognise as a blackout. It's not like fainting, where you collapse. It's when a drunk person functions fairly well physically and is able to communicate, but is totally unaware of what is going on around them. The following day the person has no recollection of what has transpired the day before. In some cases this blackout condition can last for a number of days.'

'Is that what happened to me?'

'Yes, Cliff.'

'I have just remembered that I have a home in Croydon. Helen is in St Joseph's Home for Children. We're having her weekend break from the orphanage.'

Jean smiles and says, 'I'm so glad that you have somewhere to stay. You take good care of your little pal, Cliff. Hopefully we may see you back at our A.A. meeting soon.'

After thanking both of these wonderful, kind people, Helen and I walk out the front door. Lynton pats me on the shoulder and reassures me. 'What you have been through is not uncommon, Cliff.'

'Sometimes after a blackout happens to me I wonder if I am going to die,' I tell him.

His next words are both humorous and encouraging. 'Cliff, I have been sober for ten years. But in my early days I felt the same, and once when I asked another A.A. member if he ever had fears of dying, he said no, it's the rehearsals that upset him.'

I laugh as I think of all the times I have been afraid of dying, and then Lynton's tone changes to one of compassion. 'Son, when you get back to your home, sit quietly for a while and give some serious thought to where you're heading in life. Ask yourself if alcohol is costing you anything more than just money?' I am uncomfortable under his stare. 'If your answer is yes, then I suggest that you consider coming back to another one of our A.A. meetings.'

I shake his hand and mutter, 'Yeah, thanks, Lynton.' At the same time I am thinking, Me, an alcoholic? Rubbish! I can stop any time that I choose.'

Sunday afternoon I feel safe nestled back in our little 'castle' at Croydon. There is a knock at the door. It's Fred. 'Where have you been?' he says. ' I came down last night and this morning but you were not home. I was starting to get worried that something may have happened to both of you.'

I tell him some story about staying with Ella's friend overnight at Glebe but do not give him the true story. Fred is no fool and can probably guess part of what really happened. I know he is concerned for Helen and me. He says nothing further about it because he does not want to push me away by challenging me. Fred is a very wise man.

I am hitting the booze hard. Tuesday I am very drunk and by Thursday, I am almost on remote control. I finish work and tuck my pay packet safely into my coat pocket and head for the local pub in Croydon. Within two hours, I am really spun out. There is an argument with the lady behind the bar, because she doesn't want to serve me any more alcohol. Shortly afterwards I enter the invisible black hole of oblivion once again.

My eyes open slowly. The vision before me is that of an angel. She has the beautiful face of one of God's angels and is dressed all in white. Crowning her head is a snow-white veil that comes down to her shoulders.

Her face is only a few inches from mine. My first words are, 'Shit, I've gone the wrong way. I'm in Heaven!'

My angel, who turns out to be a nursing sister at the hospital, pulls up a chair alongside my bed and enquires, 'How are we feeling?'

'I can't answer for you, but I'm bloody well aching from head to foot. What happened?' I ask.

She informs me. 'I was having my tea break when you arrived on Thursday night around 11.30 p.m. You were in a highly inebriated condition. The ambulance driver told me you had been hit by a three-tonne truck on Liverpool Road at Croydon. She overheard the truck driver being interviewed by police. Apparently he was not speeding and you seemed to appear from nowhere. Luckily he saw you step off the footpath about one hundred yards ahead and he applied his brakes on the old truck.' She pauses for a moment, puts a thermometer in my mouth and continues, 'I should not be telling you this information. Later on today you will be interviewed by the resident psychiatrist to see whether or not you tried to commit suicide. I have probably told you far too much already. Make sure that you do not divulge to anyone what I have told you, otherwise I could be in a lot of trouble.'

'I am relieved to know what has transpired. Thanks for being such a good sport,' I say. 'By the way, what day is it and what's the time?'

She glances at her watch. 'It is 5.15 a.m., Friday morning. You are a very lucky man. Apart from a few abrasions and a small cut on the side of your leg, you are in good physical condition. Apparently you either stumbled or you deliberately threw yourself under this truck. The police allowed the truck driver to go, assuring him that he was not to blame for this mishap.'

'How long will it be before I can go?'

'You just relax.' She pats me on the arm. 'I'll be going off duty soon. Good luck with the shrink!'

'Thanks a lot for all your help.'

She gives me the thumbs up and says, 'You'll have them eating out of the palm of your hand. Good luck.' She winks and quietly walks away. I am very fortunate to have had this person enlighten me about my misadventure, she has given me the chance to devise a story which can save me from going to the local funny farm. Most nursing staff would not have disclosed any information to me at all.

In the early afternoon, a man enters my room, accompanied by the matron. He is tall, very thin and so pale that he looks as if he needs a blood transfusion. The chubby little matron introduces him to me as the psychiatrist. He resembles a long funnel web spider as he sits down on the chair by my bed, dressed in a black suit with his legs crossed and arms folded. He finally speaks. 'Now, what's this all about, young man?'

I hesitate slightly as I collect my thoughts. 'Doctor, this is a terrible situation for me to be in. Can I have a telephone to call my wife and let her know what is happening?'

Dr Death gives me a stern look and replies, 'No, not at the moment. Now tell me exactly what happened yesterday. I want you to explain the events that led up to your movements last night.'

I pause as though in deep thought and answer, 'Well, late yesterday afternoon I crossed paths with two former army comrades. It has been several years since we last met. Naturally, with all the excitement of being in each other's company, we had a few beers and talked about old times. They informed me that a third member of our battalion, Dudley 'Irish' Callahan, was waiting for them in the city. Irish is a very close pal of mine and was leaving for Victoria late last night. Realising my remote chances of seeing him again, I decided to accompany them to the arranged meeting place.'

The washed-out eyes of Dr Death show no response. I cast my eyes downwards. It is very hard to meet the cold, unfeeling stare of this man. 'Carry on,' he says as he unfolds his arms and clasps his hands together. He holds his outstretched fingers in a tent-like shape underneath his nose, and I continue, 'I phoned my wife to explain what was happening, that I was going to have a few drinks to celebrate possibly our last reunion. I told her that we would be having dinner and not to wait up for me.' I look at Spiderman for some recognition or a sign that he believes my story. No such luck. He just takes off his glasses, slowly wipes them with his handkerchief and continues to gaze at me. He deliberately says, 'Well, go on.' I feel uncomfortable and continue, 'After our meal the four of us went into the bar for an after-dinner drink. I'm usually a teetotaller. I became quite light-headed from the alcohol. My mates thought it was hilarious. They drove me to the railway station around 9 p.m. The last thing I can remember is boarding the train to take me home.' I take a deep breath and wait.

'Have you ever had suicidal tendencies?'

I give my best, horrified look, 'Good Lord, no! Absolutely not.'

Unwinding his legs he looks straight into my eyes and asks, 'What are your feelings right now?'

'I'm feeling very sick and sorry, sir, but not as sorry as I'll be if I don't contact my wife.'

He beckons the nursing sister. 'I understand that apart from a few abrasions and a small cut on his leg, this patient has no other physical damage. Is that correct?' The nurse checks my chart at the end of my bed and answers. 'That's correct, Doctor.' He decides that most of my 'marbles' are still intact and gives me a cursory nod of the head, then walks out of the ward.

The nurse returns and says, 'Let's get you out of bed. Walk around the ward and I'll see if you have any problems. I suppose you would like to get out of here.'

'I certainly would,' is my enthusiastic reply.

'When you are dressed you are free to leave,' the nurse tells me as she hands me my clothing. 'Your clothes are in a hell of a mess.'

I look at my clothes. One sleeve of my shirt is missing. Grease and oil stains adorn my trousers. One leg has a rip at knee level, the other is ripped from top to bottom. My jacket is a complete write-off, it is torn and totally saturated in oil and grease from underneath the truck. The nurse informs me that the driver of the truck could not stop in time. He braked suddenly to avoid me but the old truck skidded sideways and I was thrown underneath. When the truck came to a halt I lay there motionless as oil leaked all over me. I hand my jacket back to the nurse to be disposed of. 'Can I please have a pair of scissors?' This request is promptly granted, and my tailoring skills with the scissors transform my state of dress. The shirt is now sleeveless, minus the collar. The trousers are transformed into a ragged-edged pair of shorts. Fortunately, my well-worn shoes have not been damaged by my altercation with the truck.

Around 3.30 p.m. I leave the Western Suburbs Hospital and walk about five hundred yards to St Joseph's. I do not go home to change because I am already over thirty minutes late to pick up Helen. I rub some of the grease and oil off my shorts onto my hands, smear it over my face, forehead and my forearms before I ring the door bell. The door starts to slowly swing open, revealing one of the younger nuns dressed in snow-white. At first glance she takes a small pace backwards, and before she can utter a word I rattle off my story. 'Sister, please forgive my appearance. I've been working on a car. I lost track of time and that's why I am running late to collect Helen. I do apologise for looking such a mess.'

She eyes me up and down, then says, 'Yes, I see.' She turns around and calls out to people on the upper level, 'Tell Helen Nichols her father is here.'

Down the winding staircase Helen comes, looking as fresh as a flower. When she sees me, her usual self-discipline flies out the window. Her eyes open wide as she comes closer. 'Daddy, you're filfy.'

I grab her hand, wave a thank you to the nun, then hurry out of the place. I find a public telephone box, dial my place of employment and explain, 'Yes, an accident. No, no damage done. Yes, I'm all right. Just a few cuts and bruises. I'll be there for work on Monday.' Deep inside I am aware that my life is out of control. I know something is wrong yet my denial about my circumstances, drinking and attitude towards life prevents me from seeing my problem.

One week later, when I arrive to pick up Helen from St Joseph's, I am informed that Mother Superior wishes to see me. After being directed into her office I sit and wait for the boss lady. I feel unworthy. Finally, she arrives and sits herself opposite me. She is a resplendent figure dressed in white. Her stiff white collar gleams and highlights the sky-blue ribbon around her neck. From this ribbon dangles a crucifix, which causes me to feel that my breathing is a mortal sin. 'Mr Nichols, I'll come straight to the point,' she begins. My mind is confused as she continues, 'A married, childless couple, who are members of our congregation, have asked permission to take Helen on a seven-day holiday to the Gold Coast.' She pauses and adjusts her rimless glasses back onto the bridge of her nose. 'Both of these people are trusted volunteer workers and very good Christians. They often take our children on day or weekend outings. They are impressed with Helen and would like to give her a special treat. So what do you say?'

I lower my head and think for a moment about this request. I know that this is common practice at St Joseph's. I realise the couple come with excellent references from Mother Superior and that this is a wonderful opportunity for Helen to have a much-needed break from St Joseph's. I know I cannot afford such luxuries for her so I then reply, 'Mother Superior, I'll talk to Helen and give you my answer on Monday morning.'

When Helen and I arrive home I explain the situation to her. 'There is a lovely couple in the church, Brian and Julie, who don't have any children. They are wondering if you would like to go for a holiday on the Gold Coast. It will be good for you to have a break from St Joseph's for seven days.' I hold up her seven fingers for her to count. 'After seven days you will then come back to Pa Pa and I. What do you think, darling?'

She ponders for a short time and then asks, 'Will it be good, Daddy?'

'I'm sure it will be, love.'

Helen decides to go and Mother Superior is informed the following Monday. Brian and Julie give Helen a wonderful time. She returns with a suntan and many expensive clothes, hats, shoes and toys. I give her a big cuddle when I see her and she gladly snuggles into my arms.

Three weeks after Helen's holiday I am once again summoned into the office of Mother Superior. She has a very serious look on her face and says, 'Sit down, Mr Nichols.' She is very direct. 'How do you feel about Brian and Julie adopting Helen?' A bomb explodes in my head and for some unknown reason I gaze straight at her crucifix attached to the blue ribbon. 'Mr Nichols. Mr Nichols, did you hear what I said?'

I feel like I am on the receiving end of an invisible knockout punch. 'Ah, yes, I did hear you.'

'Both Brian and Julie are financially comfortable. They have a magnificent home on the north side of the harbour. Helen will not want for anything. She will have a good education, opportunity later in life and security.' Her voice softens as she leans closer to look into my eyes, 'Let's face it, Mr Nichols, the future for Helen does look bleak. Be honest with yourself. You have none of these things to offer your child.'

I stand up and feel lightheaded. All I can say is, 'I'll speak with Helen.'

I talk to Helen about Brian and Julie's offer, telling her, 'You will not have to live at St Joseph's. Your new home will be a big house with a swimming pool. You will have lots of new clothes and toys.'

She looks at me and asks, 'Will you live in the house with me?'

'No, sweetie.'

Immediately and emphatically she says, 'No! I want to stay here with you and Pa Pa.'

I hug Helen and say, 'Well, that's where you will stay.'

I inform Mother Superior regarding Helen's decision the following Monday, and add, 'I realise that there is something, madam, that far outweighs material things and opportunity. It is the bonding of love.'

She stares at me with her mouth wide open and is probably thinking about how much my priorities in life are out of order. I continue, 'Yes, unbelievably, despite all of the pain and heartache Helen and I have endured, we love each other very much.' Once more I look at Christ on his cross hanging from the blue ribbon around her neck. I lean towards her and add, 'Mother Superior, isn't it true, that God is love?' I then depart.

The Kindness of Kath

S ince my encounter with the three-tonne truck I am very aware of how my drinking threatens not only my life but also Helen's. I realise that I may lose her if I don't begin to control my drinking and get my life in order. When Helen has a three-week holiday break from St Joseph's I take my holidays at the same time. Fred visits every day and our little trio enjoys a peaceful life together.

One Saturday morning I decide to take Helen for an outing. While waiting for a train to the city, Helen proudly displays her new shoes and little handbag to the smartly dressed woman sitting alongside her. 'Do you like my new shoes?'

'Must be a big day out,' the woman smiles.

'We're going to the Sydney Cricket Ground to watch the football match,' I volunteer. Helen and I continue conversing with this lovely woman and learn that she lives close to us in Croydon. Suddenly the electric train slithers alongside the platform and many people jostle to get aboard. I call out loudly to the woman, who is now caught up in the throng, 'We should be back around five-thirty this evening.' I point to the Croydon Hotel up on the hill and add, 'If you care to, perhaps we could meet, have a drink and dinner.'

Just as she is about to disappear into a carriage she calls back, 'That would be nice.' She nods her head up and down in case I haven't heard her.

At the football I only have a single glass of alcohol. This is a rare occasion for me. I don't want to be intoxicated and make a fool of myself when I meet this woman later at the hotel. I consume at least six meat pies in the space of four hours and Helen devours two. I know that eating a meal generally stops me from drinking and it works today. Many times the reverse has occurred: drinking alcohol has stopped me from eating.

When we arrive at the Croydon Hotel, I scan the sea of faces in the lounge area. The place is crowded and my concern is that I may not be able to find the woman I've come to meet. I see waving arms across the room. Two ladies are beckoning me from the back of the room, 'Over here.' I cannot recognise either of them. When I see the third woman, Kath, sitting at their table I realise the other two women are Kath's friends. I feel nervous as I approach the women. Kath is very kind and makes me feel comfortable. She introduces Helen and I to her friends, then shouts us both a drink. We all converse very freely and it is not long before I feel comfortable. I shout the next round of drinks and then

Kath suggests I take Helen to the hotel's playgroup for children. Helen is excited to be placed in the playroom with other children. Kath and I drink moderately as we chat. At 7 p.m. Helen and I are invited to Kath's home for dinner. I am far from hungry after my pie-eating marathon, but feel it will be nice to enter a normal household.

Kath's small, semi-detached house is not unlike our old home in Glebe. It has the same cascading sand and mortar pouring from the walls. I guess some bricklayers used little cement when laying bricks in these houses. Kath tells me how she has raised two sons alone after her husband deserted her. She introduces Colin, who is sixteen and Laurie, who is fourteen. Both her sons make a great fuss of Helen, especially Laurie.

Kath and I begin meeting regularly and Helen looks forward to the weekends when she sees both Kath and Laurie. Fred and Kath bond from their first meeting, too, and quickly become good pals. Kath is a tall woman about five feet, ten inches—she mostly wears flat heeled shoes when she is with me. She has a soft, warm face coupled with a brilliant smile. Her hair is fair and her eyes are twinkling blue. She has a wonderful singing voice and is one of the kindest human beings I have ever had the privilege to know. Her tolerance and compassion for others has to be seen to be believed.

My job at the chemical company is still intact, thanks to Kath. Monday to Friday at 5 a.m., she now walks to my house to wake me up for work. She even prepares my breakfast before returning home to tend to the needs of her sons. One particular morning I am shaking badly and feel quite ill because I was drinking heavily the night before. It is almost impossible to get my eyes to focus and I'm concerned about getting to work. Kath sits me down at the table with a hot cup of coffee. My eyes are closed and I am filled with self-pity because of my state of mind and body. The clump of a plate being set down before me causes me to open my eyes. I'm horrified at what I see and yell, 'Kath, my bloody eyes have fallen out!'

'Don't be silly,' Kath says as she laughs. 'It's just two poached eggs.' I feel rather stupid and embarrassed at my over-the-top, paranoid reaction. I realise I am in a very fragile state. Kath finds this incident very humorous and often relates it to others.

Around this time Fred decides that the strain of travelling from Glebe every day is too much so he moves to Croydon. Allan's Private Hotel is to be Fred's new address, his room is in an outhouse shed in the backyard, which has been converted into living quarters.

Summer slowly departs and the fresh winds of early April greet us. One evening I am having a drink at the local pub with Fred when he makes an unexpected statement. 'Cliff, why don't you ask Kath to marry you?'

I nearly choke on my beer. 'What?' I reply as I wipe my mouth with my handkerchief.

My father is very serious. 'Kath is a wonderful woman. She thinks the world of you and Helen. Maybe this could be the answer for you to settle down and get your life in order.'

I'm speechless for a few moments, then say, 'I'll think about it, Fred.'

I'm afraid my proposal to Kath is not very romantic. It comes about over a meal of curried sausages and mash at Kath's place. When I ask her how she feels about getting married she looks surprised. I am even more surprised when she tells me she'd love to be my wife. I am too mentally ill to make a romantic occasion out of the proposal.

Late May, 1964, Kath and I are married at the Registry Office in downtown Sydney. The wedding does not make the social pages of the newspaper but Helen is certainly one happy little girl. I, unfortunately, am lost in alcohol addiction. I become selfish and take for granted the many good deeds done by people trying to help me, especially Kath. She is a person with great faith and believes if I am given time and love I will eventually come to my senses and stop drinking. The debt I owe this woman can never be repaid. She is there for me, even when my survival is under threat. Without her love and support, I firmly believe that I would not be here today.

The devotion and kindness that she pours into Helen is also never ending. One afternoon Kath arrives home with a surprise for Helen. Huddled in her arms is a pure bred boxer pup. Helen is wildly excited to have her own friendly, loving playmate and asks me to give him a name. I call him Cassius after the great American boxer. She spends hours playing with her new companion. I know my little daughter loves Kath dearly and I watch great warmth and affection develop between the two of them.

One day late in September, I spend all day Saturday at the local pub. I drink and gamble on racehorses, thinking life is wonderful because I am winning. At dusk, I stagger down a small lane and head homeward clutching an armful of bottled beer. When I arrive home Kath is shocked. But her comment on my drunkenness goes in one ear and out the other as I pull out a large wad of money and place it on the table. 'That's for you Kathy, my love. It's been my lucky day. Let's have a drink to celebrate.'

She is dumbfounded. 'Goodness me, Cliff, how much did you win?'

I look at the pile of money. 'I dunno. Hundreds or more, maybe millions. C'mon open a bottle of beer and we'll celebrate.'

To keep the peace Kath joins me for a glass of beer as we count our fortune on the table. 'Nine hundred and forty-five pounds Cliff! What do you want to do with all this money?'

Looking at the loot, I reply, 'It's all yours, Kath. Buy yourself a fur coat.' Kath tries to get me to lie down on the bed to sleep off my inebriated state but I say, 'C'mon, Kath, have a drink to celebrate our good luck.' She has another small beer then retreats to the front room with Helen, to watch television. I enter into another blackout.

Sitting alone in the kitchen, I drink, sing and talk to myself. This causes a sudden wave of self-loathing and disgust to come over me. I begin to cry and call out, 'I am a failure at life.' Between sobs, I mumble, 'All of life's opportunities have passed me by. If people and circumstances were kinder, I would be somebody today, a star to be acclaimed and loved by all.' Then, as if controlled by some outside force, I rise from my chair and stagger towards the kitchen window. My upper body is clothed in a short-sleeved shirt. With one great yell of, 'I'm damned,' I plunge my arm through the glass of the window and instantly withdraw it. When Kath and Helen hear the crash of glass both of them rush into the kitchen. I am standing there with blood pumping from my arm. There is a huge, deep gash about five inches long on the inside of my lower arm. All I can feel is joy as I start singing 'Carolina in the Morning' and dancing around the kitchen. My inner thoughts at this insane moment are that as soon as my life blood runs out, I can find peace and there will be no more pain.

Kath dispatches Helen to a neighbour's house, with a message to come quickly. This woman is a nursing sister and arrives within moments. She stops the flow of blood by binding torn, strips of clean sheeting around the deep gashes. Before she leaves she says, 'Kath, take him to hospital immediately because stitching is vital.' The nurse does not have a car and neither of Kath's sons are home, so Kath and Helen hurry to seek help from another neighbour with a motor vehicle. But I cannot wait around. I start the journey on foot and head in the direction of the hospital. When they return I am gone. Everybody becomes frantic, wondering where I have disappeared to. They think I am unable to walk far from home, because I am too weak from loss of blood. People search shrubbery at the house, next door and every area within a hundred yards of home. Finally, one of the searchers suggests that I might have walked the ten-minute journey to the Western Suburbs Hospital. The neighbour then decides to drive Kath and Helen to the hospital.

There I am, as large as life, in the casualty ward. I am sitting alongside another wounded drunk, who is in great pain. Kath walks towards me as I ask my fellow drunk, 'How long have you been here, mate?'

'A bloody long time!'

'What's wrong with you?'

'I think me bloody arm's broken.'

The words of this man filter through my confused mind. 'A bloody long time with a broken arm!' I leap to my feet, push open the large doors leading into the treatment room and yell, 'I'm not waiting here all bloody night for you bums. Give me a needle and cotton and I'll sew the bloody arm up myself!'

All hell breaks loose in the treatment room and voices ring out through the hospital—'Who let that idiot in here? Get him out of here, right now!' A solidly built nurse, with a stern face, yells, 'Get out of here immediately.'

I return to my seat. After waiting a few minutes my patience runs out and I demand to be taken home. Kath tries to convince me to be patient and wait for the necessary treatment. My mind is made up and I insist on going home. I leave Kath no alternative and she walks me home. Kath is very concerned and encourages me to rest. It is not long before I drift off into a deep sleep.

The following morning, when I gain consciousness, every part of my body aches and my head seems to contain bars of lead. Every time I move, the bars clang violently within the casing of my skull. The pain in my arm is secondary. The horrors take over and I feel the familiar, frightening enemy advancing. There are millions of them. 'The Germs' start to attack as they always do after a heavy bout of drinking. I feel them munching on my innards. I know they are going to eat right through my belly. I need a drink. I must drown these bastards. I must have a drink to drown them, now! My skin is clammy as I huddle under the blankets. I call out, 'I'm cold, Kath. God, it's freezing.' Within a few seconds I am on fire and start to kick the blankets off. I see my wrist and stare at the dirty, dark, blue-black sheeting wrapped around my upper wrist. Nausea sweeps over me. My fingers touch a dark-brown patch, which is rock hard. I realise it is congealed blood and my stomach turns over again. I scream out, 'Kath, please get me a drink.'

This wonderful lady returns to my side with a large glass of cheap brandy. Placing one hand behind the back of my neck she slowly raises my head. The lead bars within my head crash forward onto my forehead. I shake, take a deep breath and grab for the tumbler of brandy in Kath's hand. Ignoring the dribbles from the corner of my mouth, I take a few great gulps of the liquid. I cough, then groan about the burning sensation within my chest. Slowly I lie my heavy head back down on the pillow.

For three long days I lie in bed sipping on the cheap brandy, wondering when my heart will stop beating.

I feel that soon I will die. On the fourth day I try to wean myself off the booze. Sleep is almost out of the question because the pain in my wrist is shooting right up to my armpit. I start to unravel the solid black sheeting around my wrist, it is very sticky. As I peel the layers away, I see that the once white sheeting is saturated in a dark, crimson colour. I gently try to pull the last layer of the bandage from the wound. It will not budge and with every reasonable tug the material holds fast. The pain is excruciating. Kath brings in a bowl of warm olive oil. I soak the last piece of material on my wrist for some time. We then try to pull the last blackened piece of bed sheeting from my wound. I ask Kath to give the bandage one reasonable tug, hoping it will come out. I steel myself for this horrific moment. 'Now,' I order. Kath gives one good yank. The only thing we succeed in doing is lifting me nearly six inches off the bed as pain radiates goes to every part of my body. I nearly pass out. The bandage stays firmly in place. I now know it is time for me to see a doctor.

The receptionist in the doctor's waiting room directs me to a seat. My eyes wander around the room. Whoever did the interior decorating must have been on a budget of no more than ten pounds. In one corner of the room a bowl of artificial flowers stands on a small coffee table. On the opposite wall hangs a large painting of a black cat. Its wicked green eyes keep staring at me. A large round table in the middle of the room is stacked with outdated magazines and pamphlets advising us all about how to lead a healthy life. Looking at the faces of the daily decoration of human beings seeking help is enlightening. One person sits with his eyes closed as though he is not really there. Another thumbs her way through a magazine, rapidly flipping one page after another. At this rate she will go through at least six magazines in the space of five minutes. Fear and anxiety is obvious by another person's body movements. If a patient's eyes meet with another's, there are no words, just a smile transmitting a message of reassurance that we will be out of here soon.

A squeaky voice interrupts my thoughts: 'Mr Clifford Nichols.' I follow the doctor into his surgery. He is a thin man, about thirty-five, has a ruddy complexion and is dressed in regulation uniform—white jacket, dark trousers and the badge of honour dangling around his neck, the stethoscope. 'Now what do we have here?'

I gingerly hold up my arm and inform him that I have accidentally fallen through a window. Looking intently at the mess before him he enquires, 'How long ago did you do this?'

I feel ashamed as I say, 'Four days ago.'

Straightening up with a look of horror on his face his voice booms, 'Good God! Four days ago and you have only just decided to seek help!' I do not want to hear his next words. 'No wonder you can't remove the bandage. The wound has been healing over it.' He opens his door and calls to another doctor, 'Charles, have you got a moment, please?'

When Charles realises what has happened to my arm, he mutters, 'Goodness gracious.'

My doctor then says, 'Would you mind staying with me for this one please, Charles?'

'Not at all. I think you are going to need my help.'

My doctor then turns to me. 'This is going to hurt, old chap, so steel yourself for this rag to come out.' My doctor prepares himself by taking a deep breath. 'Are you ready?' I fearfully nod my head. The bandage is finally tugged free and an enormous thunderbolt of pain shoots from my toes to my head. It is accompanied by a great gush of blood that flies up the wall, all over the doctors' white coats and the white-sheeted bed. I pass out.

On awakening I have regained some composure. The wound is dressed and my doctor, who looks concerned says, 'The wound required ten stitches. Can you slowly move your fingers?' I cannot. The doctor then asks me to move my right hand back and forward from the wrist. There is no movement. My doctor looks worried. 'I want you to come back three times a week so I can follow your progress. You are not out of the woods yet. I need to monitor your ability to move your hand. I don't think you have cut through the tendons but you have gone perilously close. Hopefully you've just shaved them.'

After four weeks of perseverance, movement gradually returns to my fingers and hand. Almost six weeks pass before the flexibility of my right hand returns to normal. I realise how fortunate I am. Nearly losing use of my right hand causes me to live a very quiet, peaceful life from Christmas, 1964, until the end of 1965. I somehow know that the curtain is coming down on the horror show of 'Let's Destroy Cliff'. I hardly touch alcohol because I am sick and tired of being sick and tired. Helen and I begin to get to know each other better and our relationship starts to blossom. Kath is finally getting some peace of mind. Even Cassius the dog seems to greet me in a different manner.

Many inhabitants of planet Earth come under the label of Escapeaholics. This is the word I use to describe someone with an overwhelming need to escape from life's daily routines and stress. The inexplicable feeling of being trapped in a revolving door compels people to look for a way out. Escape comes in many forms, some harmless and others quite destructive. Some people use various vehicles of destruction to transport themselves into another world, and when people begin the journey to destroy self they stand at the crossroads of life. Here people can look up at a huge signpost, which indicates the different directions they can take. The various signs point to Alcohol Road, Drug Street, Poker Machine Avenue, Anorexia Parade, Overwork Boulevard, Gambling Crescent, Sex Lane and many other escape routes. Each of these destinations can allow the escapee to change identity and become anyone rather than him or herself. My escape is alcohol.

Years ago a man told me a story about a father and his ten-year-old son. The boy had a jigsaw puzzle. On one side was a map of the world and on the reverse side was a picture of a person's face. The boy could always work the jigsaw out in a few minutes. His father, however, tried countless times but could never finish this complicated task. One day, in frustration, he asked his son how he was able to finish the intricate jigsaw so quickly. The lad answered, 'It's simple, Dad. I work out the easy side with the person's face on it first. Then I turn it over. Once you have the person right, then the world just falls into place.' I need to stop escaping into alcohol and get myself right, then maybe my world will fall into place. I have tried to stop drinking but it is only ever a temporary solution. I have no idea how to refrain from drinking for the rest of my life.

A Spiritual Awakening

From 1957 until 1966 I have haphazardly attended A.A. meetings, trying to do something about my drinking. During these nine years the longest period I have managed to refrain from drinking is six weeks. I cannot concentrate at the few meetings I do attend because I am full of fear. Afraid of being called to speak, I hide at the back of the room behind the largest person I can find. Since childhood I have been afraid of so many things and fear has caused me to become a person I do not want to be. I am a people pleaser. When two or three people have different opinions on a given subject I agree with them all rather than suffer the fear of offending anyone. I awake from my sleep at night, sit bolt upright in bed clutching my heart and gasp, 'Oh no!' These panic attacks convince me that I'm about to have a heart attack. The one word in the dictionary I find hard to say is 'no'. I am afraid I may be judged as unsociable if I say no to an invitation, a suggestion or direction—I am never able to be master of my own destiny. When I am served a nauseating meal and the waiter asks, 'Is the meal up to your expectations, sir?', I always reply in the same meek voice, 'Yes, it's fine, thank you.' I am too afraid to make a fuss or draw attention to myself. When the telephone rings I am terrified of who it will be, I become frozen with fear and unable to answer the phone. If I hear a knock at the door, I'm sure someone must be after me, I wonder what have I done wrong and hope they will soon go away. My hands shake and I want to run out the back door and escape.

Even at A.A. meetings I find it impossible to admit that I am an alcoholic. I am terrified of what people will think of me. I am exhausted by being afraid.

I talk to a wonderful A.A. member called Smokey after a meeting at Glebe one night. I tell him all about my fears and he quietly listens. Our conversation becomes very deep and meaningful and he is the first person to ever understand how I feel. We are still talking after everyone has left the hall.

He informs me that all the fears I have will never ever happen. I am totally lost by this. He then explains that what does happen in our lives is the unexpected. I am even more confused now. If all of my fears will not happen then how do I get rid of them? I realise that every attempt I make to change my pathetic, fearful, alcohol-dependent life fails. My confusion causes me to realise that no human being is able to help me either. I am filled with impending doom, the fear of dying or going insane. I bid Smokey goodnight and start to walk home. I look up to the heavens and cry out, 'For God's sake help me!' Nothing happens.

Life continues. It is simple, devoid of all drama and excitement. This existence feels too normal. When this feeling has come over me in the past, the solution was simple: have a drink of booze and mentally escape. This time I realise, for the first time in my life, that alcohol is not the answer. Early January, 1966, I say to Kath over dinner, 'I'm going down to that A.A. meeting at Stanmore tonight. It starts at 8 p.m.'

Kath smiles and gives me encouragement, 'Cliff, that is a great idea.'

Helen asks, 'What do they do there, Dad?'

'I talk with some nice men and women, who help Daddy to stop drinking alcohol.'

Her face breaks out into the widest smile and she says, 'Good.'

When I enter the meeting room I hear a familiar voice say, 'Well, look who's here.' It's Jack, who saved me from my suicide attempt three years ago. Beside him is Lynton, who is also happy to see me. Both of these people have loved and cared for me in some of my most desperate moments. 'It's really good to see you, Cliff,' says Jack.

A voice from the front of the hall suddenly calls out, 'Take your seats, please, the meeting is about to start.'

I find a seat behind a very large woman and hide, because I don't want the chairperson to see me. As usual I am fearful he will call me to speak. My concentration level is very poor; my mind has been so ravaged by years of drinking that it is only capable of thinking about one simple idea: I have to stop drinking. I have never been able to think beyond this. But for some unknown reason, tonight I begin to think differently. My mind becomes absorbed: What am I trying to find here? I silently begin to answer my own question. I want the shaking to stop. I want to be normal. I want to go to work and feel well. I don't want to have financial problems. Yes, I want to feel good, have peace of mind, be able to breathe with ease and find freedom of self.

As the meeting proceeds, I sit with my whole being feeling totally empty. I am oblivious to all around me. My mind becomes blank. I am unaware that my destiny is about to be changed forever by a miracle and my life completely turned around. I have only one question which keeps entering my mind: What do I want?

Suddenly, the first part of my miracle comes when a small voice within answers: A way of living without drinking alcohol. I say it over and over again: Yes, a way of living without drinking alcohol. That's it. My mistake has been to look at the solution, 'I must stop drinking', rather than looking at the cause of my drinking, 'I have no living skills.'

On the wall I see a banner and read a suggestion that my life has become unmanageable because of alcohol. I think for a moment and realise that my life was unmanageable long before I took my first drink. I have been afraid of the night, the day, other people and of being myself since the day I was born. I have been the court jester of the world, entertaining people and making them laugh in order to feel loved, accepted and needed.

I have never known anything about a manageable lifestyle, communication, voicing my opinion, being responsible, making sensible decisions or having loving, healthy relationships. I have been like a leaf carried down a fast flowing river. I did not plan anything. I let other people make my decisions for me and even allowed them to select my wives. My life has always been unmanageable. When I drank to blot out my pain and inability to live a normal life, I could never guarantee my behaviour or where I would finish up. I believe my first step needs to read, 'I admitted I was powerless over life and that my drinking had become unmanageable.' That's why I need 'a way of living without drinking alcohol'.

The instant this answer comes to me, a vision appears on my left. He is a small, unshaven man with crumpled, soiled clothing. He looks pathetic and lost. I am filled with compassion for this pitiful person and stare in sympathy. He is a reflection in a plate glass window of a pawnshop. My insides scream silently in recognition when I realise the reflection is me! The vision only lasts for five seconds, then it fades; the little, pathetic, clown Cliff dies right before my eyes. I feel he is gone forever. The impact of this vision is so great that I am instantly changed from a frightened, nervous person to one with courage. I stop hiding behind the large woman and move my seat into the aisle. I am now in full view of the chairperson and hope that he will call me to speak. I am so filled with freedom and joy that I believe I am the only person in the room who knows about the wonderful phrase, 'a way of living without drinking alcohol'.

CLIFF NICHOLS

I believe I have the answer for everybody in the room and want to share it with each one of them. But the chairperson does not call me and I am sadly disappointed.

I do not disclose what happens on this night to another human being; this event is inexplicable and I am in fear of ridicule. Many years later I will tell my dear friend, Robert, a Frenchman and a member of A.A. He will tell me to never, ever be afraid of the truth, and his words of encouragement will allow me to speak without fear of what happened.

But on that Monday night in 1966 I find the experience very frightening. For a long time after the event I try to fathom it out. Initially, I put it down to my being in the horrors and that it was all in my imagination. I rule that theory out when I realise it is months since I have had alcohol. Then I wonder if I might have had a dream on Sunday night and my imagination remembered it at the Monday night meeting. Was it a trick? Did I unwittingly doze off at the meeting and my imagination take over? In time, I come to realise that it is none of these things. When I want to stand up and be counted instead of hiding in fear, my fear turns into courage. When the desire to drink is totally removed and I have no withdrawal symptoms, I have no doubt that a real miracle has taken place. It is now thirty-five years since I last tasted alcohol. In all of this time I have not given one tenth of a second's thought to alcohol, whether good times or bad. I neither hate alcohol nor love it.

This is how I explain my miracle. Prior to getting sober I am a little boy locked in a dark, black room

248

crying out for help. There is no answer. Whenever I call it is always quiet. For many years I am so alone. One day the door of the room slowly opens and a stream of light spears through. A hand appears and a soft, loving voice whispers, 'Take my hand.' Although I'm filled with terror, the fear of the dark, isolated room is greater than my fear of this hand. I don't see a face or body. All I see is the hand. I care not if the hand belongs to a woman or a man, if the skin is black or white or if the person's religious belief is Catholic, Protestant or Jewish. All I sense is that the owner of this hand has just one purpose, to love all of humanity, even me. I do not look up. I just grab hold of the hand of hope and place my faith in this power of love far greater than me. I have never let go since that day.

After this miracle I realise that I know little about life and even less about myself. I know survival skills but living skills have been nonexistent since infancy. I don't know how to live or act like a responsible human. I have been in a room of darkness, ignorance and pain for four decades. The child on his mattress on the balcony. The boy feeling deep shame at the sight of his injured, alcoholic mother in Royal Prince Alfred Hospital. The young lad escaping on a train to the country town of Leeton. The jockey who never donned silks. The soldier, bandsman, roof painter, jazz band leader, and producer and director of musical reviews. World traveller and collector of the Emperor's royal ducks in Japan. Tap dancer extraordinaire, acclaimed by footpath audiences from Bridge Road, Glebe to Hong Kong and Kowloon. The pomp and ceremony of military bands, the shame of the police cells and the drunks' tanks. The hospital handyman and drinking companion for the matron. Shoveller of horse manure with Jock, my crippled friend. Tram guard on a tightrope. Hotel entertainer at the British Lion Hotel and bottle yard worker. 'Dazzling' drummer with my dear friend Keith Gleeson at the Bourke Hotel. Guest for one week at Her Majesty's prison at Long Bay Gaol. The father wandering with his lost child in the world of skid row. Who am I?

Another Monday night while attending an A.A. meeting I find myself not in tune with the various speakers. My eyes are fixed on the word 'alcoholic' printed on a large, calico sheet hanging on the wall. I keep asking myself, What does the word mean apart from addiction to alcohol? I sit thinking about this word for some time and do not even hear the speakers at the meeting. Almost an hour passes before a peculiar answer comes into my head. 'That must be it,' I mutter to myself. The following is a description of me when I am drinking:

A
Lunatic
Coming
On
Home,
Often
Late,
Impersonating
Caesar

If that's who I am when I drink, who am I now I don't drink?

The transformation from a derelict alcoholic to a sober person is so powerful. I witness the death of Cliff, the alcoholic, and witness the birth of sober Cliff. I remember seeing a sign outside a church many years ago and it said, 'Come to me and ye shall be reborn.' I could not understand it when I first read it yet now it begins to make sense to me. I have become a completely new person. I still have the same name and I still look the same but my defects of character, compulsive drinking, fear, anxiety, paranoia and poor self-perception are completely removed.

I used to live in a room of mirrors and could only see myself and my pain. Now I have turned the mirrors into windows and I realise there are other people out there suffering. I suddenly become totally interested in other people and no longer focused on myself. The burden of hopeless damnation has been removed and I am now free, filled with hope, courage, love and a self-confidence that I have never known.

After a few months of sobriety I realise the discovery of self is an amazing journey. I feel like I have been carrying a heavy bag of iron on my back for eternity. Suddenly, the powerful hand takes the weight of life away. Instead of travelling down Alcohol Road in the self-destruct vehicle, I am now in a luxury limousine cruising down Self-Discovery Highway. I am now free to be myself. I write a poem to try and express my new incredible feelings:

CLIFF NICHOLS

I have opened my eyes to the world around,
Like a child I am learning to see.
This wonderful gift that I have found,
So new and exciting to me.

I have lived my life in colours of grey,
Black and depressive inside.
Afraid to face the start of day,
My soul I wanted to hide.

A light of freedom has filtered through,
I'm saved from the cruel, dark sea.
There's golden sun and sky of blue,
At last, there is hope for me.

Farewell My Friend

Helen is now ten and a day-time pupil at Our Lady of Bethlehem Catholic School. She is a pretty, young girl full of enthusiasm for life. Kath is at peace because she can now see the results of her wonderful patience and caring. Fred is a constant visitor at our home. The bond between him and Helen is very strong and they spend many happy hours together. He loves looking after Helen and this allows Kath and I to enjoy many social functions together. I achieve one year of wonderful sobriety and my sense of humour grows stronger. For the first time in my life I have finally achieved something worthwhile. I feel proud and elated.

At the A.A. meetings, when some of its real characters are speaking, I find myself belly laughing for the first time in years. 'Skinny Cecil' is one of these funny guys and states, 'I haven't found it necessary to drink booze for nearly a year.' A voice from the rear calls out, 'You're a liar, Cecil. You were pissed last week.' Cecil quickly replies, 'Yeah, but it wasn't necessary.' Another character, 'Shifty', tells about his doctor trying to identify dangerous periods when his patient feels vulnerable and tempted to drink. The doctor enquires, 'Can you predict a precise time when you feel you have to escape into drink? When would the danger period be—early morning, after you get your pay packet or when you are depressed or elated?' The patient ponders, then replies, 'Yes, Doctor, there is one particular time that I do think of drinking.' The medico smiles. 'Wonderful, now we are getting somewhere. When is this particular time?' Shifty answers promptly: 'When I'm awake!'

Other characters include a young lady who lived alone on a farm. She says she had reached breaking point and felt suicide was her only option. After placing the barrel of a shotgun to her mouth she tearfully said, 'Goodbye!' Suddenly she realised if she pulled the trigger she may chip her teeth. She then aborted her suicide attempt. Vanity won on the day! Another person tells of his attempt to leave the planet. Somehow he had climbed up onto a high cabinet in his shed and his head was nearly touching the roof. After throwing a stout rope over a beam and ensuring it was firmly in place, he then attached the noose around his neck. Letting out a great yell, 'To hell with the world', he jumped. Unfortunately, the rope was too long and he broke both his legs! I cannot guarantee the authenticity of these stories yet these people do go on to enjoy many years of sobriety.

A friend of mine who survived skid row and finally found sobriety tells another story. After five years of being sober he had become a successful businessman, and decided to take his wife on a world cruise. The first night on the ship the couple were guests for dinner at the captain's table. Prior to the first course being served the captain announced. 'Steward, sherry for my guests.'

My mate replied, 'Not for me, Captain. I'm an alcoholic.'

The captain looked a little puzzled and turned to the steward, saying, 'In that case, perhaps my guest would prefer a beer.'

My friend smiled and his response was to the point: 'Captain, if I have that sherry or that beer, within the hour I will be running this ship!'

'In that case, steward, give this man a fruit juice.'

My good friend, 'Feathers', who got his nickname because he was a chicken thief, is certainly one of my favourite characters. We both decide to attend the Stanmore meeting on Monday nights. Neither of us have had a good education. Feathers always maintains he failed finger painting at kindergarten and was seven years in second class. My understanding is lost when people use words with more than five letters—I actually failed sandpit. For several weeks various people at A.A. meetings have referred to the bad habit of procrastination, and Feathers and I nod our heads in agreement, not wanting the audience to know that we were ignorant of the word's meaning.

One night at a meeting I ask a mate the meaning of this word. He explains, 'It refers to a person who keeps putting things off. A good example is when we continually postpone mowing the lawn. Finally, the day comes when the grass is three feet high and only then does this person become angry with himself for procrastinating.' The meeting begins. The chairperson calls individuals to come and share their stories with fellow A.A. members. Each speaker walks to the front of the room and addresses the group. The first and second male speakers mention their bad habit of procrastinating. A well-dressed woman also admits that her greatest character defect is continual procrastination. Once she sits down a loud voice booms out, 'Do you wish to speak tonight, Feathers?'

This giant of a man then strides forward and announces, 'I have enjoyed the honesty of the people who have spoken tonight.' With his head held high and his barrel-like chest puffed out, he continues, 'I have great admiration for the previous speakers and especially admire the courage of the woman who just spoke.' In a thunderous voice he confesses to all, 'Ladies and gentleman, I too masturbate.'

For a second I could have heard a pin drop, then an explosion of laughter rocks the room. Feathers is bewildered and sits down. Later when I explain to him the meaning of the word procrastinate he looks shocked and says, 'Shit! I'm the only one to give myself up.'

After getting sober, I spend a year working for a major paint company as a phone order clerk. But eventually, I realise that I am capable of doing better than this. Inexplicably during one of my lunch hours, I find myself at the reception desk of an electrical firm a few hundred yards from where I work.

'Can I help you?' the receptionist enquires.

'I would like to see the sales manager, please. It is a personal matter,' I say.

She ushers me into his office. There, behind a large desk, sunken deep down in a leather chair, is the sales manager. He resembles a giant toad. What there is left of his fair hair is parted in the middle. Beneath the hair-line, a round florid face sprouts a bulbous, rubbery nose, with fine red lines crisscrossing its bridge. My first impression is that this guy is partial to a drop or two of the old Mr Booze.

'Sit down,' he says pointing to a chair. 'Now what can I do for you, young man?' he wheezes.

I come straight to the point. 'I would like to work for your company as a commercial traveller.'

Surprise shows on his face as he splutters, 'I had no idea we had advertised for a sales position.'

I inform him that there is no such advertisement. Before I have a chance to give myself a top-class refer-ence, he is on his feet with his arm outstretched. Attached to the end of his arm is a sausage-like fist, it has four extensions of little frankfurt-shaped fingers and a plump thumb. He offers me a handshake and a silent message of 'on ya way'.

Three days later I am back in the foyer of this company. This time the same receptionist asks, 'Do you have an appointment?'

'No,' I reply.

Mr Toad enters the foyer and sees me. 'You're very keen', he states. 'Why don't you leave your phone number and address. If something comes up we shall contact you.'

There is no premeditation in my actions. It is similar to a moth being attracted to a light. Five days later I am once more standing before the receptionist. She now has a look on her face that says, 'Hell no! Not you again.' I am informed that the sales manager is busy and I assure her that I can wait.

After thirty minutes the door of the sales manager's office swings open and the gentleman appears with a sheaf of papers in one hand, his reading glasses in the other. When he sees me his eyebrows elevate half an inch and he asks, 'Are you sleeping here? We have no vacancies, so I'm afraid the answer is still no! Why do you keep coming back so consistently?'

My reply must sound strange: 'I don't know, myself. It is as if I am drawn here in spite of myself. I can truthfully say, sir, it is not planned. It's as though some outside force compels me to keep coming back. In fact I feel embarrassed and do not blame you for thinking that I am talking a lot of rubbish.'

He puts his papers down on the desk and scratches his belly. He looks at me for a moment, then makes a decision. 'Why don't you come in and sit down.' He reaches for a telephone, and his voice is loud enough for all to hear as he speaks to the managing director. 'Do you remember the chap I told you about, who keeps coming in here for a position as a commercial traveller? . . . Yes, that's the one. Well, he's here again. I have a feeling about this whole situation. Do you wish to come

down and have a chat with him for a few moments? . . .
You will . . . Okay then . . . Yes, five minutes will be fine.'

As I wait for the arrival of Mr Big, I feel a pull at
my nerve strings, and I am filled with anticipation when
he finally appears in the doorway. He is a big man, about
six foot, four inches tall and built like a block of cement.
He extends his huge arm and my hand disappears into
his a strong, warm handshake. His voice booms, 'So, this
is Mr Consistency.' He pulls his chair right alongside
mine. After he asks a few preliminary questions, he looks
me dead square in the eyes and says. 'Perhaps we should
give you a start. What do you think, Bob? Shall we take
a chance?'

Bob moves his head in approval. I am relieved and
grateful. I would never have contemplated applying for
this position in my drinking days—not even a couple
of stiff Scotch whiskies inside would have given me
enough Dutch courage to do this. Yet, here I am, one
year stone-cold sober, doing this as if I have absolutely
no say in the matter. But I can't congratulate myself
yet. Now is the time to confess a secondary detail to
my new employers: I have never been behind the wheel
of a motor vehicle, so I don't know how to drive—quite
a handicap for a commercial traveller!

When I break the news to both men they sit motionless for a couple of seconds. Mr Big then turns to Bob.
'He is having a joke with us, isn't he, Bob?' Bob shrugs
his shoulders and gives me a sickly grin. 'Just having a
little joke hey, Cliff?'

My reply is to the point. 'No.'

Mr Big stands up, looks down at me for a moment and realises that I am serious. He sits down again on the large couch, buries his face in his hands for a few seconds then flings himself back on the lounge. His arms extend to Heaven. He lets out the greatest roar of laughter I think I have ever heard from a human being. He looks up and has tears streaming down his face. Bob joins in with his own particular brand of wheezing laughter. Both men finally regain their composure. Mr Big looks at me, bursts out into laughter once more and cries out, 'This bloody guy is serious!'

I sit there not knowing if I still have the position or not. It takes a good thirty seconds before sanity comes back into the office. Mr Big stands again and asks, 'I suppose now that you have the job you probably expect us to pay for your driving lessons?'

Not wishing to miss an opportunity my reply is, 'It certainly would help!'

Once again the big man starts to shake with laughter. Walking towards the office door to make his exit, his hand on the door knob, he looks back over his shoulder and addresses Bob. 'I tell you what, Bob, if this fellow can sell our products as well as he sells himself, then our company will flourish. Make arrangements for his driving lessons.' Looking in my direction he points his finger at me and says, 'Welcome aboard and the best of luck.' I hear him laughing as he ascends the stairs to his office.

There is another facet to this unusual pantomime. Apart from being unable to drive a motor vehicle, I have no knowledge of the company's electronic load cells or other technical equipment I will be required to sell. My experience as a handyman is zero. I can't even fix a toaster or change a household fuse. During my first few months in this position my best means of defence is to be totally honest with the clients. Amazingly, this works. Every time I openly confess that I know absolutely nothing about the product I am selling, each prospective customer is taken aback, but then, after much laughter, they go out of their way to help me. My sales are successful about sixty-five percent of the time, and I end up spending one year with the company.

In February, 1969, I am offered a position for a well-known cosmetic company. A New South Wales representative is needed to call on department stores and chemists in cities and country towns. I feel that Lady Luck has been with me as an electronic load cell expert and I don't want to tempt fate by pushing that luck any further, so I go to my employers and break the news that I will be leaving. I also confess that my electronic knowledge amounts to zero. Hearing this statement Mr Big and Bob enjoy a second round of hearty laughter and warmly wish me well in my new career.

I excel in my new position, which has me away from home midday Sunday until Thursday evening each week. I have no boss looking over my shoulder and I enjoy my freedom as I visit cities and towns I thought I would never see. I make many new friends at work and at different A.A. meetings I attend in my travels. The job is financially beneficial for both the cosmetic company and myself, and I value the three nights a week when I can be with my family.

I have previously mentioned that as a handyperson I rate as minus ten—and this situation is one which does not improve. When the power fails at home one night Kath is grateful when I offer to fix the situation. Having seen a fuse changed before I feel very confident. I locate the fuse box, pull each of the little plugs out and note the one with the broken wire. After replacing the bits and pieces I proudly walk through the front door announcing: 'Let there be light!' I flick the switch and all the electrical appliances in the house blow. I even sabotage the home next door because its power supply comes from our meter box.

My travels throughout the New South Wales countryside are not without incident either, because my handyperson skills are also less than zero when it comes to changing a car tyre. The inevitable happens: I have a flat tyre and try to fix it. Unfortunately, I position the jack underneath the rear passenger side door. All I succeed in doing after a few pumps on the jack lever is to crinkle up the metal of the door by about six inches, and it looks like a corrugated roof. I am fifteen miles out of the country town of Gunnedah and all I can see is bushland. I am a member of the state road service but they do not like changing tyres for men—in any case I cannot see a house in sight where I might telephone the service. Hell, what do I do?

Eventually, a passing motorist pulls up and asks, 'Can I help you?' After explaining my situation I ask the young woman to notify the road service that I need assistance. During this conversation I hold my right arm up at an angle with my hand formed into a claw. I point to the scar inside my wrist, which was the result of plunging my arm through the glass window years before.

'My right arm is paralysed due to a previous accident,' I explain, while pretending to brush flies away with my extended claw. She just looks at me wide-eyed.

Finally, I can see the road service guy in the distance. I wave furiously with the claw. He gets out of the car and asks, 'What's this all about?'

'Sorry to have to bring you out here, mate, but as you can see my hand and arm are paralysed.' I wave the claw under his nose.

He takes a pace back in fright, saying, 'Okay. Let's get this over and done with.'

All of the time he is changing the tyre I am wandering around with the claw, convincing him of my handicap. Even when he is on bended knee I keep waving the claw under his nose as I ask him questions. I sense all he wants to do is hurry up and get away from this weird person. Needless to say the tyre is changed quickly. As he drives off I give him a grateful wave with the claw held high in case he is looking in his rear view mirror. When I am desperate, anything goes!

I might be a total mechanical fool but I'm a very happy one. I am glad to be sober, to have a job that I love and to feel healthy. I am grateful to be alive.

Very late one Saturday night in September, 1969, there is a sudden thunderous banging on the front door. Half asleep, I get out of bed and hurry to the door. A voice calls out, 'Police here.' Two burly police officers confront me as I open the door. One says, 'Mr Nichols?'

'Yes,' I reply, bewildered.

The sergeant breaks the news. 'Is your father a Mr Fredrick Nichols?' I nod my head. 'I have been asked to inform you that he is in Prince Alfred Hospital, Camperdown.'

I feel stunned. 'What happened?'

'Apparently he has been in an accident of some kind, but I have no further details.'

Hurriedly I explain to Kath what has happened and ask her not to wake Helen or tell her anything until I find out more details. I dress and leave for the hospital. The thirty-minute drive feels like three days because I am anxious to see Fred. Memories start to flood back as I enter the old, drab, Victorian sandstone building of the hospital. It is shrouded in semi-darkness. It is here, as a young boy, that I had collected dear old Nell, with her blood-soaked bandages. It was such a long time ago. This is also where the doctors operated on my collapsed lung. Apparently it is Fred's turn now.

The light is very poor as I enter the ward and the patients on either side are asleep. There are ten beds, five on either side. I cautiously approach the nursing sister at her desk. A small, soft light reveals her face and the snow-white veil adorning her head. She whispers, 'Are you Mr Nichols?'

'Yes,' I answer.

'I've been expecting you.'

'What happened to my father?'

She slowly rises from her chair. 'Apparently your dad was walking past a lane outside Harold Park Paceway when he was jumped on by four louts. He was attacked, beaten and robbed of what little money he had. A woman driving by witnessed what happened. Unfortunately, it was too dark for her to get a good description of the attackers but she did telephone the police and ambulance, who found your dad in the lane about 11 p.m. The race crowd had all gone and the pub was closed. I'm afraid your father's hip is badly broken.'

She guides me down to the far end of the ward where Dad is lying in bed. His face is distorted with pain and it is heart-wrenching for me to hear his short sobs and moans of agony. His eyes are closed. The nurse informs me, 'He is heavily sedated and probably does not know that you are here.' I sit down, hold his hand, look at the face of my best mate and wait.

My thoughts go back over the life of this wonderful man, who fought on the shores of Gallipoli, only to return home with his health shattered. He experienced the breakdown of his marriage, through no fault of his own. I still do not understand why he and Nell parted. Nell was not drinking when I was two and she still refers to Fred as nature's gentleman. It is still a mystery to me. After the horrors of war, he has spent the greater part of his life alone, wandering around trying to find himself and a measure of peace. He has helped and had great compassion for many unfortunate people, especially women and children without means of support. He often busked with his blind dog Bob to raise money to feed and clothe them. His support through my years of insane drinking saved my life many times. He is such a wonderful friend to me and a loving, joyful grandfather for Helen. He has given so much, yet expected so little in return. It all seems so unfair. Even though Fred is seventy-seven years old he has the mind, body and spirit of a much younger man. He is very fit because he has never owned a car and has always walked wherever he wants to go.

'Why don't you take yourself home?' The soft voice comes from the nursing sister. I look at my wristwatch and realise it is 3.30 a.m. 'Your father is heavily sedated and in a deep sleep. There is nothing you can do. Why don't you go home, get some rest and come back around lunchtime tomorrow.'

Over the next few weeks Kath, Helen and I are constant visitors at the hospital. Fred's recovery is slow and it takes him three weeks to learn how to walk again. After his discharge, he tries hard to get himself physically well again. I encourage him to walk daily to strengthen his body and to get movement back into his hip. Unfortunately, it is very painful for him to walk and his hip does not heal well. I feel saddened to see this gallant man so beaten, hobbling in pain with every step. He fights all the way and tries to walk longer distances each day. He never complains and manages to keep his wonderful attitudes towards life.

After two months Fred's health is still deteriorating.

He looks very fragile and has lost a lot of weight. He goes back into hospital again. On one of my visits to see Fred I query the matron about my father's delirious condition. She then informs me that Fred has been diagnosed with cancer and his delirious state is caused by the heavy, painkilling drugs being pumped into his body. I am shocked and return home to break the news to Kath and Helen. The sad news envelops us in a blanket of gloom.

It is one week after Armistice Day, Friday, November 18, 1969. I return home from a business trip to Canberra. I drive up towards our little house in Croydon and there is Helen, waiting to greet me. She is now twelve. Her first tearful words to me are, 'Pa Pa died this afternoon.'

At first I cannot take this news in. I thought he would live at least another three to six months. I am saddened that I wasn't at his bedside when he died. But I shed no tears. All I have is a great empty feeling within my heart and soul. I have just lost my best friend. I get out of the car and wrap Helen in my arms. On entering the house Kath puts her arms around me and sobs her heart out. I am a man in a trance.

After Kath wipes her eyes she tells me, 'Cliff, Helen and I were at Fred's bedside when he died. His last words to both of us were simply, "I know that Cliff will never drink alcohol again".' I feel this trust is the greatest legacy this wonderful man could have left me.

His funeral service is held in St Vincent's Catholic Church, Ashfield, opposite Helen's school. People come from all walks of life, businessmen, a few old diggers who served with him in the war, wharf labourers, publicans, ex-boxers, nuns from St Joseph's, ladies of the night, the editor of a leading newspaper, racehorse trainers and their associates, as well as a couple of well-known Sydney crims. One thing I can say for good old Freddy is that he certainly had a mixed bag of human beings at his send-off.

After Fred's death I experience a period of time where my life partially loses direction. I feel restlessness and turmoil at the loss of my dad. He is the last remaining link to the only family support I have ever known. I have little connection to my mum. She now resides at a rest home for the aged, at Vaucluse. Poor Nell is losing her mind and can only live in the moment. I am over two years sober, yet I feel the abandonment like a small child who has just lost his daddy. I feel alone. This great loss, however, does not push me to the point where I pick up alcohol. Fred's departure leaves a huge vacuum inside of me and signals the end of an era. I am now faced with the responsibility of being an adult and this is foreign to me.

Four months after Fred's death I re-evaluate my life. He has been the pivotal point of my family life. Although I have been sober for two years and not dependent on Fred, his daily visits to our home had always given me a sense of security. I liked to know he was nearby. Now Fred is gone I feel like I don't fit in with Kath and her sons. I struggle with the truth about my marriage to Kath. Although I have the highest respect and admiration for her, my marriage to this wonderful lady has been out of necessity, not out of love. I married Kath to give Helen stability and love in her life. I realise, too, that it was Fred's daily visits that enabled me to remain in this home, and now he is gone it has nothing to offer me. I know my future is not here and I must move on.

Kath and I discuss the situation with honesty and in a civil manner. Despite Kath being saddened by my attitudes regarding our relationship, she is calm and reassures me she will be all right. She will be able to support herself, too, because she has a well-paid job as a receptionist. A few days later Kath and I part good friends. There are tears and hugs with promises not to fade out of each other's lives. Helen, who loves Kath as her mum, is also very upset, and we decide to leave Helen's beloved Cassius with Kath for company.

Helen and I become two travellers on the bumpy road of life again. Our new home is a two-bedroom, furnished apartment at Neutral Bay, just north of Sydney Harbour Bridge. The cosmetic company I am working for offers me full-time sales work in the Sydney metropolitan area. The position is 9 a.m. to 5 p.m., Monday to Friday, and means I do not have to spend nights away from home. Naturally, I accept because it also means I will be better able to care for Helen each day when she gets home from school. Helen is now my only family and the two of us continue to build our wonderful friendship. She is a very loyal daughter and I hope her future will be filled with faith, love and courage.

Counting My Losses

Helen is now fourteen and asks me, 'Dad, can I leave school?'

I am not surprised and ask the obvious, 'Don't you like it any more?'

She laughs and says, 'No. It's boring. I just want to get out into the world and do something exciting.'

'If that's what you really want,' I reply, wanting the best for Helen. 'Would you like me to organise a job for you in a pharmacy?'

She looks at me with a big smile on her face and says, 'That would be terrific, Dad!'

Towards the end of 1971, I help her secure a position at a small chemist shop in Neutral Bay, and she loves every moment of her newfound freedom and independence.

Both of us enjoy the Christmas and New Year break and soon it is time for us to go back to the daily grind of work. Around 5.30 one January evening, I complete my business at Glebe Pharmacy and then decide to walk over to the British Lion Hotel, curious to see what has changed. Perhaps fate intends me to revisit the hotel. Once inside I notice that the beer garden is almost deserted. A flood of memories rushes through my mind. But I am unaware of the tragedy that lies in wait for me. What is about to happen can only be described as one of the most heart-wrenching moments of my life. The shock and anguish are indescribable.

A middle-aged couple sit at a table some distance away. I hear a voice yell, 'Hey, Cliffy. Is that you?' I look across at the couple and walk towards them. 'You look like a million dollars, Cliff. Sit down, mate.' Harry is one of my old drinking companions. 'You remember the wife, Joyce? Can I buy you a drink?'

I break the news to him. 'No thanks, Harry. I have not touched a drop of booze for well over four years.'

His mouth drops open. 'No wonder you look so well.'

I decide to buy both of them a drink and order my usual tonic water. Suddenly, Harry points to the table where an old woman is sitting and says, 'There's an old mate of yours, Cliffy.'

I look across to where this person is sitting. She is side on to my view. What I see is a rather shabby, elderly woman, half slouched over a glass of wine. 'Who is it?' I ask Harry. 'Go over and have a look,' he half whispers. Rising from my chair, I walk towards the woman. Her head slowly turns and she looks directly at me. What I see is a pathetic, old woman with scars above her eyes, motley skin, strands of lifeless, ginger-grey hair hanging over one eye and crimson lipstick half smeared across her mouth. Watery, dull eyes stare at me and white saliva dribbles from each corner of her mouth. She gives me a crooked smile and displays her few remaining nicotine-stained and broken teeth. She croaks, 'Ullo, love.'

I have no idea who this poor, unfortunate woman is. I start to wonder if Harry is playing a practical joke, yet some inner voice keeps saying, You know her. The electric shock of recognition finally hits me and travels from my toes to my head. Words jump from my mouth. 'Christ almighty! No! No! . . . God no! It's Nicky! The lovely, wonderful Nicky.' All I can say then is, 'What in the name of hell have you done to yourself?' I am angry, confused and helpless.

She frowns and gives me a puzzled, insane stare. 'Who are you? What do you want? Piss off, mister,' she slurs as she points a nicotine-stained finger towards the exit gate.

I look directly into her troubled eyes and speak loudly. 'It's Cliffy. Cliffy, bugger you.'

Her mouth slowly opens and her eyes narrow as she tries to focus. She half cries and shrieks out, 'Cliffy, where have you been, you little bastard? Let me look at you. Just look at you. Fancy my charming boy in a lovely suit and tie. You look lovely.' She suddenly seems to come alive and half turns in her chair as if to address the world.

'Look everybody, here's Cliffy. He's shown the lot of you. Look at him. He's better than any of you bastards.' With a sigh of equally sudden exhaustion, her brain goes back into limbo land. 'Buy me a drink,' she demands as she continues rambling. 'My shoe is too tight . . . Bert's being a bastard . . . they are all a bunch of parasites . . . bloody mongrels taking my money. Where's my drink?'

I go to the bar and order a large sherry. I tell the barman I want the good stuff, not the rot gut she's been drinking. Harry joins me at the bar and fills me in on what has been happening in Nicky's life. 'She's been back living in Glebe for a few years now and has been drinking heavily for some time. The last gutter mongrel she lived with beat her many times. He was the one who knocked most of her teeth out, split her eyes, broke her limbs and kicked her. She wouldn't leave him because there was nowhere else to go. Besides, nobody else wanted her. At the moment she is living with an old bloke and his crippled son. This is about the best deal she can get.'

I return to Nicky and place her drink before her. She takes a large mouthful and a soft sigh escapes. I put my hand over hers. At first my touch causes her to jump slightly, like a frightened animal. I continue patting the back of her hand and she seems to settle down. 'Do you remember Helen, my little girl?' She gives me a puzzled look and I continue, 'Well, Helen and I have a nice little home just over the Harbour Bridge at Neutral Bay. What about you coming to live with us? You can have your own room and I know you will be happy.'

My words seem to fall on deaf ears. She must be close to having a 'wet brain', Korsakoff's disease, which is a form of alcohol-related brain damage. Her only words are, 'Get me another drink.'

I order another drink then sit down alongside her. 'Nicky, what can I do for you?'

She starts quietly laughing. I want to hit her for what she has done to herself, yet at the same time I want to cry and grieve for her. I feel so totally useless.

My mind goes back to yesteryear when I was on the verge of losing my will to live. Nicky had been there for me. I ask myself, What state of mind and body were you in, Cliff, when she rescued you? I look at her with compassion, warmth and love, and see that alcoholism has forced her onto the merry-go-round that I have left behind. I want so desperately to give her what I have found, and sit with her for almost half an hour trying to help. Sadly, I have to accept the stark reality that I can do nothing. She is too far gone.

It is well after 6 p.m. and I know I should be home for Helen. She finishes work at six and I do not like the idea of her being home alone. Before I leave I realise there is one last thing I can do for my once beautiful friend. I take out all the paper money I have in my wallet—the one hundred and twenty dollars I had withdrawn earlier this morning to pay some accounts. While she is drinking her glass of wine, I slowly slide her battered old handbag across the table, put the bag between my knees and slip the money inside. I tell myself, If she is going to die, at least she is not going to die broke.

For one last time I try to get through to her that she needs help, but to no avail. She is no longer of this planet. All she can do is laugh and keep asking for more wine. I stand up, lean over and kiss her on the cheek. 'Goodbye, Nicky love. Thank you for everything.' I'm choked up so much I can hardly breathe. I am crying soft, painful tears of grief. I don't know if she even understands what I have said to her.

Just before I walk through the exit gate of the beer garden I look back at her. What I see is remarkable. Perhaps for a few fleeting moments a flash of sanity has come into the mind of Nicky. Looking at me for the final time, she quietly says, 'Cliffy, you keep the way you are right now. Keep this way always, love.' She then gives me her favourite provocative wink of years gone by. For a period of three seconds the beautiful blonde woman from the Bourke Hotel reappears. Precious moments, then suddenly my lovely friend is gone again. She turns away. I hear her laughing in a sinister way and once more her poor face is buried in a glass of wine.

Maybe fate drew me back to the British Lion Hotel to say my farewell and to give my thanks to a beautiful soul, lovely Nicky. I hear about Nicky's death a short time after our encounter. She was only thirty-nine. Strange as it may seem, from the time of our first meeting right up until the present moment, I did not know and still do not know Nicky's surname.

The loss of this great friend causes me to wonder how much more time is left in Nell's life. Helen and I have been making monthly Sunday visits to see Nell at Vaucluse House, which is situated high on the foreshore of Sydney Harbour and was once a privately owned grand mansion. This wonderful old home overlooks magnificent views of the harbour and is now a home for women in their twilight years.

Every time I visit Nell, she asks me the same question:

'How's the Poli lad?' She is referring to my father, the word 'Poli' being her abbreviation of Gallipoli. I always reply with the same answer: 'He's good. He sends his best wishes to you.' There is no point telling Nell that Fred has passed away because she would not remember.

On occasion, when I am working in the eastern suburbs area, I drive up to Vaucluse House and ask the matron-in-charge for permission to take my mum out for lunch. Nell really enjoys these little excursions. We go down to the shopping areas of either Rose Bay or Double Bay and find a nice restaurant. I escort her by the arm to her table, then order her a glass of quality sherry.

Each time, she asks, 'Do you think the matron will mind my having a little drink?'

My answer is always, 'We can keep this as our little secret. Matron does not have to know.'

Nell gives me a wink and says, 'Mum's the word.' She then proceeds to tell anybody within range of hearing that I am her 'one and only after ten years of trying'.

This woman still has her amazing sense of humour and warm spirit. All of her life, her constant companions have been heartache and pain, yet Nell has cared for others throughout, despite her alcoholism. She always gives a helping hand to those struggling. She would do washing, cleaning, ironing and even babysitting to help out. Nell always lives in her own little world. Now she has a need for help none of her friends come to her aid. They have all drifted away and forgotten her.

Mum passes away six weeks before Christmas, 1972. It is only a few short years after my dad died. Nell's tired body has finally given up. The saddest thing about Mum's funeral is that Helen and I are the only two people in attendance. I guess this is the final farewell for a lonely alcoholic.

Only later in my life have I come to understand her. She is a mother who loved her child so dearly. She supported herself and her 'one and only' by scrubbing other people's floors and doing their household chores. During the Depression years, many children were put into Government homes or orphanages because their parents could not feed or clothe them. When I was a child, Nell's devotion and hard toil always placed food on our table. It was never necessary for me to utter the words, 'I'm hungry, Mummy.' I have never had the opportunity to say these words to you before, Mum, so I'll say them now. Thank you for all your unselfish devotion in caring for me as a child. I understand today how hard you worked to keep me out of orphanages. When I was a young man, lost in the sea of alcohol and pain, you were always there. I remember the times when I saw you at the Glebe Post Office on Aged Pension day. You would always go in and draw your money out, then give me part of your pension so that I could survive perhaps another day or so. I'm sorry that I did not understand your great love for me until now. How sad it is that we did not have the opportunity to get to know each other more. Mum, I love you. God willing, you will hear me today from your high position in Heaven.

One week before Christmas I am still grieving the loss of my mother. I decide to drive over to Vaucluse and park my car overlooking the ocean. It is midday and the sun is giving birth to thousands of tiny, sparkling diamonds on the water. My thoughts are of my early life. The vision of many people's faces come into focus. I miss my mother and father, who have died, and take a moment to remember all my friends who have passed away. The parade seems endless, as I sit in peaceful surrounds.

I see Bandmaster Pearson and Bob Rowan from Eastern Command Band. Bob passed away at the young age of thirty-eight. Colonel Croft, who allowed the jazz band to operate within the regular Army. My duck-hunting mate at the Emperor's moat in Japan, Roy Le'Minn. Mrs O'Leary from the rooming house in Leeton. Jack from A.A., who saved me from suicide. Alf, the flea-carrying pipe layer in that itchy house in Surry Hills. Rona, the pianist, and the wonderful Bruce on banjo. Ray Warren, my friend and sergeant major in the Signal Corps. The beautiful Nicky. The Duchess and Mad Molly. Good old Jock Nicholas with his manure truck—if they have a race called the Indy 500 up there, I bet he is leading the field. Keith Gleeson on piano at the Bourke hotel. Ella of Glebe and house-party fame. Finally, my father, Fred, and mother, Nell. I feel extremely grateful that they have all crossed my path in life. Each one of them has given me a mixture of love, kindness, laughter and even a lifeline when hope was almost gone.

Another Lost Soul

It is April, 1974. Helen is almost seventeen and we are still living in our home at Neutral Bay. She has grown into a beautiful young woman. Her shoulder-length blonde hair is always immaculately groomed, her blue eyes are alive and full of mischief. She has developed bodily into a nicely proportioned teenager and is slightly taller than me. Her personality is vibrant. She always has the latest jokes to tell, and I can assure you that some of these funny stories she relates to me would not be considered appropriate humour at the local church group.

Around this time I visit a young man to help him with his alcohol-related problems. At the private hospital a friend introduces me to Sue, a young, female patient. She is just twenty, terribly thin, has difficulties handling life and has anxiety running rampant through her being. She is undergoing alcohol aversion therapy, but I feel the treatment she is receiving is of no benefit to her, because this method can only ever be temporary. It takes away one of the most precious rights of a human being: the right of decision. Her parents live over one hundred miles away in northern New South Wales, but she does not wish to return home and has no other place to stay in Sydney. After visiting her a few times, Helen and I decide to try to get her out of the hospital and bring her back to our home. When we make the offer for her to stay at our place she says, 'Yes, please.'

Helen and Sue share the same room, each having their own single bed. They live in harmony, almost like sisters. Sue starts to put on weight and her body begins to develop a healthy shape. Her skin improves dramatically and her blonde hair starts to shine. Sue is petite, around five feet, two inches tall. Eventually, she begins working at the pharmacy where Helen used to work. Helen by now is second-in-charge of a large pharmacy in the heart of the city. I encourage Sue to go out socially with Helen, feeling that a twenty-year-old should be enjoying the company of people her own age, rather than joining me, a man of forty-seven, in my social circle. After many attempts to encourage Sue to go out with Helen, my daughter finally informs me, 'Dad, Sue is not enjoying our outings or the younger guys we go out with. She tells me that she would rather socialise with you.'

Sue loves my carefree attitude towards life and my sense of humour. She is always asking to come with me whenever I go out. I do not hesitate to grant her request because I love having the company of such a vibrant, attractive young woman. Our social life becomes one of going to theatres, restaurants, race meetings, dinner engagements, A.A. meetings and entertaining at home. Our workday life is squeezed in between these events. Sue shows interest in the work I am doing so I assist her in gaining a position in the perfume and cosmetics company that I work for. We then begin working as a team calling on pharmacy and department stores in the Sydney region. Eventually, we form our own company calling on various country stores throughout the state.

Sue and I have now been sharing a romantic life together and running a business for six months. Helen is thrilled and says, 'Dad, now you have someone in your life and will not be alone, I would like to leave home. I want to start a new life with Kim, if I can find her. She is sixteen now and by law she can leave home without Toddy interfering.'

I am happy that Helen has the opportunity to find her own independence. I think it is wonderful that she is reaching out to create other family bonds. I know she is making a positive decision and I have no doubts that this lovely, vibrant girl will avoid the same mistakes I made at her age. I reply, 'If that's what you want, love, then I'm right behind you. Keep in touch or I'll come around and haunt your house.' We both laugh.

It is not difficult for us to find Kim, because she is still living with her grandmother, Toddy, who was responsible for sending me to prison thirteen years ago. I have only seen Kim twice since then. Once, when Helen picked her up from Toddy's house so that we could spend her twelfth birthday with her. The other occasion was when Kim lived with Kath, Helen and myself for four weeks, when she was about seven. When Toddy took ill and Shirley was unable to care for Kim, Kim came to live with us. I thought it was very kind of Kath to have both my daughters under her wing. Kim began school with Helen at Our Lady of Bethlehem Catholic School. After one week Kim told me she had had enough because the nuns terrified her. I took her straight out of the school and put her in Croydon Public School. I felt like this was history repeating itself, thinking of how Nell transferred me to a public school in Glebe when I was terrified of the Christian Brothers.

About a month later while I was away working, Toddy arrived at our house to see Kim after school. She told Kath and Kim that she was very lonely and wanted Kim to come home. She then looked at Kim and told her she could have the beautifully dressed doll in a cane basket that she was holding in her hand and a new bike if she came home with her. Kath was wise and sensed what was happening. She discussed the matter with Kim. Kim was attracted to the doll and promise of a new bike and agreed to go with Toddy. Kath and Helen were devastated and felt powerless to change Kim's mind.

Kim had lived with Toddy for over five years and perhaps that was the only home she knew. Returning to Toddy's home meant that Kim would live in a two-roomed flat, which cost two pounds a week to rent. It was small and infested with many cockroaches but it was all Toddy said she could afford on her pension. Kim's personal hygiene was a weekly bath in an old iron tub, which was filled with saucepans of hot water heated on the stove. On weekends Toddy and Kim's aunt often attended the local two-up game and gambled until the early hours of the morning. Before they left the flat they made sure that Kim was fast asleep then left her on her own. Sometimes Kim woke up around 1 a.m. and realised she was alone. She was always scared on her own. Many times she asked God to let it rain so that she would not feel so alone. Sometimes it did rain and the gentle noise on the roof enabled her to feel less afraid and she fell asleep.

When I arrived home I saw how upset Helen and Kath were. I cuddled them both and learnt of what had happened. I was instantly angry at the cunning way Toddy came to the house and took Kim back. Kath tried to get me to settle down and informed me that it was Kim's choice to go. I was angry that a young child was given little time to think about or discuss the matter with her father. I felt robbed of the opportunity to be a father for both Kim and Helen together yet again. Kath explained to me that Kim had been with Toddy for over five of her formative years and that it was probably the only home she knew. I wanted to go and talk to Kim, I was not convinced, yet I knew the odds were against me now. To visit Kim and risk crossing paths with Toddy while I felt like this or any other time was not a good option.

Once again Toddy placed me in a bind. I was trying to get my life in order and I knew this woman was simply someone I could not afford to deal with, sober or not. I realised that I needed to leave well enough alone. It caused me a lot of grief to know that Kim and I had to have more time apart.

If it had been possible for me to have seen Kim on a regular basis, I would have done so. Visiting Kim at Toddy's home would have meant bloodshed. Toddy would not hesitate to call the police. The friction between Toddy and myself was explosive, whenever we crossed paths. I knew nothing would have changed.

It is not until 1975 that I get an explanation from Kim. Helen is still living with me and comes home one afternoon with a lovely surprise.

'Guess who I have here,' says Helen, as she opens our front door. Behind her is a young, sixteen-year-old woman, the same height as Helen, but that's where the similarities end. Kim's dark-brown hair is just below her shoulders and her brown eyes twinkle. My first thought is, God, she looks like me. I am speechless. We cuddle each other yet both of us are like strangers. I am very excited and invite her in. She talks as rapidly as I do and has my same quick, nervous laugh. We have another big cuddle and talk for hours. Three days later, in October, Helen and Kim find a two-bedroom furnished apartment just a twenty-minute walk from where I live. The Dashing Duo move in together.

The time rushes by 1975 . . . 1976 . . . 1977. Sue and I have shared some wonderful times living, loving, laughing and working together. As we build our company I train Sue in all aspects of the business. She is eager to learn. We act as agents for cosmetic companies, and call on pharmacies and department stores in city and country areas. We continue to see Helen and Kim on a regular basis. Both of my daughters have become women of the world. Helen is twenty, a qualified cosmetician and manager of a very large pharmacy in the city. Kim is eighteen and manages a small department store, also located in the city.

'Guess what,' Sue says at the dinner table one night.

'What?'

'I'm nearly three months pregnant!'

To say I am surprised is putting it mildly. 'You mean you are having a baby?'

She laughs. 'I believe that's what the term pregnant means.'

Now, this type of news comes as a surprise to any young, red-blooded man. In my case, I am neither young nor red-blooded. I am fifty years of age and feeling a little anaemic. But even still, excitement flows through me and the first words to jump out of my mouth after the initial shock are, 'We'll have to get married.' Sue agrees. Everything seems to have been going well between the two of us and marriage seems the logical thing to do.

The wedding is held in the grounds of a friend's home and there are about fifty guests, including Helen and Kim. Standing before the celebrant to take our vows, I am aware that there are actually three of us—Sue, myself and our unborn baby. Little Jody Antoinette is born on June 20, 1977, at King George V Maternity Hospital. She weighs in at a healthy seven pounds, has a mass of black hair and the most beautiful brown eyes. She is lively and certainly has the Nichols' colouring.

When Jody is five months old, Sue informs me that she is pregnant again. I am very surprised and reply, 'Didn't your doctor tell you that you could not get pregnant while you were breastfeeding?'

Her reply is emphatic. 'Well, he was wrong. According to my calculations, this new baby is due August next year.'

Kelly Lee Nichols makes her entrance into the world on August 4, 1978. She is a blonde beauty with brown eyes—and a ferocious appetite. Her hair stands up on end, similar to that of a punk rocker, and I nickname her 'Spike'.

I am excited about the birth of my two daughters and have always loved being a father to my children. Unfortunately, I have not always been able to be the ideal father for Christine and Kim, so this time round with Jody and Kelly becomes very important and precious to me. I really appreciate being a sober father and being able to be there for my children. They become my little playmates rather than my children. But having two babies places an enormous workload on Sue, and I am totally ignorant of her situation because I am on the road five days a week. Sometimes work takes me away from home for up to ten days at a time, and Sue finds it hard to cope on her own.

Sue calls on local pharmacies while her mother, who lives nearby, babysits the children. She also does the administration for the company from home. She tries to tell me how hard it is to cope with a business and two small children. I'm afraid I listen but I do not hear. My mind is caught up in planning the following week's country visits and liaising with importing companies and pharmacies.

In 1977 Helen decides to go to Perth because she wants to see more of Australia. Helen, more than anyone else, knows what I have been through in life and is thrilled that my life with Sue and our new business are going well. I think she feels relieved that she can spread her wings and fly, now she knows I will not be alone. I realise that my little girl is now a woman.

My heart sinks at the thought of her living so many thousands of miles away. Even though I have three other wonderful daughters, it is my little travelling mate, who did all the hard yards with me, that I am now thinking of. She is excited about her new venture as it draws near and also no longer having responsibility for her dad's welfare. I am proud of this warm, loving, witty, self-confident woman, who seems very happy within herself. I wish her well and it is a very sad moment, the day she departs.

Helen has never had trouble finding employment because she has excellent references and soon finds herself a position as a cosmetician. She is very pleased when she learns about Jody and Kelly, her step-sisters, being born. Not long after being in Perth Helen meets Joe and settles down to married life. Sue and I visit Helen when she is pregnant with her first child, Jamie. She gets to meet Jody and Kelly for the first time and is enthralled by them. Katie is born about fifteen months after Jamie.

Kim is still managing the small department store in Sydney. I talk to both of my daughters regularly.

After a few years of many long hours and hard work, our business begins to expand. Sue and I now import goods from overseas and our company is flourishing. I am on the road travelling and calling on clients all along the east coast of Australia. I also visit isolated inland places like Cunnamulla in Queensland and Cobar and Bourke in far-western New South Wales. Sue handles all of the office administration and cares for the children. Although life is hectic, success continues to come our way, and we decide to investigate the untapped market in Queensland.

In 1982, we move to Brisbane, set up a warehouse, office and showroom, hoping to expand our market opportunities in Queensland, and after a shaky start the business quickly gains momentum. We move into a lovely four-bedroom house, with a swimming pool, in the northern suburbs of Brisbane, certain that we are now on our way to even greater success. Sue organises babysitters and a woman to do the household chores so that she can focus more on work. Soon she is continually caught up with appointments and dinner engagements, which seem necessary to create a super successful business, and she becomes trapped in a nonstop world. Sue's work just never seems to end and neither does mine. It seems as though we are doing everything right except paying attention to each other. Any romance and fun that was in our lives has waned to such an extent that our only passion is being consumed with work and more work. As both our lives crank up a notch in pace our communication suffers. My work often takes me away from home for long periods, as I travel miles, over gruelling country highways and roads, promoting our business and selling products. Despite my busy life, though, I know it is important for me to still go to A.A. meetings, and I attend many meetings in isolated country towns to offer my support.

On rare occasions I get a break from country travelling when I call on Brisbane pharmacies, and this means I can be home at night with Jody and Kelly. My little playmates have their own distinctive personalities. Jody has very warm, attractive looks and mannerisms. She has rich, dark-brown hair and eyes, and is very much like Kim. They both talk and move very fast, have very vivacious, outgoing personalities and wonderful senses of humour. In fact, Kim and Jody look like mother and daughter. Kelly Lee is also attractive with blonde hair and lovely brown eyes. She moves through life at a slower pace and always seems to be in a world of her own. But she also has a gregarious side and a great sense of humour. Whenever she is asked to sing or dance she is transformed into a human dynamo with all of the energy and passion that can be summoned from her small body. She has absolutely no fear. No matter how large the audience, she does not show the slightest sign of being selfconscious.

I love to drive them to and from school. Sometimes after school, I take them to one of the major department stores for afternoon tea. Other times we go down to one of the many fun parlours where they can play pinball machines to their hearts' content. While driving in the car, we sing songs and make up silly little poems about each other. On Sundays I take them into the city centre. They always enjoy our little expeditions to the city square where we arm ourselves with scraps of bread and feed the pigeons. I love to hear their squeals and shrieks of laughter as the pigeons land on their heads and shoulders. These are wonderful times.

My state of mind is that of a much younger man. Despite my success, happiness and wonderful freedom from alcohol, I am only just learning basic living skills that most men have learnt in their youth. I have no idea that relationships need constant nurturing.

Separate Ways

The demands of running a business and raising a family become excessive for Sue and me, and the strain of working long hours starts to take its toll. We begin to disagree about everything. I gamble excessively on racehorses, trying to escape the pressures of life. Deep inside I know something is wrong but I don't want to look at it. I am not aware of the dangers of this escape or its effect on my family. I see nothing wrong with having this diversion from my everyday problems and stresses. I cannot recommend this pastime. Sue, especially, is spreading herself too thin by trying to handle business dealings with associate companies as well as our own. The shouting and verbal abuse increases and I eventually realise it is not good for us or our children. Our marriage collapses. I move out of the family home and temporarily live in a small, one-bedroom unit. Both children are devastated. After the breakdown of our marriage comes the inevitable collapse of the company. Reconciliation between Sue and me is impossible and the only option is to divorce.

I sit in a square room with twenty others, who are looking straight ahead as if waiting for a slow walk to the gallows. From the look of the people in the waiting room, it seems that divorce court appearances must rate at the top of the list of stressful situations. I am oblivious to the surroundings, however. I could have been waiting for a bus. I am not stressed at all.

After twenty minutes Sue enters the room and asks me, 'Do you have legal representation, Cliff? My solicitor would like to speak with your representative.'

'No, I don't have representation.'

She seems a little puzzled. 'Are you going for custody of the children?'

'No.'

'What else do you want?'

'Nothing, Sue. In fact I think you should sack your solicitor. It is just a waste of money.'

She departs, saying, 'I'll be back in a moment.' Then returns and says, 'Cliff, my solicitor would like to speak with you.'

After being introduced, the solicitor asks, 'Is it true that you are not going to contest custody of the children or any material items from the home?'

'That's right, mate. All I want to do is get this mess over and done with.'

He looks at Sue and smiles. Then he looks at me once more before turning back to Sue. He exclaims, 'Why are you divorcing this fellow? He seems like a rather good bloke?' Sue looks stunned and says nothing.

Our appearance before the judge is brief. Divorce is granted and we are out of the building in a matter of fifteen minutes. Sue and I meet up with Patricia, Sue's friend, who has been waiting in the foyer downstairs. The three of us step out into the sunlight. I make a suggestion that a cup of coffee would be nice and we all head for the nearest coffee lounge. Patricia seems astonished at the conversation going on between Sue and me. We console each other as if we had just lost a hundred-dollar note, rather than experienced the trauma and grief of divorce. When it is time to depart Sue has tears in her eyes. Instinctively, I move towards her and put my arms around her. More tears flow as I softly rub her back. Looking over Sue's shoulder I can see Patricia, dumbfounded, with her mouth and eyes wide open. Her face seems to be saying, 'What the hell is going on here? Are they really going their separate ways or are they making up again?' We go our separate ways.

My feelings relating to the divorce are lying dormant within. It seems like they are on a time-delay. But within days of the divorce Sue notifies me about her new executive position with a major company—which means she and the children will be moving back to Sydney—and my feelings are suddenly no longer dormant. The impact of no longer having my children, as well as the trauma of divorce, makes a lethal, emotional combination. The realisation that once more I am alone fills me with a mixture of fear and anger. Thoughts of revenge even start to surface. My mind is in turmoil. Why? How can this happen? These questions repeat themselves continuously in my head, day after day. I need answers.

None are forthcoming. The pain reminds me of the time I was dismissed from the band and left to paint the roof of Victoria Barracks. Now it is grief over losing my family. It's as though any chance I have of belonging to a family and being with loved ones has been smashed to pieces; my pain crashes like waves on a rocky coastline. Somehow my family has been washed away with the tide, to disappear into the vast expanse of ocean, gone forever. Although I don't understand why this has happened, I know enough about myself today to realise I must look for clues inside myself. Was my marriage based on ego when I strolled down the street with an attractive, twenty-year-old blonde's arm linked through mine? Was I, a middle-aged man, silently telling the world to look at me and see that I am somebody worthwhile? I wonder if this is the reason I feel so depressed. Is it my ego getting in the way? Confusion is my daily companion as I search for answers. I realise ego is only a small part of my problem. Losing my daughters is the biggest part, followed by the loss of the business.

I am almost sixty and my chances of gaining employment are near impossible. The collapse of the company leaves me unemployed and without a credit rating. I no longer have a motor vehicle and all I have is a few dollars in my pocket. Added to my woes is the frightening fact that now I am unable to afford my rent. I pack my suitcase and begin to walk. I find myself standing on a street corner at a busy five-way intersection at Albion, on the fringe of Brisbane City. Alongside me on the pavement is the suitcase containing all my worldly belongings. I start to ask myself if I am back on skid row. A voice from within tells me to just start walking. Let go, trust in God and all will be well. I am grateful there is still a flicker of faith left within! And it is miraculous that the thought of drinking alcohol does not enter my head.

My memory banks are jolted and I remember a lady whom I had visited with a friend about one year ago. She is a family friend of one of my A.A. mates—I'm sure she lives on the main road of this suburb. I begin to walk. Past the Albion Hotel, I see the green and white two-storey block of flats where she lives. Desperate times now call for desperate measures, so I climb the rear outside wooden stairs leading to her door. Calling upon whatever courage I have left, I knock three times.

The door opens and I am greeted in a warm and friendly way. 'Hello! Clive, isn't it? You and Kev came here one day to check on my wellbeing.'

I smile and correct her. 'Actually, Cliff is my name.' After explaining my plight she tells me I am welcome to stay in her small, spare bedroom until I get on my feet. I assure her that once my unemployment cheque arrives, I will gladly pay her fifty dollars per week for the room. (My God, I'm on the dole!) Ailsa is the name of my benefactor and I am her guest for six weeks.

On the fourth day with Ailsa, I make a decision to snap out of the grief. I arise early, dress in my business suit, take a deep breath and walk out onto the main street. Once again I am a man on a mission—I need to buy a car—and eventually find myself entering a major car sales firm.

'Take a seat,' says the young accountant. 'Now what can I do for you?'

I explain what has happened in my personal life, the company collapse and my loss of credit rating. Turning to his computer he says, 'Now, let's see just how bad this credit rating is.' He looks at me with a furrowed brow. 'Dear me, you are right in regards to your credit rating.' Then he changes the subject. 'Why do you wish to start all over again? You did say your age was sixty?'

'That's right. I am not yet ready to lie down and die. I want my independence back.'

The young accountant asks me to wait a moment, and picks up his telephone. After a pause of five seconds, he then speaks into the mouthpiece, 'Roger, I have a gentleman with me who is sixty. He recently had a domestic upset and a company collapse, which created a poor credit rating. Roger, I have a strong feeling that we should go ahead with this application. Although he is sixty he is still willing to get up and have a go. What do you say?' There is a pause and he says, 'I'll ask him.' He holds his hand over the mouthpiece and asks me, 'Can you go down to the finance company in person?'

Within the space of thirty minutes I am in Roger's office. He is the loans officer of a large finance company. After another long period of interrogation, I am finally rewarded with a positive, 'Yes, your application for a loan is approved!' I excitedly hurry back to the car company, thank the accountant several times and assure him that I will not let him down. I keep my word and pay this loan off twelve months before the due date. The finance company actually owes me seventy-four dollars when I make the final payment.

My car is seven years old but to my eyes it is the most beautiful, modern limousine in the world. After contacting former business associates I begin calling on chemists and department stores again. I leave Ailsa's little home and lease a flat in Clayfield. The flat is part of a long, single-storey building divided into three sections. Each unit has its own separate entrance with three wooden steps. The tin roof makes living in this building equivalent to being in a foundry. I call it my tin shed. My income is low and the rent is cheap, but at least I have some form of independence.

Over the next two years Sue flies Jody and Kelly up to Brisbane three times a year. I look forward to seeing my daughters and love being with them. But their return to Sydney is always a moment of sadness and I often have tears in my eyes as I bid them farewell. In 1988, I receive the sad news that Sue has accepted an offer to manage a firm in Taiwan. This means that Jody and Kelly will also move overseas. Sue and I make a verbal agreement with Jody and Kelly: if one or both of the children do not like Taiwan after six months, then they can return to Australia and live with me. My heart is heavy as I bid my playmates farewell this time. It will be quite a while before I see my daughters again and share in their fun and laughter.

About the same time the children leave, I am compensated by Helen moving from Perth to Brisbane. She brings my two grandchildren, Jamie and Katie, with her. Unfortunately, my wonderful travelling companion of bygone years has also gone through the traumatic experience of a marriage breakdown. Once again it is time for the pair of us 'to keep our chins up high'. We are a great source of strength and comfort for each other.

I often cook Helen's favourite meal, beef curry, and have her over for dinner. Neither of us dwells on the past because we have learnt to never mind about the problem but get on with the job of living. There are many times of telling jokes and laughter as we both begin to get on with our lives. Both of us look forward, not back, and begin to enjoy jazz concerts, theatre and social outings.

One month passes and Helen calls to take me to see a show at one of the leading clubs. I have no idea of the secret Helen is keeping. I am surprised to see that my old friend, Enzo Toppano, is one of the stars of the show. The other is his wife Peggy, who I have not yet met. I have not seen Enzo for thirty-two years and hurry to meet them after the performance. Enzo is astounded when he sees me. It's as though he is looking at a ghost. The last time he saw me I was a derelict sprawled out on a bus seat near the Glebe Town Hall. He is so emotional and amazed that I am still alive that he wraps his arms around me and hugs me tightly, then introduces me to Peg and insists on taking Helen, Peg and I to a restaurant. We talk until the early hours of the morning, and both Enzo and Peg insist that I put pen to paper and record my life's story. I cannot understand the importance of carrying out this assignment and I am confused by their insistence. Enzo speaks to me in simple terms, 'Trust me, Cliff. This story must be told. This is a story of hope for many people, not just those with a drinking problem.' I begin to think about what Enzo is saying. 'Okay. I'll give it a lot of thought.'

When I return to the 'tin shed' I start to write this book. For many nights the ritual of putting pen to paper goes on long into the night. Sometimes I find myself still writing when the sun comes up. I am sixty years old and feel like my life has reached its end. There are moments of self-pity and great sadness. Each day I am virtually living an hour at a time, yet somehow, somewhere within me there is a small voice constantly telling me, 'All will be well.' I keep writing.

After attending numerous interviews for employment, I finally run out of options. I have lots of energy and motivation yet my age prevents me gaining suitable employment. By February 19, 1990, I am sixty-three, unemployed and receiving a pension for a chronic lung condition. My allowance is not a fortune, yet it is enough to survive on. Even though I am unable to get a job, I decide that I can still get a life and retire gracefully. Retirement is paramount in my mind now. Not wishing to live in Sydney or Brisbane, I decide to go to Surfers Paradise, on the Gold Coast.

By now Helen has been married for a while to a young man, Evan, who I had befriended and helped in the past.

He is a warm, compassionate person and I am grateful that Helen has found love and happiness.

I am in paradise when I obtain a nice, one-bedroom beachside unit at Palm Beach. This new Housing Commission unit is like a castle after living in the dark, tin shed. I feel like a king when I sit on my balcony, feel the cool ocean breezes and watch the colours of the sunset.

Within two months Helen's second marriage ends. Although they loved each other dearly and Helen is pregnant with her and Evan's first child, Evan has unresolved issues, problems which Helen feels she can no longer handle.

Helen and her children move to Tweed Heads and rent a three-bedroom townhouse. They are only fifteen minutes' drive from my home. When Helen gives birth to a second daughter, Nicole, I offer her my support and attend the birth. This experience further deepens my relationship with Helen and it is a very moving moment for me. I am pleased that I am sober and able to support my daughter. Nicole's perfect features make her the most beautiful child that I have ever laid eyes on. Helen and I both feel safe. The fact that we are close by gives us both a warm, secure feeling. I love being a grandfather to her children and often spoil them. Life is kind to us both once again.

My Greatest Gift

Mid-morning one day in April, 1993, there is a knock on my front door accompanied by a soft voice, 'Is anybody home?' I am in the bathroom with one side of my face shaved and the other still covered in white foam. My attire is comprised of an old white singlet, a pair of baggy shorts and a red thong on my right foot. I can't find its mate. Filled with curiosity, I open the door. Before me stands a lovely young woman. She has short, dark-brown hair cut in an Audrey Hepburn style. Her large blue-grey eyes dance as her smile reveals perfect white teeth. Her blue jeans are tight fitting and accentuate her shapely figure. The sudden shock of having such a beautiful caller makes my voice jump a couple of tones. 'Yes, what is it?'

She points to the ground some twenty feet below. 'Hello, I'm your new neighbour. Would you be able to help the guy below carry my refrigerator up to my unit, please?'

From my third-storey balcony, I look down upon a man standing next to a massive white monster. I shudder and respond, 'I'm sorry dear. I have a lung condition and it would be impossible for me to help you.'

She gives me an understanding smile. 'Oh, never mind. I'll see if I can find someone else.'

Then she is gone. I feel so useless and worthless not being able to help. I am a very lonely person, starved for company, and a twinge of sadness comes over me as I realise I will probably never communicate with this warm, lovely person again. If I am fortunate, I may get the occasional 'hello' or 'have a nice day'.

But one week later when I go downstairs to collect my mail, she seems to materialise out of nowhere. Opening her mailbox, Dian introduces herself and we converse for a short while on trivial matters. Our conversation becomes very interesting when she mentions that she was born in the country town of Leeton. I tell her about my days in Leeton when I was a lad. We have something in common and begin discussing familiar people and incidents. I enjoy our conversation and continue telling Dian about amusing incidents that happened to me in Leeton twelve years before she was born. Excited, I fire questions at her. Is the Hydro Hotel still standing? What about the Wattle Café? Is Nick Scanlon's pool hall still there? After twenty minutes of stimulating conversation Dian remembers that she has an appointment. Suddenly words jump out of my mouth. 'Do you like beef curry, Dian?' And just as suddenly I feel foolish.

She smiles and shyly says, 'I love beef curry.'

Nervously I continue, 'I'm cooking one of my special curries tonight for dinner. If you have nothing better to do, I would appreciate your company.'

Dian does not answer immediately. I begin to feel even more foolish. My thoughts are that I'm a silly old fool and I should not have asked her.

Then she surprises me. 'I would love to have dinner with you this evening, Cliff.' And she is gone.

I spend the next few hours preparing dinner, wondering if everything is perfect for my guest. Dinner is very successful and I am highly complimented by Dian. After dinner we both feel relaxed and at ease. Dian settles for a glass of fruit juice and I have a mug of steaming hot coffee. We communicate as if we have known each other for years. Dian asks about my life experiences and I open up to her about my life. She hears about the whole mess, the years of alcoholism, the loneliness, my failures and successes. While she sits and listens I realise that she is genuinely interested. Experience has taught me that only people who have suffered great pain, fear and heartache can ever fully understand my life story. I feel brave enough to ask, 'What about you? Do you feel like telling me about Dian's journey?'

She looks down at the glass in her hand and then starts to speak rather softly, 'My family lived in the Leeton area until I was nine. In 1963, my parents made a decision to pack up and move to Coleambally, about seventy kilometres south-west of Leeton. There are five members in my family, my parents, older sister, twin sister and myself.'

Noticing Dian's empty glass I interrupt, 'Would you care for another fruit juice?' I sense she is feeling uneasy so I give her time to compose herself.

'Yes, please.'

I refill her glass and pour myself another coffee. Once more we settle and Dian resumes her story.

'Life was very rugged in Coleambally. The whole family were like pioneers, clearing and fencing virgin bushland on the eight hundred acre farm. The two main crops were wheat and rice. We also had about one thousand sheep. The living conditions were equivalent to that of early Australian settlers. There were five people living in a tiny tin shed. We had no running water, electricity or phone. The only sewerage was a pan behind a gum tree. The year was 1963, yet it seemed like 1863.

'Monday to Friday my sisters and I would ride our pushbikes to Argoon School. It was a makeshift school, located in the cookhouse of an old, deserted station homestead. Come the weekend we had little time for play. My father had no sons to run the property, so Saturday and Sunday were work days for us. My twin sister, Margo, liked working inside the house helping Mum with cooking and other household chores. My other sister, Joanne, and I loved the outdoors and did various chores on the farm. I loved working with sheep and had a highly intelligent, black and tan kelpie called Nip. She was brilliant at the intricate sheep work. Even at the age of ten I could control the dog well. In fact, neighbours borrowed this dog many times to round up their own sheep.'

Dian hesitates for a moment, then continues, 'My father became friends with a neighbouring farmer, who was better off financially and owned more property and equipment than us. He ran very large flocks of sheep on leased land. He was married, had three children and was a highly respected member of the community.'

There is silence and I sense Dian is struggling with something. She gathers her thoughts, and continues, 'You know, Cliff, I learnt very early in life that success has nothing to do with wealth. I also learnt that wealth can hide a multitude of sins in some people. No-one saw what was happening to me because wealth somehow gives people status, respect and community standing, regardless of what acts the person performs.'

I start to wonder what Dian is about to say. She seems so open and honest, yet struggles to get these next words out.

'My father's so called friend would often request that Nip and I help him muster sheep on his isolated properties. Unfortunately, his request was granted. Initially, when I was sent out with this man it was a family outing with his sons. Eventually, this man manipulated the situation so that I was alone with him droving sheep. I was a young, shy ten-year-old. The properties were remote, uninhabited and a long way from my home.

'These trips to round up sheep began to reveal how cruel and sick this man was. His domination of my life became so great that he took unspeakable liberties with me and told me not to open my mouth to anyone. Sensing his insanity, I feared for my life and kept my suffering, violation and pain a secret. At times I would be so gripped with fear that all I could call upon was God and the beauty of bush. My nightmare continued for eleven years. My fear was reinforced by this vile man telling me what he would do if I ever told my parents or anybody else what transpired on these "work expeditions". I feared for all my family's lives.'

I am glad of the break in our conversation when Dian asks for another cold drink. My heart is like lead and emotionally I am very shaken. After offering Dian her drink, I say, 'I cannot begin to imagine how you survived this trauma, but believe me I do relate to the fear and pain of abandonment you must have felt.'

When Dian hears these words she looks at me with tears in her eyes. 'Cliff, I know you understand how I felt and that's why I can speak to you about it now.'

The clock on my wall shows 11 p.m. We have been talking for five hours. I encourage her to continue.

'My life was always on the run. He waited outside school, drove up and down the road outside my home and continually haunted me wherever I went. When I was successful in obtaining a scholarship to Teachers' College in Adelaide I thought my nightmare was over. It was not. He followed me to Adelaide and interrupted my studies. I forfeited any hope of graduating by running away once more. I crossed the Nullarbor Plain in the clothes I was standing up in, hitchhiking from Sydney to Perth, thanks to the kindness of truck drivers. I have slept on the grass beneath the shadows of the Sydney Harbour Bridge and even huddled on deserted beaches to escape this man. I often went without food and shelter. I had many jobs but could never settle, with this man hot on my heels. My feelings resembled a large black hole and were hidden deep inside me. I felt robbed of my right of decision, my womanhood, self-esteem and dignity. I felt like this revolting man was piling invisible layers of putrid shit all over my being, even covering my mind and body. Not long before my twenty-first birthday this evil person murdered his wife and committed suicide. I felt relieved that I was finally free. But I was also very angry, because I was robbed of the opportunity to kill this bastard myself. Prior to his death I was planning to kill him, because I could not take any more abuse. I figured it was better to go to gaol for murder than to live in the prison this man was keeping me in.

'I was numb for many years after this event. My life had been that of a person going through the motions of being normal, when really, inside, I was traumatised by the years of violation. The harsh judgement and contempt from community, friends and some relatives left me unable to express an opinion without fear they would reject me. My need for understanding and love was so great because of what I had suffered. When this man first violated me I was a child. He continually told me that I was to blame for his actions. I have never known what it is like to feel safe enough to be loved by a man or for me to return that love. I feel as though I have been lost and alone, floating way out in the universe.' She pauses and drinks her cold juice.

I nod my head, understanding the feeling of being lost

in space. I then utter words that have great impact on Dian: 'You must have felt so alone!' We both cry.

She confesses to me a little later, 'Do you know, Cliff, I was so alone during those years and you are the first person to ever understand the depth of my loneliness. Thank you for being so understanding and caring.'

I then say, 'Always remember one thing, Dian. The raping of one's body is a serious physical offence but no-one can ever touch your soul. That belongs to you. Whenever you find true love you will be able to offer your heart and soul by exercising your own right of decision.'

She thinks for a moment and replies with tears in her eyes, 'That's so true. The bastard was never able to touch my soul.' Dian pauses for a moment, then continues. 'My adversity has given me a great appreciation for the simple things in life. I still appreciate having sheets on my bed and being able to sleep without the bitter chill of winter reaching my bones. When it rains I am grateful I am not huddled under some bridge to keep dry. I love having a choice of food, after having times without. After having no rights, I cherish my own right of decision and that of others. Despite my great misfortune, Cliff, I have overcome so many odds against me. After his suicide I just wanted to live life. I re-educated myself to post-graduate level and had a ten-year career in the public service. I went from casual typist to registrar of a large college. I then became a staff trainer and finally a personnel manager. I did voluntary work with teenagers and people struggling with life. This whole tragedy taught me about the meaning of success. Society tried to teach me that it was all about power, status, greed, self-ishness, money and material possessions. Success, to me, is nothing to do with these things. It's to do with how I overcome the odds in front of me by loving and trust-ing God no matter what. It's to do with giving to others less fortunate than myself without expecting anything in return. It's about respecting people's rights and knowing my own. It's all about loving.'

It is after midnight when Dian and I finally say good night. Before Dian leaves she turns and says, 'Cliff, you are the most successful person I have ever met.'

I feel rather embarrassed because compliments are a rare thing in my life. We shake hands and Dian returns to her own flat. I lie awake in bed for a long time think-ing about what Dian has told me. I try to envisage her pain. All I can feel is confusion. How can anyone commit the act of rape? I feel deep sorrow for what has happened to her.

Over the next few days I cannot help but wonder how Dian could have ended up in a Housing Commission unit. The next time I see Dian she invites me over for coffee. I cannot help myself and ask, 'Dian, I have been thinking about what you told me the other night and I can't help wondering how you went from being a personnel manager to a person living in a Housing Commission unit?'

She laughs. 'Life is full of surprises, isn't it? In 1989 I was living on my own and working in Orange. I had just bought and renovated my first home. After a relationship breakdown I decided to rent my home, resign from my job and move to Townsville. I managed to get a job initially as a cleaner, then night fill person in a supermarket and finally a position as an office administrator. Unfortunately for me I was exposed to chemical sprays, which I am severely allergic to, contracted glandular fever and was unable to work. Interest rates for housing loans skyrocketed so I was forced to sell my home in Orange for little profit. I also ended up with Chronic Fatigue Syndrome and was forced to go on a pension to survive. I soon after moved to the Gold Coast to be with family, and was eventually able to gain my independence when a Housing Commission unit became available here.'

I am amazed at Dian's strength to enjoy life and to remain positive in the face of adversity. She still has a wonderful sense of humour and does not seem bitter or angry about the hand she has been dealt in life. I begin to admire this wonderful new friend and learn that we have a lot in common.

For many months I continue to regularly visit Dian, cooking meals and offering encouragement because there are times when she has great difficulty with daily tasks. We always enjoy each other's company and a great bond forms between us. The following year there is a marked improvement in her health. In 1994, I plan a surprise fortieth birthday party for Dian and her twin sister. It is wonderful to see Dian so vibrant and healthy. Our friendship is purely platonic for a long time; she does not want a relationship with a man twenty-seven years her senior, and I feel she would be better off with a man her own age. I try to match her up with some of my younger friends, but she is not very impressed with my efforts; she tells me she is able to choose her own companions, so I give up being the matchmaker. But we grow closer. She becomes my best friend, and we are inseparable. I always sense Dian is afraid to trust because she has been so hurt in life. Sometimes, when she feels safe enough, she says to me, 'Will you just hold me while I cry.' Hold her I do and her cries come from deep within her soul. I try to offer Dian the help that I have been given throughout my life. I want so desperately for her to experience:

> Healing
> Energy
> Love and
> Peace

because I realise she has experienced a lot of pain and torment through her life. Our friendship continues to deepen.

The following week I receive a letter from Helen. Within the envelope is a small reprint of a photograph of Helen when she was five years old. I hurry over to Dian's unit and talk with her for hours about the memories the photo has triggered. I tell Dian that I have not been to my old home in Glebe for many years and she suggests that I should revisit my home. I am a bit sad because I realise that I cannot afford it. Dian is very positive and tells me, 'If you want to do something badly enough, then I know you can save the money.'

I feel a sudden surge of excitement and bravely ask her, 'Would you consider coming with me?' Her warm eyes look at mine. 'I'll have to give that some thought.'

I give Dian a copy of my autobiography manuscript and ask her if she would like to read it. She is excited to be able to get to know me through the pages of my book.

A little over a week later, Dian suddenly disappears for a period of six long days. I anxiously await the return of my friend. I feel so lonely when she is not around. Each day I walk out onto my small front balcony, cast my eyes down the street, hoping to see her car appear. Every time I hear the sound of a motor vehicle, I think it may be her returning. I do this about twenty times a day. My torture is relieved one morning when her old blue car comes into view. She gets out of the car, waves and gives the most glorious smile. Now I am really confused. Dian comes up to my open front door, walks in, puts her arms around me and holds me for a very long time. Unexpectedly, she tenderly kisses me. This first kiss sends tingles through my whole body. At sixty-six I feel the chances of finding a love in my life are over. What does her kiss mean? Do I dare to think there could be a future for the two of us? Dian's kiss births hope for a new beginning.

She then explains, 'When you asked me to go to Glebe with you, I had to get away for a while, so I stayed at my girlfriend's place. I sensed you had strong feelings for me, so I needed to sort out how I felt about you. I was worried about the age difference and whether I could handle another relationship. I have been hurt so many times. While I was away I missed you very much and realised you are the greatest friend I've ever known. I have hurried home to tell you this. I have also decided to help you save up so that we can both go to Glebe.'

I am overwhelmed with her news and can't believe what is happening to me. We sit down and talk for hours. Dian tells me that my old, hand-typed autobiography manuscript has great potential, and it would be a good idea to have it typed onto computer and stored on a disk. She gives me great encouragement and we pay for a little to be typed each week. I get overwhelmed to see it so neatly presented several months later.

We continue to see each other and out of desperate, dark times something rich and wonderful blooms. I feel the resurgence of my vitality as I realise it is possible to start again. Thoughts of future loneliness begin to fade. I look out and up, instead of down and within. For the first time in my life I feel truly loved and in turn can give love back.

Prior to meeting Dian the only love I had ever known was from people wanting to love and rescue me: Fred, who wanted his son to become a man, and Helen, whose loyalty and love hoped for a father to emerge. All had hoped for me to become someone, someday. This new love Dian offers goes to a depth far beyond the boy on the balcony's final barrier of feeling unworthy. I have never known anyone who is truly my friend. All I have to offer Dian is myself and that's all she ever expects. This in itself breaks down the barrier of feeling unworthy and finally gives birth to a safe, loved and secure man. I am sure that God has directed his best angel to me in human form because her love is so unconditional. I now know that this is what I have searched for unknowingly all my life.

I begin to laugh at little things and there is a spring in my step. When people comment regarding our age difference I do not care. My search is over. After finding my true friend and love, nothing else matters. We both continue to discover the secrets of life by loving and accepting each other for who we are, feeling grateful for finding one another and appreciating our good health.

We save money and eventually move out of our respective one-bedroom units, and into a lovely two-bedroom unit right near the beach—an ensuite, large living area, garage and huge bedrooms are a luxury for us. We also save enough money for our trip to Glebe. The trip is fulfilling for both of us.

Helen and her children are now just five minutes drive away. They all love Dian and enjoy her company. Dian and I often babysit Nicole while Helen lets her hair down or works. It is lovely to have family so close.

We have very few material possessions, so we dispose of the worn-out furniture we both possess, and completely refurnish our new home, courtesy of time payment or as I refer to it, 'uneasy terms'. Financially, we are on the lower end of the scale but emotionally we are way above the multi-millionaire class. We are fortunate enough to have been given gifts that all the money in the world cannot buy. These include peace of mind, love, contentment, laughter, friendship and freedom to be ourselves. Perhaps the years of pain we have both endured are our down payment for the future.

A fellow member of A.A. once told me, 'Faith alone may not open the gates of Heaven and let us in, but it will most certainly open the gates of Hell and let us out.' Dian and I are grateful we got out.

The Unexpected

It is New Year's Day, seven weeks before my seventieth birthday. After returning from my walk to the corner shop, Dian greets me at the front door. She informs me that an old friend has arrived. When I enter the lounge room I observe a man around fifty with a woman in her mid-forties. All I can say is, 'Hello there.'

Dian laughs and says, 'I bet you don't know who this is.'

I am totally confused and don't like the guessing game being played.

Dian can no longer hold her excitement within. 'It's Christine, your daughter you haven't seen for forty-three years.'

My body is transfixed to the floor. I think this is some type of pathetic joke. Christine speaks. 'It's true. My husband and I have been searching for you for years.'

My response is brief, I can hardly speak, 'Sit down. Dian, will you make some coffee, please?'

I can barely take in the conversation over the next fifteen minutes. It seems as if people are playing out a drama and I am the audience, and that the whole show will disappear in a puff of smoke at any moment. Arising from my seat, I walk over to the kitchen sink. I turn around to look once more at the three people, deep in conversation. I see a middle-aged, fair-haired woman, who is beautifully attired. Her face shows a mixture of kindness and humour. I hear her say that she has two sons. I can see she resembles her mother, Daphne, yet the Nichols' humour seems to come through with her words and actions.

As I walk slowly back towards my seat, Christine stands up, walks towards me and suddenly she puts her arms around me. I hug her as her tears come in a great flood. I am held so tightly that I have difficulty breathing. She holds on as though she will never, ever let me go. Over and over she repeats the words, 'Those wasted years . . . those wasted years.' I can see her husband, Gordon, and Dian, watching this happy drama. Gordon goes to hold his wife but Dian puts her hand on his arm and whispers. 'Let her cry. She has waited a long time for this.'

Christine continues to hold me, looking into my face every now and then. By the time we all resume our seats I am totally drained. Christine, Gordon and Dian are all chattering away. Amid the odd burst of tears is more crazy, happy laughter. I sit there completely exhausted, nursing my bruised ribs and trying to stop the room from spinning. Even a smile makes me ache and for once in my life I am speechless.

Six months earlier Dian and I had been searching for Christine on the electoral roll. We managed to locate her Uncle Martin and sent him my address and phone number. Apparently he passed the information onto Christine, and Gordon encouraged her to visit me. I feel relieved the search for Christine is now over.

Early the following year I also renew contact with Kath, the wonderful woman whom I had married in 1964. I have managed to keep in contact with Kath over the years every time she visits Helen. It is lovely to see her each time even though it is several years between visits. I have never forgotten her kindness to Helen and me during my drinking days. Kath is now not in good health so we keep in touch by telephoning regularly.

One of our conversations goes for nearly two hours. She laughs about the old days and says, 'God, the first time I saw you drunk I wondered what the hell I had gotten myself into!' We laugh and reminisce about our many escapades. She adds, 'Remember the time you won all that money and told me to buy myself a fur coat? Well, I did buy a very nice fur and I still have it to this day.'

The latter part of our discussion is on Kath's health. She is on constant medication for fibroids in her lungs. These have been caused by the asbestos her house is made from. I realise that we may not be making many more telephone calls and say, 'Thank you for all you have done for me, Kath. I know I would probably have died without your love and caring. Helen loves you as her mum because of all the love and kindness you have bestowed upon her. To this day if a stranger asks what her mother's name is, she has no hesitation in saying Kath. Neither of us will ever forget your kindness.'

She replies, 'I thank you, too, Cliff. The most important thing you taught me was not to worry. You also taught me the difference between a problem and an inconvenience. I have never forgotten that.'

Kath still lived in Croydon on her own, constantly visited by her children, Laurie and Colin. Since Helen and I left Kath, Helen always maintained contact with Kath and visited her at every opportunity. However, towards the end of 1998 Kath passed away and joined my mother and father in her rightful place, the highest point of the kingdom of Heaven. Kath was eighty-two years of age.

My mind reflects back to the wonderful blessings I have received and the gifts of human nature from people like Kath, who were there in my hour of need. My much-loved father, Fred, and daughter, Helen, who travelled my journey with me. All the others like Nicky, Nell and the other unloved battlers, who offered food, money, a place to stay, the warmth of friendship and, most of all, hope. I am grateful for my sobriety and the gift of Dian, my soul mate. This gift all the wealth of the world could not buy. I appreciate having my family around me, my own peace of mind, a faith I did not know I could have and, most of all, a contentment with life and myself. Today I really like me.

Remembrance

In September, 2000, I witness the closing of the twenty-seventh Olympiad. What a resounding success Sydney has presented to the world! Sydney, my old birthplace, where many good and bad memories were made. It is almost thirty-five years since my first experience of total sobriety. Throughout this period I have not had a reason to drink alcohol or take any mind-altering chemical. I am both grateful and fortunate to have a new beginning every day.

Dian has been my soul mate for seven and a half years. To this day my love and devotion for her has not wavered. In fact my feelings have grown stronger with the passing of time. One evening I take Dian for a very romantic dinner for two at a top-class restaurant. After our meal I propose. When Dian accepts I inform her that it is now time for me to give her a ring. I put my hand into my coat pocket and grab a toy mobile phone. I hold the phone to my ear and push a button that makes it ring. Dian cracks up into uncontrollable laughter and our evening progresses into a fun-filled, memorable occasion. We decide to make this coming Armistice Day—also known as Remembrance Day—a day to remember. On the eleventh hour of the eleventh day of the eleventh month in 1918 world peace was declared to end the hostilities of World War I. Dian and I choose this date for our marriage, because our wars with pain and isolation are over.

Our wedding is a small, no frills, intimate occasion filled with love. It is held in our new home at Banora Point, near Tweed Heads. The ceremony is performed by a marriage celebrant under a beautiful tree in our backyard, and we have written our own vows for this special day.

Dian looks directly into my eyes and begins, 'Cliff, I am grateful that God has given me the gift of you.' Tears of gratitude fill her eyes. She pauses, takes a deep breath then continues, 'You came into my life when all around me was darkness, loneliness and pain. Your love overwhelms me at times and your wonderful friendship is like a bright, beautiful light that takes the darkness away. It allows love to shine. Your love, thoughtfulness, kindness, wonderful sense of humour and zest for life have become my precious diamonds. To find my soul mate, who adds sunshine, companionship, challenge, beauty, loyalty, love and meaning into my life, has ended a long search and gives me a special reason to live. For the first time in my life I feel safe enough to pledge my heart, my loyalty, my truth, my friendship, my love, myself. These are my diamonds which I offer you.'

I am deeply moved by Dian's sincerity and her vow. I then take a deep breath and begin mine, 'Dian, you came into my life when I was surrounded by loneliness, heavy heart and memories. You came in the form of brilliant light. Your face gave out the aura of kindness, love and hope. Because of you I can once more see the flashing diamonds on the water on a brilliant sunny day. Once more the fragrance in the air is sweeter. I can touch the hand of hope. I can now walk with a spring in my step. You have given me the bouquet of song, laughter and flowers. Now I know the full meaning of love. You came into my life and you gave me the answers to life itself. You made me aware of the reasons why I was born and the reasons of who I am. You have given me the bright flame of love, warmth, faith and friendship. Dian, you are my miracle, my gift from God. I promise I will love and cherish you forever.'

We then exchange rings and are pronounced husband and wife. That night when I hold my new bride in my arms I tell her, 'Finding you is the highlight of my life. I compare my life's journey to sitting in a movie house. There are two movies being shown. The first one is about living through the worst kind of horror show. When interval comes, I walk out into the light. After intermission, I return for the second movie, which is a bright, colourful musical with love and laughter. This second half need never end. Dian, I now have every reason to live.'

All My Love

Christmas 2001 is only a few months away and for the first time all five of my daughters will be gathered around the Christmas dining table. This will be a precious and moving moment for me. I'm so looking forward to seeing them all. Having Dian by my side will make my circle of love complete. This is all I need for Christmas, and more than I'd ever hoped for.

Helen, my wonderful wandering pal of bygone days, is back living in Perth with her children. Jamie and Katie are both working for law firms. Nicole is now a gorgeous little nine-year-old. She is named after our wonderful friend, Nicky, who saved our lives yet died so tragically because of alcohol. Unfortunately, in 1998, Nicole's father fell to his death from the top of a high-rise building in Sydney. It left us all shattered because he was another caring, warm soul whose life was sadly lost.

Kim now holds an executive position with a casino and we phone each other regularly. I am very proud of her. Christine, whom fate declared should live through 'those wasted years', holds a top position in a real estate firm. Her two sons, Adam and Jarrod, are fine young men who have also lived through some rugged times. Adam lives and works in Brisbane. Jarrod has a little daughter called Tahlia-Lee, which now makes me a great-grandfather. This in itself is a miracle. Early in my life, I never thought I would live long enough to be a grandfather, let alone be a great-grandfather. Christine and Gordon live on a property outside of Brisbane and often travel to Tweed Heads to socialise with Dian and me.

Daphne resides with Christine and Gordon in her own separate unit. Though we have not met after all these years, I wrote a letter to Daphne some months back trying to make amends for the past. On April 24, 2002, I was informed by Christine that Daphne had not been in good health. As it was just on fifty years since we had last communicated, I took the risk of being either ignored or abused and phoned her. Miraculously, we conversed for just on forty-five minutes in a warm, civilised manner. This was a great relief for me.

Jody, my little playmate, has finished her education at the University of Oregon and is currently working with a leading advertising company in the United States. We are in contact by phone, letters and emails.

Kelly Lee has been back in Australia for three years, and is living in her own unit in Tweed Heads. She speaks Mandarin fluently and is currently studying office administration. She still loves to sing and dance.

Alcoholics Anonymous is my extended family and I still attend on a regular basis. I get a wonderful feeling when I see people of all ages trying to take responsibility for their lives. Sobriety is the wonderful adventure we call life. I still act as secretary for an A.A. group that meets once a week, and I try to pass on the wonderful advice and wisdom I have learnt over the years.

As we draw closer to my seventy-fifth birthday, I give thanks to my friend God, for the miracle of my salvation. Despite having been beyond all human help, I am still here on this great planet of ours. Many people may wish to be recognised as religious or Christian. I am not a religious man. I prefer to say that I am spiritual and that my God, as I understand Him or Her to be, is a God of love, not a God of fear. Somehow, through all my days of darkness and doubt, I have always had an inner feeling that there was a reason for my nightmare journey. This God of love did not desert me. Instead, love released me from my anguish, healed me of my pain and gave me courage instead of fear. Because of love, I have been given the freedom to enjoy life and finally find inner peace.

The special love that Helen and I have for each other is still as strong and real as ever. How can I be sure? The answer is simple; greeting cards from Helen for my birthday, Fathers' Day, Christmas and Easter have been arriving in my mail regularly for many years. The one card that leaves no doubt about her feelings, though, is that special card she sends to me every Mothers' Day.

Postscript

If I had not held the hand of hope that day back in 1966, this story would never have been written. In fact I believe I would not be here.

Prior to gaining this hope, I found it impossible to find the courage to admit or accept I was an alcoholic. One of my greatest fears was people finding out the truth and shunning me because of the stigma associated with alcoholism. Fear prevented truth from becoming my ally. While attending A.A. meetings I was admitting that I was an alcoholic, but if I was having lunch with some work-mates a few days later it was a different story. When the normal question arose, 'What are you having, Cliff? A beer, Scotch? Name your poison!' then my response would be, 'Just a mineral water, thanks.'

'Don't you drink booze?'

'No! Actually, I have an ulcer!'

My mates would look at me in astonishment. Other times my excuses were that I had had a lung operation or was on medication. All I felt was fear, dreaded fear. I feared my employment may be in jeopardy if my employer or workmates found out I was an alcoholic attending A.A. meetings.

I discovered a new way of dispersing my fears and anxieties. I learned to let go of fear and let God, whoever or whatever He or She is, give me courage. I learned that when I hand my whole life over to this power up among the stars my life began to improve one thousand percent. When I am in control and running my life, it is chaotic, to put it mildly. But I liked this new manager I had appointed and I began to learn about faith:

> Freedom
> After
> Introduction
> To
> Hope.

Since becoming sober I have learned that I must not break another member's anonymity and that some people need to remain anonymous because of society's ignorance regarding alcoholism. I, however, felt uncomfortable about lying and eventually realised that my need to remain anonymous walked hand in hand with my old fear and shame. I decided that now my faith must walk hand in hand with my truth. I did not want to hide my secret any longer when I realised that I had the right to choose who I told about my alcoholism.

I was put on the spot one day when a valued workplace

client invited me to have a few drinks after work. Several other buyers and staff members were also invited. I felt uneasy as I entered the club, because I knew my moment of truth had finally arrived. There were six people sitting at our table. 'What are you having, Cliff?'

'Mineral water, thanks,' was my timid response.

The client laughed. I squirmed in my seat. 'Come on! What do you really want?'

The next three seconds seemed like an eternity. Taking a deep breath, I stated: 'I can't drink alcohol. I'm an alcoholic.'

My secret's out. There was stunned silence. I knew they would all walk away in disgust now.

'You can't be serious, Cliff. You're too well-dressed and such a great worker,' someone says.

One of the other buyers then asks, 'Can you explain to me what you have just said, Cliff? I am genuinely interested.'

I was surprised at his response. Suddenly my fear turned into courage and I told them about my life's journey with booze. Instead of walking away from me they were very curious. 'My sister drinks every day and the family feel there could be a problem there,' said one of the buyers. Questions came thick and fast. I felt so relieved. Telling the truth allowed me to be myself. Shame and fear melted away. I felt so free and it tasted sweet. From this point on I tell myself I have nothing to hide and hide from nothing. And I seemed to have put a false scare into my new drinking partners—the last round of drinks consisted of seven mineral waters.

How unfortunate that lack of knowledge and understanding about alcoholism and many other illnesses often isolates a sufferer. As a boy I overheard many whispered conversations based on ignorance. For example, when I was ten I asked my Mum, 'Where is Uncle Jack? I haven't seen him for a long while.'

The Victorian attitude of the day was obvious as Nell leaned over and spoke quietly into my ear. 'He is in a place called Callan Park, a mental hospital.'

'Is he nuts, Mum?'

'No. He is suffering shellshock from the Great War.' A worried look came over Nell's face as she added in a serious tone, 'Don't you tell a living soul what I have just told you, otherwise I will skin you alive!'

This condition was known in later years as war neurosis; today it has the sophisticated title of post traumatic stress disorder, and people tend not to be 'locked up' for such conditions.

I remember Nell and a neighbour talking another day about why poor Mrs Smith was carted off to hospital. The neighbour told Nell, 'She has, you know, that dreadful thing.'

'What dreadful thing?'

'You know, Nell. Good God! Can't you work it out? It starts with C.'

My mother put the flat of her hands against the sides of her head. 'God help her!'

Neither were able to say that dreaded word: cancer.

And my mother was judged harshly by people's ignorance. When neighbours stopped me in the street they would always ask: 'How's your mother, son?'

'All right,' I would mutter.

'It's a shame your mother drinks the way she does,' was their judgemental response. Anger would fill my being. Everybody knew about my mother's drinking problem but no-one stopped to help. I always felt they gossiped about other people to hide any secrets they might have had themselves. Both Uncle Jack and the woman suffering with cancer were isolated and misunderstood, just as my mother and I were because of our alcoholism.

My dream is that perhaps the day will eventuate when society will not be ignorant regarding people's illnesses. Scientific people talk about how the sound barrier has been broken and the hope of one day breaking the light barrier, yet the greatest barrier of all to break is unheard of—the barrier of denial. For me to speak freely about my alcoholism I had to break through my own barrier of denial. It took a spiritual awakening to do this. When I asked God for help I was given courage to conquer my fear, truth to replace my denial and hope instead of defeat. My mind and soul are finally free. I have become the person I always wanted to be—myself. This is my choice, perhaps it can be yours, too.